Media Representation and the Global Imagination

Global Media and Communication

Media Representation and the Global Imagination

SHANI ORGAD

polity

First published in 2012 by Polity Press

Polity Press
65 Bridge Street
Cambridge CB2 1UR, UK

Polity Press
350 Main Street
Malden, MA 02148, USA

ISBN-13: 978-0-7456-4379-3
ISBN-13: 978-0-7456-4380-9(pb)

A catalogue record for this book is available from the British Library.

Typeset in 11 on 13pt Adobe Garamond Pro
by Servis Filmsetting Ltd, Stockport, Cheshire
Printed and bound in Great Britain by the MPG Books Group

For further information on Polity, visit our website: www.politybooks.com

To Yoav and Assaf, whose imaginations extend far beyond the globe

Contents

Contents

Figures and Tables

Figures

Tables

Preface

This book reflects on the images, stories, accounts and voices that we encounter daily on television and the Internet, and in advertisements and newspapers. We take these representations largely for granted; they function as a kind of background to our social lives, but they shape our individual and collective imaginations in consequential ways. My primary concern is to explore the symbolic 'work' that media representations do in inviting us to relocate to distant locales and contexts, and to 'meet' people that are remote from the contexts of our daily lives. In particular, I examine how this invitation is played out in today's highly complex and networked global media environment through the centrality of intimacy in media representations, and I consider its implications for how the media feed the way we see, think of and feel about the world, about our relations with others and about our place in the world. The book explores these issues across five central sites where the work of media representations occurs, namely imagining others, imagining ourselves, imagining possible lives, imagining the world, and imagining the self.

This book should be of interest to students of media and communications, cultural studies and globalization, but need not be reserved to those privileged to read it as part of formal study of their subject in school or at university. I hope that the book will be of interest and relevance to a broad audience, at least among people living in stable societies, but also perhaps people in other parts of the world, whose imaginations feed on the representations circulating in the media.

Acknowledgements

Many people have encouraged and helped me to write (and complete!) this book, and also, no less important, reminded me that there's a world and life out there, beyond the book.

I am grateful to my research assistants, Kerry Arnot, Dorota Kaczuba and Yinhan Wang, and especially to Ryan Cunningham, Stephanie Dixon and Esther Etkin, for their invaluable intellectual and practical contributions and for their genuine enthusiasm for the project.

Several people have generously given time to read and/or comment on parts of the book and I would like to express my gratitude for their helpful feedback. Special thanks to Stan Cohen for his, as ever, incisive comments on earlier versions of chapters 2 and 3. Amnon Aran made a number of insightful comments on different parts and has encouraged me throughout. My colleagues at the London School of Economics and Political Science, Robin Mansell, Sonia Livingstone, Linje Manyozo and Charlie Beckett, have been helpful and supportive at different stages of the book-writing process. My discussions with Richard Sennett were formative and helped me hugely to focus my thinking and articulate the story of the book.

I was fortunate to have some early conversations with Roger Silverstone, at the embryonic stages of the project, from which I benefited a lot. Roger's intellectual spirit left a heavy imprint on my intellectual development and I have more than once imagined his (critical!) comments and suggestions on different parts of the book. I can only hope I got it right. His posthumous *Media and Morality* has been a huge source of inspiration and guidance, and a constant reminder of how much I miss him.

Cynthia Little is the best proofreader and language editor I could wish for. I cannot thank her enough for her meticulous reading and care. Cynthia is also a good friend and I thank her for her generosity and friendship. Fi Carroll also deserves special mention, for the tremendous support she has been giving as well as for her useful advice on the musical aspects in chapter 2. I am grateful to Philip Davies for his work on the index.

The book emerged from my teaching the topic as part of an LSE Masters course, in the years 2005 to 2011. I was extremely fortunate to have very interesting and interested and engaged students. The seminar discussions, in which students drew on their diverse cultural and personal backgrounds and experiences and shared their critical thoughts, greatly contributed to my thinking on the subject.

I have benefited from LSE's excellent library and Heather Dawson's expertise and help about where to find what. Our department's administrative staff, Cath Bennett, Jean Morris and especially Vanessa Cragoe, have been supportive and helpful, and I thank them for this. I am grateful also for the financial support I received from LSE to carry out the research for the book.

Several parts of this book were written (and rewritten) at the Giraffe and Maison Blanc cafés in Muswell Hill and I am grateful to their staff for nourishing me (literally) so I could write about the nourishment of the imagination.

My dear friends Ros Gill, Bruna Seu, Hila Shkolnik-Brener, Irit Segal and Avital Shaal were unstinting in their tremendous ongoing encouragement, support and love, which have nourished not only my thinking and imagination but also my confidence, happiness and sanity! Eileen Aird is a fundamental source of support and guidance whose voice I have carried with me: I am deeply indebted to her.

I am grateful to Polity Press and would like to thank Lauren Mulholland, Helen Gray and particularly Andrea Drugan for their enthusiasm for the project, and Andrea for her encouragement and very useful advice and assistance. It has been a true pleasure to work with them.

Finally, I am hugely indebted to my family: my loving precious mother, Atalya Wolf, my darling father, Nechemya Orgad, Kobi Wolf, and my dear brother, Itamar Orgad, and his family. You are far away, but only geographically. Huge thanks to my family in London: my husband, Amnon Aran, for his love, patience and help, and especially my beloved boys, Yoav and Assaf, to whom I dedicate this book. They are the purest joy and light I have ever known. I am forever caught in the elastic love trap they weave with their incredible imaginations.

Introduction

Almost seven decades ago, the American Allen B. DuMont Corporation launched a remarkable advertising campaign for its television technology. An advertisement put out in 1944 promises a prospective consumer of the DuMont Television-Radio Receiver that:

> **YOU'LL BE AN ARMCHAIR COLUMBUS**
>
> You'll sail with television through vanishing horizons into exciting new worlds. You'll be an intimate of the great and near-great. You'll sit at speakers' tables at historic functions, down front at every sporting event, at all top flight entertainment. News flashes will bring you eye-coverage of parades, fires and floods; of everything odd, unusual and wonderful, just as though you were on the spot. And far-sighted industry will show you previews of new products, new delights ahead.
>
> All this – a world actually served to you on a silver screen – will be most enjoyably yours when you possess a DuMont Television-Radio Receiver. It was Dumont who gave *really clear* picture reception to television. It will be DuMont to whom you will turn in peacetime for the finest television receiving sets and the truest television reception . . . the touchstone that will make you an armchair Columbus on ten-thousand-and-one thrilling voyages of discovery! (*Billboard*, 19 August 1944: 9; emphasis in original)

This text appears under the image of a man in an armchair, on a fireside rug (signifying home), gazing at a huge DuMont television screen, watching what looks like a scene from the Olympic Games, of a woman performing a back-flip dive. The backdrop to these images shows examples of what presumably are the 'odd, unusual and wonderful': a huge ocean liner, a group of cabaret artists singing to an invisible audience, and two horses, racing neck and neck, clearing a hurdle in front of the grandstand.

The advert is designed to sell a product, a specific communication technology. But it is also selling the fundamental promise brought by media and communications to a post-war world:[1] a promise to annihilate time and space by connecting the viewer, through mediated representations (images and narratives), to events that are occurring miles away and to distant others whom the viewer will likely never meet. Fulfilling this promise depends on media and communications technologies: they provide a platform for experiencing the world 'just as though you were on the spot' and they create this experience. Media and communications are both the facilitators and the vehicles of the constitutive experience of globalization: the 'disembedding' and 'lifting out' of social relations from local contexts of interaction and their restructuring across indefinite spans of time-space (Giddens, 1990). Disembedding of social relations is the basis for 'the intensification of worldwide social relations which link distant localities in such a way that local happenings are shaped by events occurring many miles away and vice versa' (Giddens, 1990: 64). Importantly, the process of 'disembedding' of social relations is inextricably connected to, framed by and dependent on the production, circulation and consumption of commodities in the global market. In this process, media representations not only project and promote 'new products' and 'new delights', for example, in the form of advertisements, but themselves constitute commodities that are produced, disseminated and consumed in the market-dominated media environment.

In this DuMont ad, it is the enormous television screen that 'lifts' the small-sized viewer out of his local daily experience, 'planting' him in 'exciting new worlds', signified by media events such as large-scale sports events (women viewers notoriously are excluded, characteristic of discourses of technology at that time).[2] This technologically deterministic and utopian language, typical of advertising discourse, reverberates in today's commercial discourses, as well as political, popular and scholarly debates on communications technologies. For example, recent discussions in the press and academia about the use of social media in the Arab world are characterized by a considerably utopian and celebratory fervour about the determining role of Twitter, Facebook, mobile communication and blogs in transforming politics and connecting remote protesters in the streets of Cairo, Benghazi, Tripoli, Rabat, Sana'a and Manama (to mention just a few) to millions of viewers across the world.

However, the disembedding of social relations does not occur automatically by virtue of the technological capacities of the medium. Rather, 'symbolic dislocation' (Thompson, 1995), the capacity to relate to distant events and distant others in locales and contexts that are remote from the contexts in which we live out our daily lives, relies on viewers' acceptance of the *invitation* issued by media images and narratives to dislocate; the *proposal* to think and feel 'as if' and 'just as though you were on the spot'. To put it differently, symbolic dislocation and the disembedding of social relations, which are constitutive of the experience of globalization, are predicated on and enabled by the capacity to *imagine*, to make-believe, 'to see in a thing what it is not, to see it other than it is' (Castoriadis, 1987 [1975]: 127).

The capability to imagine is not 'produced fully fledged as a result of some kind of spontaneous generation' (Boltanski, 1999: 50); nor is it, as

Appadurai (1996) observes, solely a personal, private creative faculty of the mind. Rather, imagination must be nourished by personal experience, but also, fundamentally, by collective cultural representations. 'In order for imagination to play its role in the coordination of emotional commitments, different persons must be able to nourish their imagination from the same source' (Boltanski, 1999: 50). The 'stretching' of social relations across time and space relies on the generation and fostering of a collective global imagination: a sense of ourselves and far-away others traversing a common global social space; a sense of distant places, people and cultures being relevant and connected to us, here and now. The central concern of this book is the cultural role that media representations fulfil as imaginary institutions (Castoriadis (1987 [1975]): how they feed a global imagination and 'stretch' relations across time and space.

Media Representation and the Global Imagination explores the images, stories, voices and accounts that appear in the media on a daily basis and feed the ways in which we imagine the world: how we come to see, think of and feel about the world, and our place and relations with others in this world. In particular, the chapters in this book address the following questions. What do contemporary media representations tell us about the world we live in? How do media representations call on us to imagine our lives and those of others in a world characterized by rapid processes of globalization? What 'scripts' are being produced by current representations, which, in turn, inform the way we imagine our and others' lives in the world today?

Global imagination refers to a collective way of seeing, understanding and feeling, at a global level, to a sense 'of who we are, how we fit together, how we got where we are, and what we might expect from each other in carrying out our collective practices that are constitutive of our way of life' (Gaonkar, 2002: 10). This is not to say that global imagination is a monolithic, homogeneous or fixed symbolic faculty. Nor does it abolish or swallow other imaginations, personal or collective. Rather, the global imagination is enabled through, cultivated by, and emerges via an ongoing process of symbolic construction of the real and the possible in image and narrative. It interacts and competes with other collective and individual imaginations, which may call into question the very possibility of a global imagination. The symbolic process of representation, on which the global imagination feeds, takes place largely in the media, in the ongoing production and circulation of images and stories. Media representations, therefore, are key everyday agents of imagination; they constitute fundamental resources and facilitators of this collective imagining (Frosh, forthcoming).

This view, which I develop throughout the book, suggests that representations are immensely powerful: that they nourish a wide and deep understanding and feeling that guide and frame people's actions and practices. However, there is an important caveat to this assumption. The power of media representations as agents of imagination is conditional: the representations circulating in the media have to be *meaningful* to their viewers. Representations must be efficacious, they must 'work' and must accomplish certain things (Illouz, 2007), for the man sitting in the comfort of his armchair and watching far-away spectacles, and for the many other men, women and children who consume (and produce) media representations in increasingly diverse, fragmented and unpredictable ways. Global imagination is far from being a deterministic view of media representations as conditioning or simply cultivating certain ways of imagining the world, which audiences are implied unproblematically to embrace or mirror. It is understood in this book as a complex, unfixed process that is fashioned in and through interaction and contestation among views, narratives, images, statements and voices – contestations in which their audiences take an active part. Thus, the notion in this book of 'media representations' refers to images and narratives that originate in different places and have different sources, including media consumers themselves, whose voices and accounts become increasingly visible components of the global field of media representations.

That said, an exploration of audiences' reception of media representations is beyond the scope of this book. It would be fascinating and very valuable to explore whether and how audiences recognize, accept or reject the invitations of contemporary representations to imagine the world, and to imagine their and others' lives (see, e.g., Seu and Orgad, in progress). However, the chapters in this book focus on the realm of representation: how the symbolic production of images and narratives in the global media constructs certain 'scripts' and calls viewers to imagine the world in certain ways. This study of representation, I believe, is a vital (though not the only) step towards a better understanding of the meaning of the media and how they shape and orient social life.

Although the DuMont ad was produced seventy years ago, the story it tells of communication technologies and globalization, and the implied centrality of mass media to collective imagining, are pertinent today. At the same time, media representations and the global imagination have undergone substantial transformation since the 1940s. Thompson (2005) usefully describes the transformations in the mediated and larger political and cultural environment, in which images and narratives are produced, circulated and consumed, as 'the age of new visibility'. He observes that twenty-first-century contemporary media, and especially the Internet and networked media, have enabled a new form of visibility which has become a pervasive feature of the world in which we live. Three central features distinguish the mediated environment of the new visibility from the past:

> It is more *intensive* in the sense that the sheer quantity of information flow is much greater than before, as more and more organizations and communication networks make available an ever-increasing volume of symbolic material. It is more *extensive* in the sense that the range of individuals who are drawn into these networks of communication and are capable of receiving the output of media organizations is much greater than it was a century (or even several decades) ago, and in the sense that the geographical spread of these recipients is much wider: today, information flows very quickly through networks which are not only national but increasingly global in scope. And the information environment is *less controllable* in the sense that, given the proliferation of mediated forms and networks of communication, it is much more difficult for political actors to throw a veil of secrecy around their activities, much harder to control the images and information that appear in the public domain, and much harder to predict the consequences of such appearances and disclosures. (Thompson, 2005, pp. 48–9, emphases in original)

The Abu Ghraib photos that were circulated in 2004 in newspapers and on screens across the world, which depicted the hidden practices of US military and paramilitary personnel in the closed-off world of Iraqi jails, and the release by WikiLeaks in October 2010 of almost 400,000 documents from the Iraq War Logs, are vivid illustrations of how the rise of digital technologies has amplified the significance of new forms of visibility. The wide circulation of images and accounts renders it much more difficult to control the flow of symbolic content. It is far more difficult for those in power to ensure that the images made available to the public are those they wish to see circulated (Thompson, 2005: 38).

The concern in *Media Representation and the Global Imagination* is with the 'work' that media representations do (Hall, 1997) in the age of new visibility: that is, the work they do as resources that feed individual and collective imaginations in a highly complex and networked global media environment. Two aspects of the 'work' of media representations are particularly important in this context.

First, intimately linked with the notion of the new visibility, is the idea that the work of media representations is characterized by contestation: players (institutions, groups, individuals) increasingly compete for visibility and a voice, through the projection of symbolic representations on to the global media space. Visibility in the media, in image and narrative, is a means of claiming recognition and exercising power. Contestation of representations, fuelled by the competitive logic of the market that dominates the mediated space, carries huge promise for the expansion of collective

5

and individual imaginations. Exposure to a growing range of competing stories, images, feelings and points of view is key to opening up people's imagination, in particular, to thinking and caring about people and issues that are beyond the self, and are remote from our local contexts and lives; to cultivating an outward orientation to the other and to the world; and to fostering more ambivalence and complexity in terms of how we feel and think about the world, about others, and about ourselves. Much of the debate on the role of social media in the 2011 uprisings across the Arab world, for instance – photos of Egyptians storming Tahrir Square in Cairo circulated on Facebook and tweets from Libyan protesters taking the streets of Benghazi and Tripoli (despite their respective governments' attempts to block the Internet) – speaks precisely to this promise. At the same time, in a global mediated space defined so intensely by contestation, visibility can easily become 'the source of a new and distinctive kind of *fragility*' (Thompson, 2005: 42; emphasis in original) – as illustrated by the Abu Ghraib and WikiLeaks cases. Furthermore, the sheer diversity of voices contesting each other in the global media space neither means, nor in any way guarantees, interaction and exchange of ideas, understanding or the enhancement of imagination. *Media Representation and the Global Imagination* seeks to engage with the ways in which the global imagination in the early twenty-first century is carried through contesting media representations, and to highlight the potential of this process as well as its limits and dangers.

Second, a key feature of the new form of mediated visibility is the development of 'mediated intimacy at a distance' (Thompson, 1995: 219): a form of mediated intimacy with others who do not share one's own spatial-temporal locale, and which does not involve the reciprocity of face-to-face interaction. This feature was already present in the 1940s, as evident in the promise to viewers of the DuMont advert that they would become 'intimate[s] of the great and near-great'. Another advert that was part of the same publicity campaign evokes intimacy even more explicitly, through the sexist message from American actress Betty Hutton, whose face on an image of a television screen is accompanied with the quote, addressed to the (imagined male) viewer, that 'I'll be practically in your lap . . .!' The rise of digital technologies and the growing importance of social media, interactive mediated and networked communicative forms, together with other broader cultural and political developments (e.g., the increasing centrality of the therapeutic narrative and psychological language in public discourse, the emphasis on personalization in such realms as politics and the workplace),[3] not only have created new ways for developing and expressing mediated intimacy, but have substantially *amplified* the importance of intimacy at a distance, as the fundamental and prime mode of relations to far-away people, events and experiences in the media. This is neatly captured by the 2010 Sky UK advert for its High Definition news channel whose slogan reads: 'Nothing Gets You Closer'. Beneath the caption is an image of a blonde woman wearing jeans, T-shirt and socks, viewed from behind, standing in a desert battlefield alongside a military aeroplane, looking at some soldiers (wearing uniforms of UK or US forces) on a military operation.

The differences between the Sky ad and its 1944 (DuMont) counterpart are telling. The medium, the technology, which in the 1944 DuMont ad is the television screen, does not appear in the 2010 ad. The viewer in the latter is a woman, whose representation is the same size as that of the mediated strangers (the soldiers) and who occupies with them a singular symbolic space – the desert battlefield. The viewer in the DuMont advert is clearly separate, and represented in miniature, compared to the huge screen and the events that extend from the screen. The slogan on the Sky ad reinforces a sense of intense proximity between viewer and distant other: its message is that the essence of accessing mediated representations is to get as close as possible to the far-away events and the far-away others. The image of a woman viewer gazing at male soldiers (signifying masculinity and hero-ism) heightens the centrality of intimacy in the ad, by alluding to its sexual connotations, which compound the emphasis on intimacy and closeness. Mediated intimacy is no longer articulated as an imaginary possibility ('as though you were on the spot', DuMont ad); it is 'real', it is fact: the viewer's comfort and safety zones and the distant others' danger zones merge to become one: 'Nothing gets you closer'. The centrality of mediated intimacy in today's media and imagination and its implications are at the heart of the book's exploration, specifically, how intimacy is articulated and enacted in the media representations' invitation to imagine the world, others and ourselves.

Significantly, the global mediated environment of the new visibility and its features of contestation and intimacy outlined above are not simply a structure or a context already fixed, against which this exploration of media representation is set. Rather, the new visibility describes a media environment that is constantly at work, and in which media representations are integral to its constant state of 'becoming'. Put differently, media represen-tations do not simply reflect the already existing process of globalization and the conditions of the new visibility; nor are they merely shaped by it – rather, they simultaneously shape and are constituted by this process.[4]

In undertaking an exploration of media representation and the global imagination, this book seeks to contribute to two key fields: research on media representation, and debate on globalization and the media.

Representations have been studied and explained predominantly in relation to national communities and/or their role in feeding collective and social identities, such as ethnicity, race, sexuality and gender. More recently, scholars have been looking systematically at media representations in a global context (e.g., Chouliaraki, 2006; Couldry, Hepp and Krotz, 2010; Machin and Van Leeuwen, 2007; Nash, 2008; Robertson, 2010) and the way they intersect and interact with local and national contexts and with dimensions of identity and difference. The book aims to advance this research strand, in accounting for the work of media representations as major cultural resources that nourish the global imagination. I argue that media representations cultivate an imaginary of the world as a common space peopled by strangers; they bring us closer, symbolically, to distant others and they propel the imagining of the possibility of pursuing alternative lives in a different place. Chapter 1 situates the book within the field of media representation research and discusses the traditions and paradigms that it builds on. It also highlights aspects that depart from the existing literature and the ways the book seeks to advance discussion in the field.

This book contributes also to research on media and globalization. Considerable discussion in this field has focused on how, and with what consequences, media and communication *technologies* have extended the *quantity* and *reach* of messages, the *velocity* of their transmission, and their *networked* character across the globe, particularly under the influence of the fundamental globalizing force of capitalism (e.g., Castells, 2001, 2009; Flew, 2007; Herman and McChesney, 2001; Schiller, 1999; Thompson, 1995). However, little attention has been paid to representations as texts, and to exploring how and whether media representations extend not only global reach, but also imagination and understanding. Silverstone (2007) adds a concrete question to the agenda: do the media provide us with tools and ways to think and make informed judgements about issues, people and places that we will likely know only through mediated representations? The stakes for addressing this question are high: we are increasingly dependent, often exclusively, on what we see, read and hear in the news, in our favourite television drama series, in advertisements, radio broadcasts and over the Internet. We rely on media representations to make sense of our lives and our world. They shape, inform and orient the way we see and judge the world, others and ourselves, and how we imagine real and possible lives.

However, as Silverstone (2007: 51) notes, 'in the mediated space of appearance we no longer need to, nor wish to, nor are for the most part capable of, doubt'. In other words, though media representations have a potentially huge power, and far-reaching consequences for our and others' lives, we tend to take them for granted. In our daily lives, for the most part, we do not pause to ponder media representations or to question their power. They function as a kind of 'background' to our social lives, in the sense that Heidegger and Wittgenstein refer to 'background'; the ongoing flow of mediated images, narratives and information that shape and inform a complex, unstructured and not fully articulated understanding of life and the world we live in. *Media Representation and the Global Imagination* seeks to help generate some doubt and provide the tools to develop critical under-standing of media representations. By doubt, I do not mean necessarily, and certainly not only, negative suspicions and criticism of representations; nor do I question whether representations are 'truthful' or 'accurate'. Rather, by generating doubt I mean achieving a degree of distance from the familiar, taken-for-granted images and stories encountered daily, in order to realize the crucial role that they play in describing the world, but also, fundamen-tally, in informing the way we regard, think, feel and make judgements about the world; the way we imagine people, places, cultures, habits and behaviours in today's age of new visibility.

Before outlining the book's structure, I want to add a note about its global perspective and its use of the notions of 'we' and 'today'. The book deals with media representations in the context of globalization and, there-fore, adopts a global perspective throughout, incorporating examples of media representations from different countries and cultures. While it is impossible fully or adequately to cover representations from all over the world, the intention is to demonstrate the significance of examining texts and images from various local, national and international contexts, and from across a range of discourses, media, genres, themes and forms. This emphasis is a response to the growing technological convergence and the increased blurring of the boundaries between different media, public and private, information and entertainment, which have been accelerated by the expansion of new media technologies, specifically the Internet and mobile communication. The emphasis on the meaning of media representations in a global context and the need to study them across technologies, genres and themes, is aimed also at tackling what I regard as the main weaknesses of current studies of media representations, namely, that they are 'stuck in time' and highly compartmentalized, issues I discuss in chapter 1.

However, although the book stresses a global perspective, the 'average reader' and the 'we' in this book refer generally to people living in stable societies. As Cohen (2001: xiv) notes in the preface to his book, 'we are the objects of some chapters; but mostly we gaze at distant others in poor, unstable and violent places'. In part, what I discuss as occurring within the current media environment is that this ethnocentric, largely western 'we' is changing, specifically because groups and individuals who previously were excluded from the public media space are gaining visibility and voice, a process which is calling into question the symbolic frontiers between 'us' and 'them'. Nevertheless, the book was written in London, UK, and although I tried to engage with a range of representations from across the world, I cannot completely avoid the imprint of my geographic, cultural, political and theoretical locations.

If the use of 'we' locates my account in terms of place, the word 'today', which I use repeatedly, locates the book's exploration in terms of time. In this book, 'today' is used to draw attention to a period of high media visibility that has been significantly transformed since the rise of the Internet and networked technologies. It is impossible – and unhelpful – to point to a particular year or even a particular decade as the beginning of this age, since many of the phenomena that we are witnessing in the second decade of the twenty-first century, and that are discussed throughout this book, represent the continuation of a process that was set in motion in much earlier decades and centuries. However, in other respects the work of media representation that is explored in this book represents a new departure, situated predominantly in the last decade of the twentieth century and the first decade of the twenty-first century. When I talk about representations 'today', I mean particularly to invoke Thompson's (2005) discussion of the new visibility, in order to refer to a mediated environment that is more intensive, more extensive and less controllable than in the past.

Structure of the Book

Following this Introduction, chapter 1 reviews the central premises and concerns of research on media representations. The chapter discusses key theoretical traditions and approaches in studies of media representations, and highlights aspects in the literature that are particularly relevant to the current global media environment. I reflect in chapter 1 on the challenges and tensions in the field of media representation studies, and conclude by introducing global imagination as a concept that could be used to address some of these challenges and to account for the work of contemporary media representations. Chapter 1 establishes the theoretical and conceptual framework for the book's exploration of the ways that contemporary media representations cultivate a global imagination.

Based on this theoretical exposition and critique of the research field, I develop the argument that the main work of media representations today is the cultivation of global imagination, through the construction of particular explanatory frameworks and scripts about the world, about ourselves and about the place of others in it. Those explanatory scripts are proposals, which, if recognized, accepted or rejected, inform and orient the way we see and judge others and the way we see ourselves. I suggest that global imagination crystallizes around five particular sites, which are closely inter-related and often overlap: imagining others; imagining ourselves; imagining possible lives; imagining the world; and imagining the self. This distinction is helpful for analysing the operation of media representations and how, by virtue of them, global imagination is developed.

Chapters 2 to 6 explore some of the scripts and imaginaries that are offered at each of these sites, and how they are constructed for people to draw on in imagining their lives, imagining others and the worlds they live in. Each of the succeeding chapters centres on one site of imagination and uses a particular thematic focus to illustrate and elucidate a broader argument about the work of representations in nourishing the global imagination.

The thematic focus of each chapter and the specific examples used help to bound the discussion empirically and provide an opportunity to practise the skills of analysis, which can be applied to other instances and cases. For example, the discussion in chapter 2 focuses on the representation of natu-ral disasters, but it discusses concepts, ideas and analytical tools that relate more broadly to media representation of distant others. The intention is to provide the reader with tools that can be applied to analysing the represen-tation of sufferers in similar and other contexts, as well as to analysis of rep-resentation of other types of 'distant others', for example, migrants. In each chapter of the book I develop also a broader theoretical proposition about the work of representation: a claim about the practice of representation, the possibilities that it creates and at the same time closes down, in nourishing a global imagination.

Chapter 2 explores central scripts on distant 'others' that are available in today's media space. To interrogate and illustrate how distant others are constructed in the global media, the discussion focuses on the representation of natural disasters. We tend to think of the visibility of natural disasters in the media and the response it engenders, as distinct features of our times. Chapter 2 challenges this view by starting the analysis with a discussion of representation of the first global media disaster event: the 1755 earthquake in Lisbon, Portugal. Set against the eighteenth-century representations of this event, we examine representations of recent natural disasters: the 1985 televised 'We Are The World' video clip and song in response to the 1980s famine in the Horn of Africa, and Ethiopia in particular, and the remake of this song and clip in 2010, distributed on YouTube and other digital platforms, in response to the earthquake in Haiti. A detailed analysis of these three case studies provides an opportunity to evaluate the continuities and changes in the imagining of distant others and to highlight the tensions invoked by media representations' construction of others – tensions that are developed further in subsequent chapters.

Chapter 3 turns the gaze on 'ourselves' as the site of imagination and, specifically, the ways that contemporary media representations construct, deconstruct and reconstruct the nation as a symbolic category of belonging. Using the example of the representation of the 2005 urban riots in France, the discussion examines how representations of national conflict are produced, disseminated and consumed in a changing context of 'the new visibility' (Thompson, 2005) and highlights the contesting ways of imagining the nation that the global media encourage. The chapter theorizes this contestation as an axis between two modes of relation to ourselves as the nation: at one end of this axis is attachment and at the other is estrangement. The analysis explores the work of national, transnational and global media representations in symbolically producing, reproducing and reinforcing conflicting positions along this axis. Chapters 2 and 3 are complementary in advancing our understanding of the ways in which contemporary representations inform, guide and concurrently orient us – to the other and to ourselves.

In contrast to the representations of past and present in chapters 2 and 3, chapter 4 focuses on imagination of life in the future: on the pursuit of 'possible lives'. Drawing closely on Appadurai's (1996) account of mass media, migration and the force of imagination, chapter 4 explores some central scripts on migration that are offered by media representation and constitute a springboard for people's imaginings of how they or their children might live and work in places other than their place of birth. I investigate what the 'store of possible lives' (Appadurai, 1996) consists of and what frames of understanding are proposed by media representations of migration. The analysis in chapter 4 shows that although mediated discourses on migration are largely polarized between 'dream' and 'nightmare' scenarios, there is room for more ambivalent representations within this field, which can be opened up and enabled especially by new media platforms. The final part of the chapter examines an example of a mediated site that allows more ambivalent, incomplete and potentially complex imaginings of possible (and impossible) lives.

How the world we live in is imagined and how viewers are called to imagine it in current representations is a question that runs as a thread throughout the book, and on which chapters 2 to 4 reflect from different angles. Chapter 5 takes representations of the world as its explicit focus and examines a particular instance of the world as it appears on our mediated screens: that of New Year celebrations. New Year celebrations constitute a media event that constructs a particular understanding of what the world is. The chapter analyses the production of 'geographical knowledges' (Harvey, 2001) in the construction of 'the world' in international news broadcast reporting of Christian New Year celebrations. It shows how this media event reinforces a celebratory account of the world as united around sameness, occupied by similar people in similar spaces, and joined by the same ritual and by reverence for the spectacle. At the same time, this image of the world, which is constitutive of the global imagination, simultaneously contains and enacts that which it wants to exclude: it promotes competition as the primary relation through which people, cities and countries interact with each other, establishes symbolic exclusions, and emphasizes hierarchies. Following this exploration, the chapter investigates representations of New Year that may be seen to offer different 'cartographic consciousnesses' (Harvey, 2001) of the world.

Chapter 6 is concerned with the centrality of the self in media representations and, inextricably, in the global imagination. The self has come to constitute a primary site for the cultivation of a global imagination and chapter 6 explores articulations of this and considers their implications. Chapter 6 is different from the preceding chapters in that it does not explore the theoretical subject of imagining the self by analysing one particular theme of representation, but rather analyses four 'mini-cases' of representations of self that correspond to the four sites of global imagining explored in chapters 2 to 5. It shows how imaginings of the other, ourselves as the nation, possible lives and the world, are produced symbolically by focusing on the self and, in turn, how calling us to imagine these sites renders the self the object of the imagination. Many of the issues and tensions discussed in chapters 2 to 5 converge in the discussion in chapter 6, which leads to the book's conclusion.

Chapter 7 is the conclusion to this book and draws together the various strands to provide a critical summary of the work done by contemporary media representation to nourish a global imagination. In light of the arguments developed in chapters 1 to 6, chapter 7 also reflects on the qualities and characteristics that may be seen as desirable for media representations in the future, in order to enhance collective and individual imaginations that are more complex, more ambivalent and more relevant to the 'modern liquid world' (Bauman, 2010) and the 'liquid times' (Bauman, 2007) in which we live.

All the chapters in this book employ an interpretative qualitative method of analysis that is inspired by Critical Discourse Analysis and visual analysis. The specific theoretical and methodological traditions of media representations research that inform the analysis are discussed in chapter 1. The formats and styles of analysis in the chapters in this book are deliberately different; they exemplify different ways of analysing media representations. Chapter 2 examines representations of three global media events of natural disasters from a historical perspective. Chapter 3 is based on the analysis of a case study (representations of the 2005 French riots). Chapter 4 identifies three types of 'scripts' of migration – 'dreams', 'nightmares' and 'ambivalence' – by examining a considerable range of representations across different countries, media, platforms, genres and contexts. Chapter 5 focuses on a specific media event – New Year celebrations – first analysing one broadcast news report in depth to illuminate the production of geographical knowledges in a particular representation of the world, and then examining three international and new media representations of the same event. Chapter 6 (as described above) is structured as an analysis of four mini-case studies, each focusing on a particular example related to the broader sites explored in chapters 2 to 5. Chapters 2 to 6 are all empirical insofar as the argument they make is grounded in particular examples. The selected examples do not claim to articulate an eternal truth or to be 'universal', but nor are they totally arbitrary:[5] they exemplify and shed light on broader, more general characteristics and patterns of contemporary representations, discourses and explanatory and imaginary frameworks that circulate in the media space.

Hall's (1997:9) reminder provides a helpful setting for the reader in engaging with the analyses presented in this book:

> It is worth emphasising that there is no single or 'correct' answer to the question, 'What does this image mean?' or 'What is this ad saying?' Since there is no law which can guarantee that things will have 'one, true meaning', or that meaning won't change over time, work in this area is bound to be interpretative – a debate between, not who is 'right' and who is 'wrong', but between equally plausible, though sometimes competing and contesting, meanings and interpretations. The best way to 'settle' such contested readings is to look again at the concrete example and try to justify one's 'reading' in detail in relation to the actual practices and forms of signification used, and what meanings they seem to you to be producing.

I do not suggest that my analysis of representations in the following chapters is 'correct' and that the meanings that I argue are generated are 'true'. The book is intended to open up and invite contested readings of the media representations it discusses, and of the many other representations encountered in our daily lives.

1 Media Representation and the Global Imagination
A Framework

This book argues that in today's global age, to understand media representation we have to include in our study two key concepts, namely, globalization and imagination.

Representation plays a central role in constituting and framing the experience of globalization, the symbolic stretching of social relations across time and distance. Concurrently, media representations increasingly are dependent on and determined by the networking of different social contexts and regions on a global scale. However, there has been little theoretical and empirical attention paid to the link between representation and globalization. Media representations have been studied and understood largely and sometimes exclusively in relation to national contexts. A central strand of research focuses on how the meanings of the texts and images that circulate in the media rely on, negotiate and/or reproduce national frameworks of understanding, memories, narratives, ideas, stereotypes and symbols. In that research, the significance of representations is theorized primarily in relation to national identity and culture. Another strand focuses on the significance of representations for other identity dimensions, such as gender, sexuality, ethnicity, class, or in relation to units and communities of belonging beyond the nation, for instance, consumer culture, which is not bounded nationally. Nevertheless, many of these accounts suffer from 'methodological nationalism' (Beck, 2003): their analysis of the meanings of media texts and images is informed by an implicit assumption that the nation is the primary social and political form in the modern world. Even when the analysis draws on empirical examples from across the globe, it tends to privilege the nation-state and national identity in explaining their meanings.

However, in an age of accelerating globalization, driven by economic, political, cultural and technological forces, the national is no longer the only or necessarily the dominant context within which representations are produced, disseminated and consumed, and within which they acquire meaning. Globalization is transforming social interaction and communication in radical ways (Thompson, 1995). These transformations substantially shape and are shaped by representation – the process of producing meanings through the creation of symbolic forms and content. Thus, studying

15

media representation demands that the analysis accounts for the complex nature and consequences of interactions and communication in the context of globalization. Chapter 1 seeks to establish the foundations for this project by bringing together and offering links between key debates and concepts in the field of media representation research and theories of globalization as a social process and a cultural phenomenon.

A second concept, which I would argue is vital for producing an analysis appropriate for understanding the work of media representation in the twenty-first century, is that of imagination. Drawing on Appadurai's (1996) account of imagination as a key dimension in the experience of globalization, and on Taylor's (2002) and Castoriadis's (1987 [1975]) philosophical discussions of the concepts of imagination and the imaginary, imagination is offered here as a way to help address what are perhaps the most difficult questions for research on media representations (and media more generally), that is, how to understand the power of media representations, and where this power is located. While central approaches and traditions in the study of representation provide some compelling accounts that seek to address these questions, they concurrently produce some tensions and difficult problems, especially in relation to explanations of the power and impact of representations. The concept of imagination does not provide a 'fix' for these tensions; however, I argue that it can be instrumental in theorizing the power of media representations in today's global age.

Thus, this chapter sets out to establish a conceptual triangle in which representation, globalization and imagination become the framework for the exploration in this book. The discussion begins with the object of this study, representation. Section I provides a 'map' of some of the central ways in which representation has been theorized and studied. The literature on representation is reviewed in light of three questions: what are media representations; what work do they do; and why do they matter? I am interested in particular in highlighting the relevance and value of existing accounts for exploring media representation in connection with globalization. Section II discusses some challenges and tensions in the field of media representation studies, specifically those that arise when existing theorizations seem insufficient to account for and offer tools to understand media representations in the current media environment. This critique forms the basis for the discussion in Section III, which introduces imagination as a concept that could help to address some of these challenges. In particular, the concept of global imagination is proposed as a framework to account for the work of media representations and inform their analysis. The theoretical discussion in this chapter informs the succeeding chapters and is intended to provoke broader critical thought on the subject of this book.

I Premises

This section provides an overview of some of the central 'stories' in research on media representations. It provides a selective map of some key accounts, organized around three questions, on which the discussion in the literature centres: (1) what are media representations? (2) what work do media representations do (what do they accomplish)? and (3) why do media representations matter? The answers to these questions vary and rest on diverse and conflicting epistemological, theoretical and analytical premises. The point is not to argue that one account is better or more 'truthful' than another, nor to suggest that we should somehow integrate all approaches and reconcile the tensions that are evoked by their juxtaposition. Rather, the purpose is to provide an account of the central ideas and claims that inform the research on media representations on which this book draws. I highlight the relevance and utility of certain well-established theories and concepts for exploring the 'work' of media representations in the contemporary global media environment, as well as pointing to some of their limits.

What are media representations?

Representations are images, descriptions, explanations and frames for understanding what the world is and why and how it works in particular ways (Hall, 1997). Of course, cultural representations have a long history and can be seen in the form of totemic objects created by religious societies as projections of their values and beliefs. In broad terms, any object, for example, a building, an item of clothing, an artefact, can be seen as a representation that carries meanings beyond its immediate function and use. What distinguishes media representations from these other representational objects is that their essence is to represent. In other words, their main function is to produce meaning, to capture in some way 'reality' in signs.

When we talk about media representations we are referring to *texts* (in the broad sense, which includes images) that circulate in the media space and carry symbolic content: news photographs and articles, advertisements, radio programmes, YouTube videos, blogs, Facebook pages, etc. 'Representation' refers to the *process* of re-presenting, the process by which members of a culture use systems of signs to produce meaning. This highlights that representation is an active process of meaning production, the products of which are media representations, that is, texts and images. The study of media representations brings together these two meanings: it centres on analysing representations as *texts*, by looking at their textual, auditory, visual and discursive properties, in order to establish a better understanding of the 'work' (Hall, 1997) that they do, that is, the *process* of producing meaning.

What 'work' do media representations do?

The process of meaning production through signs has been theorized in two main ways: the reflectionist (or mimetic) approach, and the constructionist (or constructivist) approach. Both approaches are underpinned by a radically different view of the relationship between the thing that is being represented – 'reality', and the act of representing it – or representation. Consequently, how they conceive the 'work' of media representations and their approach to how it should be studied and evaluated are also substantially different.

The reflectionist approach

Rooted in the Greek and Renaissance legacies, the key idea of the reflectionist approach is of mimesis, the notion that language (and by extension any medium of representation, e.g., photography) functions like a mirror that reflects true meaning as it already exists in the world (Hall, 1997: 24). The reflectionist approach assumes that reality is accessible through representation, thus the task of representation is adequately to reflect pre-existing meanings of 'the real'.

This approach is epitomized by the notion of the historical truth value of photography: the idea of a photograph as 'proof' that something *really* happened, and belief, which runs deep in modern thinking, in the photograph as an inherently objective medium of representation. A notion of the media as reflecting reality is perpetuated in popular discourse, policy and political debate. The media themselves repeatedly endorse a reflectionist claim, as manifest, for example, in the title of the UK newspaper *Daily Mirror*, or in news outlets' slogans that describe their commitment to current readers – providing 'the whole picture' (1986 *Guardian* campaign),[1] or 'hunting down the news and beating the truth out of it' (UK Channel 4's *10 O'clock News* campaign, February 2011). Media professionals, especially those working in the news, largely endorse the reflectionist view. Schlesinger (1987 [1978]) shows that news professionals have a deep-seated belief in their capacity to achieve impartiality and reflect the truth, a belief informed by the pluralist idea that one can present different points of view and achieve an accurate (reflective) representation of the range of voices and opinions in society.

The media landscape has changed dramatically since Schlesinger's late 1970s study, and both media consumers and producers are increasingly aware of the problematic nature of the notion of representation as reflection. In particular, the ability to access representations originating from different sources and places (e.g., by watching reports of events on different national and international news channels and on the Internet) highlights the simple but fundamental point that representations never simply mirror reality (otherwise representations of the same happening would be identical). Nevertheless, a reflectionist belief remains central to the thinking, discourse and practice of news. For example, in 2006, following a report by the gay rights group, Stonewall, accusing the BBC of having a 'derisive and demeaning' attitude towards gay people and rarely referring to lesbians, the BBC responded (emphasis added): 'We are committed to finding ways of *reflecting* the audience's daily lives in our programmes' (Brook, 28 February, 2006). Similarly, in a panel discussion on reporting of the 2008/9 Gaza War, journalists from Al Jazeera, BBC and the UK's Channel 4, admitting the difficulties of achieving objectivity and balance in war reporting notwithstanding, unanimously reiterated a view of their objective as of 'seeking the truth'.[2]

Much of the critique of media representations is similarly underpinned by the idea that the task of representation is to *reflect* reality. Various media monitoring projects (e.g., Global Media Monitoring, Media Monitoring Africa, Media Monitors Network) and research by national media regulatory bodies frequently are premised on the idea that the media should somehow mirror the society on which they report. They include criticisms along the lines that 'mainstream media fail to reflect social diversity existing in the communities they serve and target' (Media Diversity Institute, 2008: 2), 'television . . . fails to accurately reflect the world in which young people live' (Children Now, 2009), 'television fails to reflect the multicultural nature of Britain' (Sreberny, 1999). Similar rhetoric, predicated on the notion that the media's role and responsibility is to reflect their society, is exploited repeatedly by politicians. For instance, in a letter criticizing the media in South Africa, the country's President Jacob Zuma (2010; emphasis added) writes:

> The starting point is that media owners and media practitioners cannot claim that this institution is totally snow white and without fault. They cannot claim that the media products we have in our country today, *adequately reflect* the lives and aspirations of all South Africans, especially the poor.
>
> Can a guardian be a proper guardian when it *does not reflect the society it claims to protect and represent*?

In a world marked by the 'stretching' of time and space, in which information flows speedily across the continents, and in which knowledge of the world depends, often exclusively, on mediated symbolic content, the task of accurately reflecting reality becomes ever more fundamental. In the 'liquid times' (Bauman, 2007) in which we live, times characterized by uncertainty, the value of representation as a record of the truth which shows how things *really* are, is ever more crucial. Representation is a vital source of reassurance and a sense of certainty. But it is precisely the 'liquidness' of the global age that renders the reflectionist task of representation so challenging and problematic, if not impossible. In the global, highly competitive and porous media environment of the twenty-first century, representations can no longer be claimed to unproblematically reflect reality, since these representations are themselves a source of uncertainty, confusion and anxiety. This is perhaps most manifest in developments in digital photography and the increasingly accessible, affordable and easy-to-use image-altering software, both of which have substantially undermined the mimetic value of photographs. Cases of photos being manipulated and used as hoaxes are more frequent (memorable examples include *National Geographic* 2001 Photo of the Year of the 'Helicopter Shark', and the Reuters' photo of a scene from the July 2006 Lebanon War where plumes of smoke were enhanced to exaggerate the destruction wrought by Israeli forces). Such manipulated representations, which can be spread swiftly across the world via the Internet, satellite channels and mobile media, not only question the credibility of photographic evidence, but also cast doubt on the notion of representation as reflection more broadly. Thus, while representations may be central resources that people draw on, and which endow a degree of certainty and reassurance in their lives, at the same time they are characterized increasingly by a lack of fixity, and constitute a source of liquidness, uncertainty and anxiety. This tension is developed in the chapters in this book, and reflected upon in the final chapter.

The constructionist approach

While the reflectionist approach continues to inform and underpin the study of media representations and debates over their function and role, at the same time the idea of representation mirroring reality is the subject of ongoing critique. The constructionist approach points to the naivety of the idea of representation as a mirror; any representation, it argues, is inherently and inevitably a construction, a selective and particular depiction of some elements of reality, which always generates some specific meanings and excludes others. This view is premised on the recognition that signification systems play a central part in producing meaning:

we give things meaning by how we *represent* them – the words we use about them, the stories we tell about them, the images of them we produce, the emotions we associate with them, the ways we classify and conceptualize them, the value we place on them. (Hall, 1997: 3, emphasis in original)

The notion that representation is an act of construction is rooted in several theoretical traditions which have been discussed extensively in the literature (Gillespie and Toynbee, 2006; Hall, 1997; Lacey, 2009; Macdonald, 2003) and which I do not propose to rehearse here. I would highlight, however, the contribution of semiotics, structuralism and post-structuralism for analysing media representations, with particular mind to their application in a global context.

Semiotics and structuralism

Semiotics is based largely on the work of the linguist Ferdinand de Saussure (1974), who established that language is a system of signs. Saussure distinguishes between two elements of a sign: signifier and signified. The signifier refers to the word or image and is correlated to the signified, which refers to its mental concept. The signifier 'triggers off' the signified in our heads (Hall, 1997: 31). The relationship between these two elements is arbitrary; hence the same concept has different signifiers in different languages, that is, the same thing has different names in different languages. Furthermore, the relation between signifier and signified is not permanently fixed. Hall (1997: 32) gives the example of the word (signifier) *black*, which for centuries was associated with 'everything that is dark, evil, forbidding, devilish, dangerous and sinful'. In the 1960s, in America, the popular slogan 'Black is Beautiful' changed the connotations of the word, and *black* has come to signify the attractive, 'cool' and desirable.

Saussure contends that the marking of difference within language is fundamental to the production of meaning. Signs do not convey a fixed meaning; their meaning is produced as the difference between one sign and another. Signs, Saussure (cited in Hall, 1997: 31) argues, 'are members of a system and are defined in relation to other members of that system'. This aspect of representation seems even more salient in the contemporary global age where, primarily through media representations, we continuously encounter an ever-growing range of strangers, signified in text, image and sound as 'others', whose existence is constructed as in some way relevant to ours. The media continuously produce differences between 'us' and 'them', 'here' and 'there', through the act of representing. While Saussure was writing many years before the emergence of today's intensely mediated global environment, his theorization of the crucial link between language and difference is central to the work of media representations in contemporary times.

Semiotics consolidated the recognition that meaning is not immanent in objects, people or things, but rather is produced by systems of signification – textual, visual and/or auditory. In this context, the work of the French semiotician Roland Barthes (1977) has been immensely influential, and particularly his distinction between denotation and connotation. *Denotation* refers to a simple, basic, mostly literal or descriptive level, where there is a (relatively) value-free relationship between sign and referent. The journalistic photograph, for instance, has a strong denotative level: it is an imitative medium and its message is analogous to the referent (the thing that it represents): it appears as if a record of reality. *Connotation* refers to the level at which signs are interpreted in terms of the wider realm of social ideology; the general beliefs, conceptual frameworks and value systems of society that are evoked by the message and drawn on to decode it. For example, Barthes (1977: 15) shows how the same photograph (same denotation) can completely change in terms of its meaning (connotation) when reproduced in a communist newspaper. The titles of the publications carrying the photograph, Barthes (1977: 15) argues, 'can heavily orientate the reading of the message'.

Related to the concept of connotation is the idea that any particular representation is only meaningful within a specific cultural setting. Representations draw on certain cultural repertoires of symbols, narratives, codes and conventions, which, in turn, they reproduce and transform. For example, one may encounter a media representation, clearly intended to be humorous (e.g., a funny advert, a joke, a satirical programme), but which does not make one laugh because one does not have the cultural knowledge required to decode it. Thus, representations mark boundaries, not only in constructing certain people, certain places, ideas and cultures in terms of 'us' and 'them', 'good' and 'bad', and so on, but also in appropriating and reproducing certain frameworks, symbols and ways of understanding that are intelligible to particular groups or cultures and unintelligible to others.

However, the current age of globalization is characterized by escalating interaction between cultures and traditions, and by representations travelling across cultures and crossing boundaries. Stories and images circulate rapidly and with ease across large distances, and address audiences in different geographical, cultural and political contexts. Consequently, the same image, shown in different places around the world, will likely have different, sometimes quite fundamentally different, connotations.

A vivid example is the controversy around the Muhammad cartoons, originally published in September 2005 by the Danish newspaper

Jyllands-Posten and later reproduced in a large number of European and international media outlets. The controversy, which generated heated debate in the global media and led to a series of protests across the Islamic world, derived from the contesting interpretations of the cartoons, that is, from the different meanings, or connotations, that the same image (denotation) generated among different groups and cultures. As the case of the Muhammad cartoons illustrates so vividly, a central question concerning the significance of media representations in our global age is what happens when signifiers that originate in a particular culture and context diffuse across cultures, audiences and locales – a question that is investigated in this book, especially in chapter 3.

Post-structuralism

Post-structuralism insists that rather than reflecting reality, the work of media representations is the production and construction of understandings of the world, identities and subjectivities. This argument differs from other constructionist arguments in that it refutes the idea of a 'truth' or 'reality' 'out there': representations are not constructions of pre-existing reality, but a series of signs and symbols that pretend to stand for so-called reality.

Within this tradition, the works of Derrida and Baudrillard have been particularly influential in research on media representations. Building on semiotics, Derrida underscores that meaning can be deferred endlessly: 'meaning is never single, univocal or total, but rather is fluid, ambiguous and contradictory' (Gill, 2007: 13). Meaning is a site of constant struggle and contestation – it resists fixity. The current global media environment can be considered the epitome of a symbolic space of contestation, which makes lack of fixity of meaning more apparent and central. For example, after Hurricane Katrina hit in 2005, an Associated Press report showed a young black evacuee wading through flood water, described as 'looting a grocery store in New Orleans'. By contrast, in an Agence France-Presse report, two white people, also wading through flood water, are described as 'finding bread and soda from a local grocery' (Media Awareness Network, 2010). These two reports were juxtaposed in an online posting (Media Awareness Network, 2010) and provoked heated discussion about how racial stereotypes and judgements are incorporated into journalistic accounts, supposedly 'reflecting' the 'truth', and about how this symbolic inequality is linked to material, social and cultural inequalities in the US.

However, fully endorsing the post-structuralist argument runs the risk of regarding meaning as totally open and being endlessly deferred. If we accept that, as viewers, all we can do is gain access to multiple 'truths' that struggle for supremacy, then how can we recognize negative as opposed to positive representations, or hold responsible storytellers who represent issues in certain ways? As Macdonald (2003: 15) points out, claiming that it is impossible to evaluate the validity of specific media constructions inevitably depoliticizes the process of representation; it thwarts the analyst's impulse to seek the source of power in, and responsibility for, representation.

The notion that we cannot posit a link between representation and reality is akin to Baudrillard's idea of simulation: 'Baudrillard's concept of simulacrum removes the possibility of sign systems referring to anything other than further sign systems . . . Signs refer us to other signs, until the relation of these to the world beyond diminishes to vanishing point' (Macdonald, 2003: 15). Baudrillard's (1995) account *The Gulf War Did Not Take Place* is predicated on the idea that signs are autonomous of any system of reference, and bear little connection to everyday life. The spectacle of the war gives human misery and suffering the appearance of unreality: most of the decisions in the war were based on perceived intelligence coming from maps, images and news, rather than from actual witness-based intelligence (Baudrillard, 1995). The first Gulf War was represented on television screens as spectacle; the human misery and suffering appeared unreal. There were no depictions of hand-to-hand combat; no accounts and images on the ground. From the US point of view, Baudrillard contends, accident played no part in that war; everything unfolded according to a programmed order with the result that we saw 'a masquerade of information: branded faces delivered over to the prostitution of the image, the image of an unintelligible distress' (Baudrillard, 1995: 40). In other words, we saw not a representation of the Gulf War, nor even an approximate construction of its features, but rather a simulation of signs that bore no relation to the reality of the first Gulf War (Macdonald, 2003: 15).

The proliferation of new media across the globe and the networked character of the media today may be beginning to challenge Baudrillard's argument. At the time of writing this chapter, images of protests in Egypt against Hosni Mubarak's thirty-year regime were being broadcast live across the world, on the Internet and television. Despite attempts to block social media sites in Egypt and other countries (e.g., China), protesters' accounts get through, allowing audiences almost immediate access to events miles away. These images are radically different from Baudrillard's simulated, controlled and sanitized images of the Gulf War: they provide first-hand accounts and live images of the suffering, struggle and distress of people on the ground. Yet there is a paradox in the hyper-mediation of these images: the flood of circulating images, Baudrillard would argue, creates a sense of 'hyper-reality', a spectacle of violence and suffering. When war is 'turned into information, it ceases to be a realistic war and becomes a virtual war'

(Baudrillard, 1995: 41), and so 'the closer we approach the real time of the event, the more we fall into the illusion of the virtual' (Baudrillard, 1995: 49).

Despite this and other challenges, post-structuralism forcefully highlights the immense power of representation, and underscores that representation is not an annex to reality, but is its essence. Thus, though we may not fully embrace a post-structuralist approach, it makes two very helpful contributions to the discussion in this book. First, it points to our huge reliance on representations for making sense of the world we live in. How we understand and experience 'the world' is inseparable from its construction in images and stories. Second, the post-structuralist view destabilizes conventional notions of meaning (Gill, 2007: 12): it insists on fluidity, openness and co-constitution (through signs) of meaning, identities and subjectivities – aspects which are explored in this book, culminating in a discussion of representations of the self in chapter 6.

Notwithstanding the substantial theoretical, epistemological and methodological differences among the strands of the constructionist approach, they all contribute to establishing and confirming the idea of representation as construction. The constructivist approach is not concerned with how representations reflect or fail to reflect reality, but how they create meaning and compete over its construction.

Why do media representations matter?

Perhaps the major contribution of the rich body of research on media representations is its insistence that all representation is fundamentally and inextricably inscribed in relations of power. Power relations are encoded in media representations, and media representations in turn produce and reproduce power relations by constructing knowledge, values, conceptions and beliefs. It is for these reasons that representations matter. Most research on media representations is interested in the ways in which different types of media representation are involved, often in subtle, latent and highly sophisticated ways, in the reproduction and/or contestation of power relations and inequalities, for example, of class, gender, race, sexuality, ethnicity, age and nationality.

Conception of where power resides and the consequences of that power differs greatly in different approaches. I offer three brief theoretical accounts that highlight the embedded relation of representation in power relations. The first concerns representation and ideology, the second is Foucault's theory of discourse and power/knowledge, and the third concerns the representation of difference and the other. Rather than offering an exhaustive account of the huge body of research on representation and power, the discussion below is selective and interested. It seeks to provide a theoretical background and to highlight key concepts and questions that seem particularly useful for the discussion in the following chapters.

Representation and ideology

Thompson (1984: 5) defines ideology as 'the ways in which meaning is mobilized for the maintenance of relations of domination'. The study of the operation of ideology in and through representation is rooted in a long tradition of Marxist scholarship, at the heart of which is 'the wish to understand how it is that social relations based on domination, antagonism and injustice come to be seen as natural, inevitable and even desirable by those who benefit least from them' (Gill, 2007: 54).

In this tradition of ideological critique, Gramsci's work has been particularly influential. Gramsci contends that ideology is driven by a desire to establish a particular frame of thinking as the most powerful, most valid, or 'the truth' (Macdonald, 2003: 28). This is achieved by creating hegemony: the process through which a group or a party is able to claim social, political and cultural leadership of a society. Hegemony is not forced; rather, it relies on winning approval or consent based on *common sense*. Ideology operates through the production, legitimization and sustenance of common sense: taken-for-granted, self-evident truths, which are often accepted uncritically. It works discursively by constructing subjects, and producing discursive positions and identities to occupy. The remaking of subjectivities is a central part of winning consent and achieving hegemony (Gill, 2007).

A classic example of an ideological analysis that draws on these ideas is Dorfman and Mattelart's (1975) study *How to Read Donald Duck: Imperialist Ideology in the Disney Comic*. Along fairly typical Marxist lines, the authors aim to demonstrate the imperialist nature of the values 'concealed' behind the seemingly innocent outlook of Walt Disney's cultural representations. The Disney comic, they argue, is a powerful ideological tool of American imperialism, precisely because it is presented as naive, harmless entertainment for consumption by children (a claim later developed by Giroux, 2001). Dorfman and Mattelart offer an 'oppositional reading' of Disney that seeks to attack this veneer of innocence, in order to unveil the underlying ideological assumptions that inform Disney stories and naturalize and normalize the social relations of western capitalism (Tomlinson, 1991).

However, the current fragmented culture and media environment in which different and often conflicting voices and views circulate, is challenging this type of ideological critique of media representation. How can we establish which frames of thinking are dominant when media representations seem to offer such a huge variety of competing ideological positions, often in ironic and playful ways (Macdonald, 2003)? To understand representations of Disney, for instance, we would need to analyse not just Disney's films and cultural products, but also the numerous responses to them, including 'spoofs' and subversive representations. This makes it difficult, if not impossible, to argue that there are certain pervasive ideologies that are produced and disseminated in particular sites of meaning. Furthermore, ideological analysis begins with a specific concern, for example, gender, race or capitalism, and works back through the evidence of media representations to demonstrate the operation of the ideology at stake (Macdonald, 2003: 2). However, the current fashion in which media representations are produced, circulated and consumed is characterized by the blurring of boundaries and concerns, and by the proliferation of contesting points of view, which suggest that the divisions dictated by ideological analysis should be broken down.

Despite these and other critiques of ideological analysis,[3] it offers a valuable perspective and tools for evaluation of the power of media representations. In particular, it highlights that the power of representations to shape ideas and ways of thinking is not coercive – we are not forced to think in certain ways, representations do not determine our thinking. Rather, representations appeal to our desires, fantasies and self-interest. They shape our imagination in a subtle, ongoing, cumulative fashion. Ideological critique reminds us also that because hegemony needs to be won and requires approval, it is always temporary and contested (Gill, 2007). Thus, it foregrounds concern over representation as a process of contestation (which, however, is not to say that structural inequalities disappear) – a concern extremely salient for the study of representation in the global age.

Foucault's discourse, power/knowledge

Foucault offers a more dispersed and volatile model of the operation of power through symbolic forms, by insisting that power does not, as ideological critique would have it, operate only through repression (Macdonald, 2003). Foucault focuses on discourse as the site of political conflict. He regards discourse as knowledge: the product of specific social, historical, institutional and political conditions that render certain statements truthful and meaningful, and others false, marginalized and deviant. Discourse, Foucault argues, is what produces knowledge; it is not a medium or tool for expressing or communicating already-formed knowledge. Although Foucault refers to discourse, not representation, his theory suggests that the act of representation – producing meaning through text and image – itself transforms power relations and subjectivities and the way we experience and define ourselves. In short, that representation is constitutive of power.

At the same time, Foucault argues that bringing things into the realm of discourse works also to inscribe them in hegemonic structures and to produce self-monitoring bodies that willingly submit to and, thus, help to create and legitimate the authority of experts. On the one hand, therefore, media texts and images play a transformative, enabling role, in challenging and altering power relations. They are the sites of struggles over power relations, where challenges to dominant power relations are articulated and exercised. On the other hand, media representations work to legitimize certain discourses, and inscribe them in the mainstream, the acceptable, the legitimate. Bringing things to the realm of discourse, that is, sounding them out or publishing them on television, radio, in the newspaper or on the Internet, affirms them in the realm of the 'said'. Therefore, Foucault insists that models that assume a binary opposition between 'dominant' and 'alternative' discourse are unhelpful insofar as they simplify the unpredictability of the ongoing contest over power (Macdonald, 2003). The same representation, for example, can be both liberating and oppressive, as demonstrated by various cases examined in this book.

For Foucault, 'the question is not whether discourse is truthful but "how effects of truths are produced within discourses which in themselves are neither true nor false" (Gordon, 1980: 118)' (Macdonald, 2003: 18). Thus, Foucault's approach to discourse suggests that attempts to investigate the truthfulness of media representations are futile. The power of media representations lies neither in reflecting or distorting the 'truth' and imposing a certain view of 'reality', nor in 'softly' winning consent and establishing hegemony. Rather, their power resides in producing certain 'truth effects' and legitimizing certain discursive regimes, while rendering others illegitimate, deviant and 'false'. Our analytical efforts, according to Foucault, should be directed towards identifying how certain media representations emerge from and within 'regimes of truth', which, in turn, they reproduce and reinforce. Rather than regarding media representations as communicating already-formed knowledge, this approach stresses the constitutive role of representations in creating discourses that form and transform knowledge, and establish the truth and legitimacy of certain statements, and the illegitimacy and deviance of others.

In analysing media texts and images, a Foucauldian approach specifically encourages us to examine strategies of symbolic exclusion and inclusion: how certain people, places, social entities, objects, ideas, voices and relations are accorded visibility, authority, legitimacy and 'truthfulness', for instance, by use of experts who are constructed as authoritative, or techniques to create identification with certain characters and values. And we need to examine which voices, people, authorities, places, views and entities are excluded or rendered invisible (though the fact that a sign is not visible does not necessarily mean it is de-legitimized, and sometimes may mean the opposite). Foucault's approach is helpful also in encouraging us to situate our analyses of particular media images and narratives in the broader historical, social, cultural, political and institutional contexts within which they are produced, disseminated and consumed, and which they shape. Analysis inspired by Foucault locates the account of particular media representations in relation to discourses – the particular configurations of possibilities for making certain statements (and not making others) – which are made available and possible under certain social, historical and political conditions.

However, Foucault's approach has some shortcomings. Its concept of discourse has been criticized for failing sufficiently to acknowledge the material, economic and structural factors in the operation of power/knowledge (Hall, 1997). Its concept of 'regime of truth' and 'truth effects' has also been criticized: if the purpose is to consider the 'effect of truth' rather than the truthfulness of media constructions, it becomes difficult to see how judgements can be securely offered and relativism ultimately avoided (Macdonald, 2003: 21). Finally, for Foucault, agency is less significant than how discourses evolve over time. He is interested in delving into the implicit rules governing a statement's production, not searching for the originating source. This makes responsibility and the possibility of change ambiguous (Macdonald, 2003: 21), in terms of how and by whom certain ways of representation can be changed to become more positive and just.

Nevertheless, Foucault's work has had a major influence on the study of representation and meaning (and many other areas of enquiry). The present book is informed and inspired by Foucault, whose emphasis on discourse as a site for the production of knowledge and struggle over power seems especially apt for understanding today's media environment. However, I do not adopt a strict Foucauldian approach in that the analysis in this book lacks grand historical depth (although I discuss the importance of historical grounding in chapter 2). Nor do I elaborate on the institutional contexts or the physical materials and spaces within which representations emerge; the focus is on the discursive dimension, that is, the meanings generated by representations.

Representation, difference and the other

Unlike the approaches discussed above, here the focus is not on a particular theoretical tradition, but on an area of critical enquiry in the study of representation and power, which is influenced by various (and sometimes competing) theoretical approaches, including those of ideology and discourse. The media's primary cultural role, Silverstone (2007: 19) argues, is 'boundary work', the constant production and reproduction of difference. Representation is a site of power because at its heart is the symbolic production of difference and the symbolic marking of frontiers. Hall's (1997) writing is foundational in this context, in spelling out concerns over the production of difference and the other, and inspiring a body of work on the representation of race, gender, sexuality, ethnicity and other dimensions of difference and identity. One of Hall's most important contributions is the analytical vocabulary he has developed, which accounts for the specific representational practices involved in the symbolic production of difference and otherness. Two concepts are of particular importance to the discussion in this book: binary oppositions and stereotyping.

Binary oppositions: The meaning of a concept or a word is often defined in relation to its opposite (e.g., black/white, good/bad). Meaning generated by media representations relies heavily on this signifying practice, by which sets of binary oppositions construct opposing categories. Binary oppositions are intimately involved in the production and reproduction of power relations, with one pole signifying the dominant one against which the other pole is defined (Hall, 1997: 235, drawing on Derrida, 1972). For example, some media representations of migration construct binary oppositions that cast migrants as criminals, cunning, immoral 'invaders' versus a lawful, hardworking, and/or innocent host society (see chapter 4).

Stereotypes: These 'get hold of the few "simple, vivid, memorable, easily grasped and widely recognized" characteristics about a person, reduce everything about the person to those traits, exaggerate and simplify them, and fix them without change or development to eternity' (Hall, 1997: 258, citing Dyer, 1977: 28). Stereotyping works to maintain symbolic order, 'it sets up a symbolic frontier between the "normal" and the "deviant", the "normal" and the "pathological", the "acceptable" and the "unacceptable", what belongs and what does not or is "Other", between "insiders" and "outsiders", Us and Them' (Hall, 1997: 258).

While the concepts of binary opposition and stereotyping highlight the work of media representation as one of marking symbolic boundaries and its embeddedness in the reproduction and reinforcement of the power relations of domination and oppression, Hall (1997) points to the inherent ambivalence in representations of difference. In critiques of media representations, difference is often negative: studies consistently show how representations invest differences in people, places and cultures with negative meaning. However, Hall (1997: 238) reminds us that the representation of difference is necessary both for the construction of identity and the production of meaning, while at the same time it is a site of threat and danger, imbued with negative feelings – an observation that informs the exploration in this book.

Said's (2003 [1978]) seminal study, *Orientalism*, in which he explores the symbolic forms of knowledge that the European colonial project employed, has had a major impact on debate on the representation of difference and the other, particularly in a global context. Examining a plethora of western scholarly texts, travel writings, cultural artefacts and moral commentaries, Said (2003 [1978]) shows how Orientalism acts as a discourse and a style of thought that depends on a binary relation between 'Orient' and 'Occident'. It is a hegemonic discourse carried over and reproduced through cultural representations and, thus, sustains certain discourses and power relations. It constitutes a systematic and coherent discipline that allowed European culture to manage and produce the Orient.

Said's account is elaborate and has been the subject of numerous debates and critiques whose discussion is beyond the scope of this chapter. I would highlight three points which derive from *Orientalism* and which appear particularly pertinent to an understanding of contemporary media representations, and are illustrated and developed in the analysis of representation in this book.

First, Said (2003 [1978]) observes that the Orientalist texts emerge from the intimacy of the interaction between Occident and Orient. The significance of the 'the Other' derives from her proximity to 'us'. In modern life we interact with a vast number of others, at a distance, with whom we develop mediated non-reciprocal intimacy – a form of mediated intimacy with others who do not share our spatial-temporal locale, and which does not involve the reciprocity of face-to-face interaction (Thompson, 1995). Symbolic proximity is a central dimension and quality of the relation that viewers are called on to develop to distant others (recall the 'Nothing gets you closer' Sky advert discussed in the Introduction). However, while the media bring us closer to distant others, they also pull us apart. Various 'others', for example, migrants, asylum seekers, terrorists, distant sufferers, are cast as morally and existentially distant. This tension between the mediated proximity of distant strangers on the one hand, and their distance and distancing on the other, is at the crux of the promise and challenge proffered by media representations – a central theme that the following chapters explore.

Second, Orientalism is based on domination: its function is to establish the inferiority of the east to the west. However, rather than expressing a deliberate will or intention to control, manipulate and incorporate the other, 'it is, above all, a discourse that is by no means in direct, corresponding relationship with political power in the raw, but rather is produced and exists in an uneven exchange with various kinds of power' (Said, 2003 [1978]: 12). This view differs significantly from ideological analyses, which regard texts as having a dominant meaning, intended by their producers, which can be teased out by the analyst. Rather, Said's account draws on Foucault, who demands that we analyse media representations in terms of their interaction with wider public discourses and sources of power at particular historical moments.

Third, Orientalism is related less to the Orient than to 'our' Occidental world. The Orientalist is not concerned with the Orient except as the motivation for what s/he says. The Orientalist stands outside the Orient, existentially and morally. This 'exteriority of representation', Said (2003 [1978]: 21) argues, 'is always governed by some version of the truism that if the Orient could represent itself, it would; since it cannot, the representation does the job, for the West, and *faute de mieux*, for the poor Orient'. As this quote illustrates, Said defines the condition of subalternity as one of no access to the institutionalized structures of representation and power. The subaltern, as Spivak (1988) famously argued, has neither the epistemic capital (the knowledge and its tools) nor the political position to have a voice, because both capital and power are in the hands of the dominant. Instead of speaking, the dispossessed are spoken for. A central impetus of a postcolonial critique, significantly influenced by Said's work, is to explicate this problem of the subaltern's voice and explore the possibilities for its recovery and articulation, though for some – most notably Spivak (1988) – the notion that there is such a voice and that it can be recovered is a kind of essentialist fiction (Gill, 2007).

This huge debate about the subaltern's voice is beyond the scope of this chapter, but I want to highlight its implication for the discussion of this book. One of the central characteristics of the contemporary globalized media environment, associated largely with the proliferation and increased accessibility of media and communications technologies which allow citizens a voice to tell their stories, is that subjects hitherto excluded from the major forms of cultural representation now have the means to speak for themselves. This presents a significant emancipatory opportunity for marginalized individuals and groups to retell their stories, to recover their histories and, as a consequence, to challenge and redress inequality and injustice. New realms and possibilities for the other to speak are emerging, most notably in new media sites, bringing the potential for disrupting the binary opposition upon which Orientalism depends, and for engaging in a different kind of politics. At the same time, these possibilities and the realization of their emancipatory potential are fraught with challenges and tensions. These tensions, implicated in the ways in which and the extent to which media representations may offer alternatives to Orientalism, are a central theme of the present book. More broadly, Said's thinking on Orientalism continues to inform the critique of media representations in significant ways that are referred to in the chapters that follow.

II Challenges

I hope that the discussion in the first section gives a flavour of the richness of the field of media representation research and its plurality of approaches and perspectives. This body of work highlights the fundamental connection between representation and power and offers critical understanding of how representations can be transformed to foster more just, more generous and more inclusive frames for understanding. However, media representation research entails some crucial tensions and challenges, three of which I discuss next.

Desperately seeking the power of media representations

The first challenge concerns *the search for the power of media representations*. A fundamental justification for a critical examination of media representations derives from recognition of their inextricable relations with power, and specifically the connection between media representations and structures of inequality, domination and injustice. But what is the precise nature of this connection?

On the one hand, the semiotic tradition stresses the polysemic nature of representations, that all representations 'imply, underlying their signifiers, a "floating chain" of signifieds, the reader able to choose some and ignore others' (Barthes, 1977: 38–9). Studies show that the same representation can carry several, quite different, often contradictory meanings. For example, as I discuss in chapter 2, positive 'upbeat' images of victims of a humanitarian disaster can be seen as 'humanizing' the sufferers by endowing them with dignity and agency, while some might argue that this depiction suppresses the fact that the sufferers' predicament arises out of their vulnerability and dependency (Cohen, 2001).

The notion that representations are inherently polysemic is aligned to the emphasis on their lack of fixity and transformative capacity. Studies document how representations have changed over time and challenged frames of understanding that sustain relations of domination and inequality. For example, Gill (2007) examines how representations of gender changed and helped to undermine sexist stereotypes, but later produced a backlash that reproduces some of the stereotypes originally challenged. Liebes and Kampf (2009) show that the Israeli media's overall depiction of Palestinians during the Second Intifada was more inclusive and reflexive than the discourses and frames used in earlier decades. So a central thread in research on media representations concerns how they constitute open and changing sources and sites of meaning.

On the other hand, a considerable part of the critical force of analyses of media representations derives from being able to demonstrate that representations have 'dominant' meanings, which work to intervene in the many potential meanings of a text, and to privilege a specific one (Hall, 1997: 228). Drawing on the Marxist legacy, the Frankfurt School and ideological critiques (discussed earlier), detailed analyses of texts and images show how representations work to serve the reproduction, maintenance and fixity of the relations of domination. For instance, Hall (1997: 228) argues that in the representation of race the message is that 'even when black people are shown at the summit of their achievement, they often fail to carry it off'. This research emphasizes the conservative power of representations, that is, the power of texts and images to conserve and reinscribe power relations, and to reconstitute and re-establish relations of domination and authority through the production of meaning. Sociological and anthropological accounts have also underlined the conservative role of representations, although less from an ideological perspective than by highlighting the ways in which cultural representations serve to integrate societies and sustain symbolic order and control. The extensive research on the role of media representations in the construction of national identity (see chapter 3) is typical of this literature.

So, on the one hand, representations are seen as open to multiple readings, inherently ambivalent, and constantly changing. On the other hand, representations are seen as having 'dominant' 'preferred' meanings and carrying particular ideologies reinforcing specific ideas and values and excluding others, which works largely to reconstitute and sustain existing power relations. This contradiction corresponds to the contradictory character of the media landscape. The current complex, multi-channel media environment is conducive to *change*: it provides marginalized groups with a voice and a platform to represent themselves and to question and transform the authority of experts; it offers a dynamic context for an open and complex field of diverse and contesting representations. At the same time, the political economy of contemporary media is characterized by *reproduction of capitalism and reinforcement of existing power relations*: increasing control of media channels and platforms by the powerful few, manifested in the increasing trend towards cross-ownership and convergence. The democratization of the media and the proliferation of voices triggers attempts to reassert control and dominant narratives by powerful authorities, which suggests that as much as multiple, open meanings and change, media representations are about 'dominant meanings' and fixity. As a process, representation is both conservative, working to inscribe and reconstitute existing power relations, and transformative – subversive and challenging the familiar, established frames for understanding the world.

How can we theorize these contradictions and account for the multiple implications of representations, not losing sight of the fundamental question of power, while at the same time acknowledging the fundamental complexity and potential ambivalence and openness of representations in this 'age of new visibility' (Thompson, 2005)? I grapple with this question in the following chapters through a series of analyses of media representations of different themes and sites of imagination, and I hope that future research will engage with it further.

Research on media representations must also theorize the power of media representations against the pre-eminence of audience studies in explaining the meaning of the media. Since the 1980s, audience studies have been usefully challenging the primacy of the text that governed the early days of media and communications research. Audiences' sense-making and interpretation of media texts have come to the centre of research agendas: nowadays 'most academic writers are . . . united in agreeing that any study of meaning in the media will be handicapped if it ignores audience or reader responses' (Macdonald, 2003: 23). However, this unanimity may be rather problematic for media representations research. It can be summarized by asking: how can you claim anything at all about the meanings of media representations, if you haven't asked the audiences how *they* make sense of it? This question, frequently put to analysts of representations, seems to encapsulate a deeper questioning of the validity, rigour and objective of analysing representations on the basis of analysts' interpretation. Since analysis of audiences' reception, as Illouz (2003a: 9) argues, has come to represent the 'royal road' to the meaning of media representations, other 'roads', specifically interpretative, textual analyses, are seen at best as marginal and at worst as futile. I hope that this book will shed light on why analysis of media representations is a worthwhile and crucial 'road' to pursue in order to understand the power of the media, and how it can help establish understandings that should be in dialogue with audience research.

A compartmentalized field

A second problem in media representations research concerns this field's *compartmentalization*. Research has largely developed along separate theoretical paradigms, and thematic and methodological orientations (Macdonald, 2003). While these divisions facilitate the development of specialized expertise and a particularized understanding of media representations in specific contexts and realms, they also inhibit appreciation of how representations work to establish broader frames for understanding and feeling, and how they emerge cumulatively, across and within media, genres, themes and contexts. Three areas of division seem particularly noteworthy.

1. Reflective and constructionist approaches
The fundamental differences between the reflective and constructionist approaches (discussed earlier) have informed completely separate research endeavours, often with distinct vocabularies. An indicative example is the separation between content analyses of media representations, on the one hand, and interpretative analyses, influenced by cultural studies, and linguistic and discursive approaches to texts, on the other. Content analyses are often underpinned by the assumption that reality can be reflected in more 'accurate' and 'truthful' ways. Thus, they record trends in representations of specific issues and highlight problems, such as 'bias', 'disproportion' and 'misrepresentation', and how they change (or not) over time. Studies employing Critical Discourse Analysis and interpretative methods, however, are not concerned with the question of whether and how the truth is reflected (or not) and focus instead on how meanings are produced and legitimized, and on how power relations, hierarchies and authorities are produced, reproduced and transformed symbolically.

2. Themes
The substantial influence of ideological critique on the study of media representations is reflected in the thematic organization of the field into areas and aspects where societal power relations struggles have been central, for example, over race, gender, class, ethnicity, sexuality, etc. Research themes also mirror the categories that structure public discourse, for example, health, crime, environment, migration, and so on.

While these areas of specialization have enabled the production of focused and critical research, they have become consolidated unhelpfully into research compartments. Themes that seem different and detached, and have been studied separately, are often strikingly similar in terms of how they are represented in the media and the frames for understanding that they support. For example, Orgad (2009a) shows how a variety of representations across seemingly unrelated themes, contexts and fields, including feminist discourses on sexual abuse, the Holocaust, discourses of health and illness, and reality television, converge to support the construction of the cultural role of 'survivor' as a desirable subject position in contemporary western culture for coping with trauma and suffering. Comparison among such seemingly unrelated areas is valuable for highlighting paradigms or discourses whose power and influence lie not so much in the way a particular theme is represented, but in the way in which it emerges from a range of texts and discursive fields, to constitute a coherent form of knowledge which has clarity and visibility. More generally, critical analysis should move beyond mirroring the classification of existing categories in public and media discourse, to interrogate the division itself and what it serves, for example, how the classification of certain issues within categories of discourse of the 'personal' and the 'private' may work to de-politicize them and diffuse responsibility from institutions and society at large.

3. Genres and media

The variety of genres, media, technologies, styles, narratives and images that constitute the vast field of media representations required the development of theoretical, conceptual and analytical tools to account for the specificities of particular media and genres and their implications for the production of meaning. Specialized areas of enquiry have developed, for example, film studies, television studies, news studies. At the same time, this specialization has produced divisions, manifest, for example, in the institutionalized split between film studies (e.g., departments such as Film Studies and scholarly journals such as *Screen*) and media representations research (e.g., television, newspapers).[4] The division between the research on 'old media' and 'new media' is another example: indicatively, the term 'media representations' commonly refers to images and texts on television, and in newspapers and advertising, but not to texts and images on the Internet and new media platforms such as mobile phones.[5] It is only recently that some studies account for the relations between these divisions, for example, research on 'traditional' news coverage and representations on new media such as blogs, Facebook and Twitter.

The compartmentalized character of media representations research seems ill-equipped to address the changing media environment of the twenty-first century. The divisions discussed above, which organize the research field, fail to respond to the increasingly converged, interconnected and networked media landscape within which representations are produced, circulated and consumed. It is not sufficient to acknowledge that boundaries blur and that media and communications technologies converge; research needs to reflect this in accounting for the work of media representations and the meanings that they produce *across* technologies, genres, contexts, discourses, modes of address and forms. The highly networked and intertextual character of today's media landscape demands serious engagement with intertextuality – the notion that signs necessarily relate to each other and that to make sense of a text requires knowledge of a range of textual references. Specifically, analysis should allow for a better understanding of how ideas and frames for understanding emerge and are accumulated across different texts, and how different fields of discourse and action give rise to, and support, through a variety of representations, certain statements and ideas, while de-legitimizing others.

A good example of this understanding of representation as inherently intertextual is Silverstone's (2007) discussion of the rhetoric of evil in the US. Silverstone identifies a range of religious, popular and political discourses and representations, from Bush's political speeches, through Regan's filmic and popular identity, to the popular drama *Buffy the Vampire Slayer*, all of which converge to make the rhetoric of evil that emerged, post-9/11, appear 'natural'. Chouliaraki's (2012) work is another example: she shows how the 'humanitarian imaginary' is constituted and carried through and across a range of genres including films, online news platforms such as Twitter, Non-Governmental Organization (NGO) communications, and celebrity.

Globalization and research on media representations: Mind the gaps

In addition to the compartmentalized nature of the research field, which seems ill-equipped to respond to a globalized media environment, the study of media representation fails sufficiently to correspond to current global media and culture in other respects. First, a great deal of research on media representations is characterized by 'methodological nationalism' (Beck, 2003). Like much social science research, studies of media representations tend to privilege the nation-state as the point of reference and the context for explaining the meanings of the representations they analyse. While some research is interested explicitly in the work of media representation in a national context, other work makes universalist claims, for example, about the representation of race, gender or suffering, with little or no acknowledgement of the specificity of the national frameworks of the representations they examine and the concepts they employ for their analysis.

Second, representations can travel across cultural and national boundaries which endow them with different meanings. Diasporic and audience studies provide important insights into the processes and experiences of audiences' appropriations of texts which originate in remote places from those in which they are consumed (e.g., Aksoy and Robins, 2000, 2002; Hargreaves and Mahdjoub, 1997; Karanfil, 2007). However, there has been little attention at the level of the representation, to how meanings travel and transform. How are texts, images and discourses that originate in one locale or culture reappropriated and repositioned by a receiving medium in a different locale and transformed into a new or revised representation? How do representations from one part of the world trigger the production of representations in other parts of the world? These questions are addressed by examining specific examples in this book; chapter 3 in particular looks at manifestations of this 'travelling' of meaning.

Several cross-country and cross-cultural studies of media representations do address these issues. For example, some show how 'global' features, such as the use of direct modes of address (e.g., referring to readers as 'you'), similar adjectives, and the use of poetic devices, appear in advertising in various countries and cultures, while national versions of the same message 'localize' its meaning, for example, through the use of familiar cultural symbols that resonate with local beliefs, values and commonsensical 'ways of seeing' (Johnson, 2008; Machin and Van Leeuwen, 2007; Zirinski, 2005). Similarly, cross-cultural studies of news coverage show how national media domesticate their reporting to fit with national interests and cultural assumptions (e.g., Lee, Man Chan, Pan, and So, 2000; Roeh and Cohen, 1992).

These studies highlight the complex and dynamic tension between the global and the local, and refute charges that national frameworks and meanings are erased by multinational media corporations. However, they have some shortcomings, four of which are particularly pertinent to the discussion in this book.

First, while many studies seek to break down the dichotomous global/local construct and show how meanings travel across cultural and geographical boundaries, they are nevertheless constrained by this dichotomy. They focus on identifying how 'global' (largely understood as western and particularly American) and 'local' (implicitly conceived as national) elements exist in media texts. In retaining this conceptual division, they are reproducing the distinction that they are challenging, and are unable to offer an alternative vocabulary to capture the far more complex, messy and uneven reality of media representations in the contemporary world.[6]

Second, 'local' is often equated with 'national'. While the national imagination remains pertinent in contemporary public life, informing and shaping people's experiences, identities and thinking in significant ways, people's local realities are shaped and experienced at different levels and within different realms. People's sense of belonging to a neighbourhood and/or local community, for instance, may shape their identities and imaginations in central ways (Appadurai, 1996). Similarly, regional contexts can play a central role in shaping identities, thought and political action, as evidenced in the wave of uprisings against oppressive regimes in various Arab countries in the Middle East in 2011.

Furthermore, many studies conceive representations as 'global' because they have been produced and/or disseminated by transnational or international media, for example, advertising firms or news networks. But representations that originate in private settings and are produced by individuals and local groups can also acquire global meanings in this age of new media, some examples of which we examine in the succeeding chapters.

Third, notwithstanding the value of systematic comparison conducted by many studies, a comparative methodology almost always isolates texts from the contexts within which they were produced, circulated and consumed. Examining the purely textual and visual properties of national and local versions provides little understanding of the dynamics and relations *between* the texts, and between texts and the broader discourses and cultural contexts. It neither illustrates nor explains the contestations and interactions among representations of the same event, product or issue, across cultures, sources and places – dynamics that are important features of the media space today.

Fourth, most studies looking at how meanings travel across local, national and cultural boundaries are concerned with western representations and their adaptation, translation and reception in non-western local, national and regional contexts. This 'western favouritism' reinforces the implicit notion that 'global' is 'western' and 'local' refers to the 'east' or 'south' and that the south is the receiver that always adapts and localizes meanings produced elsewhere. As argued by several critics, it is time to 'de-westernize' media studies (Curran and Park, 2000; Sreberny, 2000; Thussu, 2009; Wang, 2010), which includes paying greater attention to non-western texts and images and the changing meanings of global and local in the field of media representations.

This section has discussed a number of epistemological, conceptual and methodological challenges that media representations research faces. Of course, no single approach or piece of research can address them all. Nor do I believe that all these tensions can or need to be reconciled; contradiction and disagreement are vital for debate to remain vibrant, relevant and useful. At the same time, it is necessary for these issues to be considered and addressed. In particular, as I hope the discussion above convinces, research on media representations needs to be able to respond to changes in the media environment, especially those related to globalization and increased networking. I want next to propose the concept of 'global imagination' as a way of addressing some of these challenges in analysing the work of media representation in the twenty-first century. While I do not claim that my suggestions are a 'fix' for the issues and tensions discussed so far, I hope to show that the concept of global imagination might provide a productive framework to account for the work of media representations and to inform their analysis.

III Global imagination

The view of the media's 'strong effects' that dominated the first decades of media and communications research has been replaced by an understanding of their influence, and the effect of representations in particular, as 'soft': as a slow, cumulative, complex, indeterminate and unpredictable process. In this view, the power of media representations lies in the creation of a certain environment of images, narratives and sensations that become the resources that shape what we know and get to know about the world. The power of media representations, in other words, resides in producing symbolic resources that feed individual and collective imaginations.

Imagination refers to the capacity to see in and think about something as that which it is not (Castoriadis (1987 [1975]), to represent 'the absent as present, with all the thoughts and feelings it would bring if it were present' (Feagin and Maynard, 1997: 41, cited in Illouz, 2009: 399). This capacity is intimately intertwined with the act of representation: the capacity to imagine relies on a repertoire of symbolic resources (representations) available to be drawn upon. In turn, representation, through signs, makes the absent present, which is the essence of imagining.

Taylor's (2002) account of 'modern social imaginaries' is instructive in accounting for the link between representation and imagination, in order to understand how media representations that circulate in global public space 'feed' collective and individual imaginations. Taylor (2002) contends that social imaginary constitutes a common understanding which makes possible common practices and a widely shared sense of legitimacy. It refers to:

> the ways in which people imagine their social existence, how they fit together with others, how things go on between them and their fellows, the expectations that are normally met, and the deeper normative notions and images that underlie these . . .
>
> . . . it incorporates a sense of the normal expectations that we have of one another, the kind of common understanding which enables us to carry out the collective practices that make up our social life. (Taylor, 2002: 106)

The social imaginary is something more than an immediate practical understanding of how to do particular things – such as how to buy a newspaper, ride a subway, order a drink, transfer money, make small talk, or submit a petition. It involves a form of understanding that has a wider grasp of our history and social existence (Gaonkar, 2002). It is a complex, unstructured, and not fully articulated 'grasp of our whole predicament, how we stand in relationship to one another, how we got where we are, how we relate to other groups' (Taylor, 2002: 107). Drawing on Heidegger's and Wittgenstein's concepts of 'background', Taylor describes the social imaginary as furnishing 'background understanding' – a wider and deeper understanding that frames society's actions and practices.

Cultural representations are constitutive of social imaginaries. Social imaginaries are shared by large groups of people and carried in images, stories and legends (Taylor, 2002). Castoriadis (1987 [1975]), a key thinker on the concept of imagination, develops the idea of representations as 'imaginary significations': rather than being grand interested and directed accounts, representations provide answers to questions, scripts that orient society's thoughts and actions:

> Society must define its 'identity', its articulation, the world, its relations to the world and to the objects it contains, its needs and its desires. Without the 'answer' to these 'questions', without these 'definitions', there can be no human world, no society, no culture . . . The role of imaginary significations is to provide an answer to these questions, and answers that, obviously, neither 'reality', nor 'rationality' can provide. (Castoriadis, 1987 [1975]: 147)

Taylor's and Castoriadis's accounts seem to provoke an important question for media representations research, namely how, alongside and in interaction with other 'imaginary significations', media representations 'condition and orient social doing and representing' (Castoriadis, 1987 [1975]: 364). In other words, how do media representations orient, shape and produce frames of understanding, narratives and 'scripts' that guide and orient the conduct of our lives?

Fundamentally, this concern with the force of imagination and representation is located in the modern age and, particularly, the age of globalization. This is not to say that the relation between representation and imagination is new; however, its qualities and consequences in modern times are radically different from how they were in the past. Drawing on an anthropological sensibility, Appadurai (1996) acknowledges that imagination is not a new social energy, but, he argues, it has a newly significant role in the contemporary world. Imagination is 'the key component of the new global order' (Appadurai, 1996: 31) and a constitutive feature of modern subjectivity (ibid.: 3). Specifically, Appadurai (1996: 4) posits that the joint forces of mass migration and the rapid flow of mediated images and narratives that mark the modern world impel the work of imagination in fundamentally new ways.

I discuss Appadurai's account of migration and imagination in detail in chapter 4. Here I draw on Appadurai (1996), Castoriadis (1987 [1975]) and Taylor (2002), to propose several characteristics of imagination that compose a framework for accounting for the work of media representation and its potential power.

Imagination is a process of negotiation and interaction between personal and collective thinking and feeling. We think about imagination – the capacity to form mental images and concepts of what is absent – as a personal, private creative faculty of the mind. However, Appadurai (1996: 5) observes that in the modern global age, imagination has been 'unleashed': from a private process, exercised in 'designated' expressive spaces of art, myth and ritual, imagination has become a 'part of the quotidian mental work of ordinary people in many societies' and a constitutive feature of modern subjectivity. The media is one of two major forces, the other being migration, that jointly have transformed imagination into the property of collectives rather than a faculty of the gifted individual. And, as Boltanski (1999: 50, emphasis in original) points out, 'imaginative capabilities are not produced fully fledged as a result of some kind of spontaneous generation. Imagination . . . must be *nourished.*'

Electronic media play a particular role in 'nourishing' the imagination, and in the re-entry of imagination into people's ordinary lives. They are:

> resources for experiments with self-making in all sorts of societies, for all sorts of persons. They allow scripts of possible lives to be imbricated with the glamour of film stars and fantastic film plots and yet also to be tied to the plausibility of news shows, documentaries, and other [. . .] forms of tele-mediation and printed text. (Appadurai, 1996: 3–4)

In this context, a particularly suggestive concept developed by Appadurai (1996) is 'local imagining'. Local imagining refers to the ways in which macro-events and broader narratives work their way into highly localized structures of feeling and into personal narratives of the local. It is at these sites of agency, where people and groups appropriate the 'big' stories of globalization and produce their own expressive forms, that globalization takes hold and becomes what Appadurai (2000) calls 'globalization from below'.

The notion of local imagining and the significance of attending to it resonate with the emphasis in cultural and audience studies on people's active reading of media texts, and what Silverstone (1994) calls 'media talk' – people's everyday comments on media texts. Local imagining echoes the processes described in reception studies of individuals' sense-making and interpretation of media narratives and images. However, a new aspect of 'local imagining' that has received little attention is that the comments of individuals and people's interpretations of media representations no longer occur only, or even predominantly, in 'the evanescent small talk of tea stalls, cinema houses, and urban gathering places' (Appadurai, 1996: 153). Rather, local imagining, which historically was mostly silent and invisible, increasingly takes place in mediated spaces visible to many: blogs, Twitter and YouTube, television, radio, magazines and newspapers. Thus, mediated sites of local imagining are becoming an integral part of media representations and, as such, contribute to and shape the resources that cultivate the global imagination.

This view of imagination and the centrality of local imagining helps break down the division in media representations research between 'public' and 'private', 'macro' and 'micro', 'political' and 'personal', and between media, themes, genres and modes of address more commonly seen as separate and detached from each other. It suggests, for example, that in order to tackle how the nation is imagined and how its meanings are negotiated in times of conflict, we need to attend to a variety of mediated sites where this process of imagining occurs: at the broader regional, national, transnational and global levels as well as the local level, for example, in national and international news reports, citizens' blogs and user-generated video clips (see chapters 3 and 6).

Attending to mediated sites of local imagining not only breaks down the private/public divide, but also helps to address the criticism discussed earlier, that textual and visual analyses tell us nothing about the 'real' meanings of representations. The meanings of media representations are increasingly discussed on mediated sites that are observable and are themselves media representations that can be studied. Of course, examining responses on blogs, Internet forums, in radio discussion programmes, social media and so on, does not replace a systematic understanding of how audiences make sense of media representations. But these mediated appearances constitute increasingly visible spaces for interpreting and engaging with the meanings of the media. Examining these sites of 'local imagining' and the representations people produce in these sites may help to address what Castoriadis (1987 [1975]: 366) describes as the problem of the 'complementarity' between social imaginary significations and individuals' own representations, that is, to account for the correspondence between, and the relevance and resonance of social imaginaries and the cultural representations in which they are carried, for people's lives, actions and understandings.

Imagination is both factual and normative, referring to both meaningful real actions and the fantastical. Imagination, the capacity to see in a thing what it is not, to see it other than it is (Castoriadis (1987 [1975]), is oriented to the future, the possible; it has a tentativeness. However, fantasy has strong connotations of private ideas or thinking which are divorced from action. This is expressed, for example, in the view of the media as 'the new opium for the masses' (Appadurai, 1996: 7), which has been influenced by the Frankfurt School's critique of media industries as integrating and pacifying the masses as consumers, and cultivating 'pseudo-individuality', 'pseudo-activity', pleasure and consensus. Conversely, Appadurai (1996: 7) contends that imagination is today 'a staging ground for [collective] action, and not only for escape'. The exploration of the possible, seeing in a thing other than it is, is key to refiguring and transcending ordinary social life. It is through imagination that collective dissent and new designs for collective life emerge (Appadurai, 1996) – a proposition that we explore in this book.

Thus, following Appadurai (1996), I reject the view that: (1) imagination is a simple escape from a world defined by more concrete purposes and structures (a claim made by some in relation to viewers' consumption of soap operas or reality television, for instance); (2) imagination is mere contemplation, thus irrelevant to new forms of desire and subjectivity; and (3) that imagination is an elite pastime (most typically associated with 'high art') and, thus, not relevant to the lives of ordinary people. Rather, Appadurai (1996) contends, imagination is simultaneously about fantasy, desire and the exploration of the possible, and is deeply connected to real meaningful action. While imagination provides 'a sense of how things usually go' (in other words, it is *factual*), it is interwoven with an idea of how things ought to go, in other words, it is *normative* (based on Taylor, 2002: 106). This account underscores the power of imagination and thus representation through which imagination is constituted: representations, in this view, are not 'just texts', insubstantial alongside the materiality of real occurrences. They are the central resources for the conduct of life, for the formation of identity and subjectivity and for the ability to act in the world.

Imagination involves thinking and feeling, and can be messy and contradictory. 'Imagination leans and relies on sensations, feelings and emotions to make present that which is absent' (Illouz, 2009: 399) at the same time as it draws on and enacts intellectual concepts which inform thinking. This observation suggests that the notion of global imagination, as developed in this book, includes what Robertson (2009) calls 'global consciousness': a continuing and increasingly reflexive awareness of the world as a whole, of the fate of the planet, of the place of the earth in the cosmos, and of the numerous and increasing risks facing humanity. However, this book expands on and departs from Robertson's account in two important ways. First, global imagination extends beyond 'awareness'. It directs attention to the affective, emotional and fantastical qualities of how we see ourselves as agents who traverse a social space and inhabit a temporal horizon of 'the world'. This centrality of emotion is missing in Robertson's (2009) 'global consciousness'. Second, while Robertson's definition stresses a sense of coherence in the way people see and think about the world, the notion of global imagination demands that we recognize the contested and often incoherent mental pictures and concepts of the world, as they appear in contemporary media representations. Global imagination is a symbolic space characterized by social imaginaries (carried largely in mediated representations), which people around the world share, but which they simultaneously compete and struggle over.

Imagination is dialectic. The work of imagination, Appadurai (1996: 4) argues, 'is neither purely emancipatory nor entirely disciplined but is a space of contestation in which individuals and groups seek to annex the global into their own practices of the modern'. Imagination is thus undetermined; it is a space for symbolic contestation. Media representation, as I show in the following chapters, is the central symbolic space through which this contestation takes place. On the one hand, representations play a transformative, enabling role in challenging and altering power relations; they constitute a site for the struggle and subversion of power relations. At the same time, media representations legitimize discourses, inscribing them in the mainstream, the acceptable, the legitimate 'regimes of meaning', to echo Foucault's view of discourse and power.

This account of imagination and representation as mutually constitutive of a symbolic space of contestation offers a way to engage with the tension discussed earlier, between the emphasis in research on the conservative power of media representations on the one hand, and on their polysemic nature, lack of fixity and transformative potential on the other. Drawing on Appadurai's account of the work of imagination in a global world, and on Foucault's insistence on the multiple and contradictory consequences of discourse, this book argues that the essence of the work of media representations is the cultivation of global imagination *through* contestation. The interest in media *representations* and their power is not in how they *either* produce and inscribe 'dominant' ways of understanding the world, *or* challenge them through 'alternative' forms. Rather, the field of media representation is seen as simultaneously liberating and oppressive, emancipatory and disciplined. The focus of this account is on how this contestation is articulated and exercised, what possibilities it opens up and the challenges it throws out and responds to. Importantly, this view does not deny that material, structural and historical power relations of inequalities matter. Rather, it is how they matter that cannot be simply mapped through fixed categories. 'Our theorizing must go beyond the repeated discovery of domination and the romanticization/fetishization of resistance in global contexts' (Shome and Hegde, 2002: 186) – a challenge to which I hope this book is equal.

Imagination is a moral force. Imagination is important because it is moral. Taylor (2002) highlights the moral force of the social imaginary: the notion that imaginaries carry a sense of moral order, which enables and legitimizes certain practices and actions as 'normal' and 'right'. This view echoes Foucault's notion of discursive regimes of truth, under which certain ideas, beliefs and claims attain the status of 'normal' and 'true' and can confer legitimacy on our common practices and pursuits and embed them in a normative scheme. The social imaginary is fundamentally moral insofar as it provides not only a grasp of the norms underlying our social practice, but also of what makes these norms realizable (Taylor, 2002: 109–10). In other words, it provides an understanding of what is possible, 'right' and desirable, as well as what is impossible and cannot or should not be attempted or aspired to.

The link between media representation and imagination as a moral force is profoundly developed in Silverstone's *Media and Morality* (2007). Drawing on Arendt (1977), Silverstone (2007) is interested in the capacity of media representation to facilitate and cultivate a cosmopolitan imagination, that is, to provide the faculties of judgement and imagination needed to pursue what he regards as more effective understanding and just participation in the highly uneven and 'liquid modern world' (Bauman, 2010):

> Imagination here is that human quality which opens the doors to understanding and in turn to the capacity to make judgements in and through the public world. Imagination, the Kantian enlargement of mentality beyond the individual and the solitary self, requires taking the position of the other, the creation of the appropriate distance to enable effective communication,

> the formation of opinion and the materialization of a political life. The enlargement of mentality involves bringing as many others into one's imagination as it is possible to do: 'The more people's standpoints I have present in my mind while I am pondering a given issue, and the better I can imagine how I would feel and think if I were in their place, the stronger will be my capacity for representative thinking and the more valid my conclusions, my opinion.' (Arendt, 1977: 241, cited in Silverstone, 2007: 46–7)

For Silverstone, at the heart of the problem and promise of imagination as a moral force is our relation to the other, specifically, the capacity to imagine oneself as another. This capacity is the precondition for empathy, compassion and care for the other, indeed for the moral conduct of our lives, especially, and more than ever before, in a world in which we encounter distant others on a daily basis, on television, in films and newspapers and on radio and the Internet. The symbolic production of difference and otherness – a central concern in the study of media representations (discussed earlier) – is fundamentally a moral practice. It offers audiences certain scripts about distant others and orients them to feel and think in particular ways in relation to those others (a central concern also in Boltanski, 1999). Indeed, following Boltanski (1999) and Silverstone (2007), one of the questions that motivated the exploration in this book is to what extent and in what ways do the images, narratives, scripts and sensations on offer in the global media space enable the enlargement of our mentality beyond the individual and the solitary self? What kind of imagination do they cultivate about the world?

However, I differ from Silverstone (2007) and contemporary thinkers such as Tomlinson (2011), and Chouliaraki (2006, 2012), who deploy the concept of cosmopolitan imagination normatively, that is, as the desirable 'yardstick' of social thought and feeling to which the media should aspire, and against which media representations should be evaluated.[7] My critique is closer to what Illouz (2003a), drawing on Held (1980), calls 'immanent critique': I analyse media representations for what they offer, for the presuppositions and claims they rest on and make, and for what they call on their readers to think, feel and perform. Inspired by Boltanski's (1999) analysis of representation as a series of proposals to the spectator, I am interested in understanding what proposals media representations present to viewers in terms of how to think and feel about the world, and their and others' lives. Cosmopolitan imagination in this view is part of the empirical object that I observe and analyse: it is one of the scripts that contemporary representations produce and promote (Robertson, 2010).

The book's enquiry into representations and their role in cultivating a global imagination centres on identifying the scripts available in the contemporary space of media representations that call actors to think about themselves and others, about current and possible lives, and about the world in which they live. I concur with the idea that cosmopolitan scripts constitute an important part of the cultural resources that cultivate the public imagination in the globally mediated public space, but I show also how they interact and compete with other scripts. It is this interaction and contestation and their potential consequences that I focus on, in order better to understand the work of media representations in the age of globalization. Hence my choice to speak about global rather than cosmopolitan imagination, because the latter may be seen as exclusive of alternative moral imaginations, and the former allows for a variety of imaginations (e.g., local, national, regional, global, cosmopolitan, public and therapeutic).

Global imagination is offered as an organizing concept that frames the book's exploration and highlights the dynamic and contested work of media representations in a global context, and their simultaneous descriptive, factual and fantastical, imaginary character. However, the concept should not be seen as exclusive of other theoretical approaches to the study of media representations, and particularly ideology and discourse.

At the same time, employing the concept of imagination to inform the study of representations differs from the concepts of discourse and ideology in four important ways. First, imagination is less structured, coherent, intentional or calculated than either ideology or discourse. Rather than full-blown ideologies, imagination can be supported by a convergence of ideological sources, discourses and influences, which may themselves compete with each other. For this reason, the book is organized by sites of imagination, rather than by themes, discourses or ideologies. Each chapter focuses on a site of the imagination and explores a variety of representations that constitute and feed the imagining in and of that site: the imagining of others (chapter 2), ourselves as a nation (chapter 3), possible lives (chapter 4), the world (chapter 5) and the self (chapter 6). Each chapter demonstrates how imagining is cultivated through the convergence and interaction of representations of different types, discourses, genres and sources, and sometimes of representations that promote competing ideologies.

Second, while the study of both discourse and ideology leans towards understanding *existing* frames of thinking and talking about the world, imagination, as discussed earlier, refers to and relies on 'how things usually go' (Taylor, 2002), but also how it is hoped they 'will go', or should be. Thus, we examine the development of global imagination within and across representations whose orientation is simultaneously the past, the present and the future, factual (e.g., news) and normative (e.g., political campaigning and propaganda), mimetic (e.g., documentary) and fictional (e.g., films), representations which claim objectivity and relevance to the public interest (e.g., news), and representations that are positioned as subjective, personal and sometimes confessional and therapeutic (e.g., blogs, personal online video clips).

Third, and connected to the previous point, media representations from the perspective of discourse and ideology have been studied largely in relation to public and often 'macro' issues, in relation to sites traditionally seen as central to the formation of pubic opinion and deliberation, most notably, news and political communication. Other works pay attention to the operation of discourse and ideology in genres and modes of 'display', which have more affective, ritualistic and imaginary qualities, for example, fictional films, advertising and talk shows. However, both ideology and discourse seem limited in their accounting for the way personal and collective/public expressions interact and compete in mediated forms. Imagination, by contrast, offers a concept that makes visible how representations in the global media space constitute a symbolic space where personal and collective thinking and feelings meet, are co-articulated, converge and also contest and challenge one another.

Fourth, the notion of imagination is intimately interlinked with the visual (see Frosh, forthcoming, 2011a, on the etymology of imagination/image) and as such is extremely relevant to an analysis of contemporary media that is dominated by the visual. Discourse and ideology lean more towards the textual. Though discourse has been applied to understanding the interaction between visual and verbal signifiers and to analysing visual representations (see Rose, 2001), historically it refers to verbal communicative strategies, and work within media studies that focuses on discourse tends to replicate this emphasis (Macdonald, 2003: 3).

Conclusion: Towards a Critical Study of Media Representation and the Global Imagination

Imagination is the foundational force and resource for overcoming the distance created by globalization, symbolically connecting distant localities and facilitating 'the intensification of worldwide social relations' (Giddens, 1990: 64). Places, people and cultures become increasingly part of an imagined space, within which they live side by side – a space McLuhan famously called 'the global village'. The global village is enabled, albeit in complex, uneven and contested ways, in and through mediated representations. Social relations can be 'stretched' and can exist across space and time, apparently 'shrinking' world societies to a single village, because people can appear to each other and imagine each other as part of an 'imagined community' (Anderson, 1983), in the 'mediapolis' (Silverstone, 2007) – the global mediated space of appearance.

The symbolic stretching of time and space is enabled through the cultivation and exercise of a global imagination. Global imagination refers to both the faculty to and the process of forming mental images and concepts of the world, and of ourselves and others as traversing this global social space. It relies on making this social space present through signs and symbols. In other words, global imagination is cultivated by a process of ongoing construction of views, images, understandings, desires and scripts about the world. In turn, this process of representation relies on and derives from the capacity to imagine.

The following chapters delve into this co-constitutive relation between media representation and the global imagination, by exploring how global imagination is expressed and carried in images, stories and discourses in the contemporary media, in five primary sites: the other, ourselves, possible lives, the world, and the self.

2   Imagining Others
Representations of Natural Disasters

'The Others are coming.'
Danielle Rousseau warning the plane crash survivors, *Lost*, Season 1, episode 23: 'Exodus'

Introduction

ABC's critically acclaimed drama *Lost*, one of the most popular television dramas in recent years, relates the story of the survivors of a passenger jet which crash-lands on an island during a flight between Sydney and Los Angeles. The survivors soon learn about this tropical island's malevolent inhabitants, the 'Others', who kidnap children and are willing to kill 'anyone whom they perceive as a threat to themselves or the island, if provoked' (Wikipedia, Others [Lost]). The Others 'take on the guise of primitive but cunning jungle-dwellers. Their disguise includes wearing primitive flax-sewn clothes and going about barefoot' (ibid.). As the drama develops, we learn that the Others are stealthy: 'They are difficult to track, leaving virtually no trail to follow. They are also able to conceal themselves quite effectively, moving within striking distance of their victims without making a sound.' The Others seem 'fanatically dedicated to protecting the island at all costs' and 'quite willing to sacrifice themselves for their cause' (ibid.).

The conflict between the survivors and the Others escalates, although the lines between groups are crossed: one member of the Others defects to the survivors and one of the survivors joins the Others. The survivors' group, which includes a diversity of genders, ages, ethnicities, backgrounds, physical looks and national identities (although the majority are American), immediately identifies itself as a collective 'we' opposed to the Others. The members of the survivors' group perceive themselves as being everything that the Others are *not*, that is, rational, humane, benevolent, civilized and honest.

The narrative of *Lost* reflects and capitalizes on the preoccupation with others in contemporary culture and political discourse, especially since 9/11. The global media overflow with others: migrants, asylum seekers, refugees, earthquake survivors, famine victims, victims of war, terrorists, and so on. Surely, their representations are not synonymous; terrorists commonly are invested with very different meanings from victims of natural disasters, for example. At the same time, as I hope to show in this chapter, there are some broader patterns and tropes that characterize the ways in which different types of 'others' are represented and which it is important to engage with. What do media representations tell us about the others in our world and how we do or should relate to them? What moral scripts are on offer in the contemporary symbolic media space, about distant others and the relations between 'us' and 'them'?

This chapter explores these questions by focusing on representations of natural disasters such as earthquakes, famine and flood. Natural disasters are increasingly frequent and destructive across the world, and have become highly visible in the global public sphere; they often constitute global media events in which distant others figure centre-stage. Their media representations, therefore, constitute a productive site for exploring broader questions of how distant others are imagined and depicted in the global media of the early twenty-first century (bearing in mind that there are also important differences between the ways in which different 'others' in different contexts are represented).

Before analysing media representations of distant others in the context of natural disasters, I introduce some of the broader theoretical debates on the representation of the other. I argue that the existing literature focuses on two narratives of the other, which are constructed in both popular and scholarly discourse largely in binary terms: the first is of the distant other, who is morally and existentially outside 'us', a site of strangeness, hostility and danger; the second is of the distant stranger as part of a 'common humanity', 'just like us', with whom 'we' (chiefly in the west) share a world and a common fate.

Global Imagination and Narratives of the Other

Knowledge about the other is fundamental for realizing and articulating one's self-identity. To understand and define ourselves, as individuals and groups (communities, nations, etc.), we need an other to relate to, and to distinguish ourselves from. This is because our ability to identify and understand ourselves largely derives from, and relies on, a sense of who we are *not*.[1] The production of meaning, as Saussure (1974) argues, depends on the marking of difference within language between one sign and another. Thus, representations of the other are pivotal resources that feed our individual and collective imaginations. Our self-understanding and how we come to represent ourselves depends largely on how we imagine others, and on who is included in and who is excluded from the symbolic realm of representations on which our imagination feeds.

However, difference has a divided legacy. It is necessary for the production of meaning, the formation of language, culture and identity, but at the same time it is threatening, a site of hostility towards and anxieties about the other (Hall, 1997: 238). Difference often translates into otherness (Pickering, 2001); the other is cast as an outsider, existentially and morally, a cultural stranger locked within reified collective categories or stereotypes such as 'criminal', 'undesirable', 'dirty' and 'irrational'. This symbolic process of 'othering' places others beyond understanding, beyond the pale of humanity (Silverstone, 2007), denying dialogue, interaction or change (Pickering, 2001). Further, as Said (2003 [1978]) argues, the function of Orientalist representations is to establish the inferiority of the Orient to the west/Occident. The Orientalist is concerned with the Orient only insofar as knowledge about it helps to establish his or her identity and superiority: 'The Other is always constructed as an object for the benefit of the subject who stands in need of an objectified Other in order to achieve a masterly self-definition' (Pickering, 2001: 71).

The media engage continuously in the representational practice of othering: they hierarchize, exclude, criminalize, hegemonize and marginalize practices and populations that diverge from what, at a specific moment in time, is seen as central, safe, legitimate, normal and conventional (Pickering, 2001). There is extensive research that documents and explains how the first narrative, of the other as a source of strangeness, hostility and danger, is constructed in the media. For example, studies show how immigrants are often stereotyped, victimized, demonized and invested through discourse and image with negative meanings (King and Wood, 2001; Van Dijk, 2000). They are deposited 'into dustbin categories labelled "social problems", "unworthy", "despicable" or "dangerous"' (Cottle, 2006: 168). Similarly, Chouliaraki (2006: 107) shows how television news reporting dehumanizes the suffering of distant others (e.g., in natural disasters or terrorist attacks), rendering them 'irrelevant to the experiential world of the [western] spectators'. Another example is a study of video games (Sisler, 2008) which shows how Muslims and Arabs are represented by a set of schematized attributes, including headwear, loose clothing and dark skin, and how the game narrative frequently links these signifiers to international terrorism. They are collectivized as 'terrorist groups' – they shout and yell, raise weapons above their heads, and laugh after killing. These and other studies explore a wide range of types of others, for example, immigrants, victims of atrocities and disasters, or terrorists, in a variety of contexts and genres. Yet they all highlight the centrality in contemporary media of the narrative of the other as a morally distant entity, and they all show that the ways that this narrative is enacted are generally quite similar.

There is a second, very different narrative, of relations to distant others, which circulates in contemporary media representations: one of living with strangers with whom 'we' share a common humanity and fate. Warner (2002:56) calls this 'stranger-sociability' – a defining premise of the modern imaginary of the public:

> In modern society, a stranger is not as marvelously exotic as the wandering outsider would have been in an ancient, medieval, or early modern town. In that earlier social order, or in contemporary analogues, a stranger is mysterious, a disturbing presence requiring resolution. In the context of a public, however, strangers can be treated as already belonging to our world. More: they must be. We are routinely oriented to them in common life. They are a normal feature of the social.

Modern publics orient us towards strangers, people we do not know and will never know, and with whom we have no shared affiliations such as family ties or intimate associations. Encounters with strangers are part of modern life: on buses, the streets and, centrally, in the media; we are required constantly to imagine others (Warner, 2002: 57). Cultural representations are central to enabling, constituting and sustaining this imagining. They are primary cultural forms that 'mediate the intimate theatre of stranger-relationality' (ibid.: 57).

The modern social imaginary of relations among strangers is intimately entwined with an image of 'the world' as a set of individuals who are all equivalent and deserving of moral recognition. As Calhoun (2008) notes, this is a historically distinctive, mainly modern way of thinking, that is, to imagine human beings in the abstract, as it were, in their mere humanity. The emphasis in this modern social imaginary is on equivalence among strangers rather than differences or particular ties, such as kinship, religion, ethnicity or nationality.

The representation of distant suffering, for example, of atrocities, war and natural disasters, is a key site in contemporary public discourse where this second narrative of a world predicated on living with strangers is produced and enacted. Sufferers figure as distant strangers in their 'bare humanity' (Calhoun, 2008), demanding care, compassion and pity. For example, a Medicins Sans Frontiers appeal shows a volunteer treating a dark-skinned baby, with the caption: 'Angolan? Mozambican? Colombian? Cambodian? Haitian? Human. Donate without discrimination'. The message is that we have an obligation to help these distant others because they are human, not because of some specific shared civic solidarity (ibid.). In this narrative, central in contemporary discourses of development, humanitarianism and human rights, strangers are integral to our lives; we depend on their co-presence. This notion is frequently coupled in contemporary thought/ discourse with cosmopolitanism and, specifically, a 'cosmopolitan outlook' (Beck, 2006), a sense of interdependence among social actors across national borders and interconnectedness among and between strangers.

Thus, the global imagination encompasses two seemingly contradictory narratives through which the other is constructed. On the one hand, there is a narrative in which strangers are others marked as different – often radically so: they are strange, morally distant and are excluded, marginalized and symbolically annihilated. On the other hand, there is a narrative of the world predicated on relations among strangers, in which others are cast as human beings, just like us, with whom we are interconnected as part of a common humanity, and to whom we are committed morally.

In structuralist terms, these narratives are binary oppositions: they are based on opposing premises. In the former, others are the social pariahs; in the latter, they belong to our world, and we are oriented to them routinely in public life. However, both narratives are often constructed and enacted simultaneously. The image of a world predicated on relations among distant strangers, global connectedness and solidarity, which transcend ties, affiliations and spatial boundaries, interacts with, and often is articulated simultaneously with, an imaginary of the other as distant, undeserving of recognition and care.

It is these dual narratives of the other and the ways they are developed in the global media that constitute the focus of the following discussion. How are these moral scripts about distant others produced and enacted in media representations of distant suffering in natural disasters such as earthquakes, famine and flood? What do they reveal about the ways in which representations invite readers to imagine distant others at the start of the twenty-first century?

Imagining Distant Others in Natural Disasters

We tend to think of the visibility of natural disasters in the media, and the responses it engenders, as distinct features of our times. The 2004 Asian tsunami, which killed more than 200,000 people, received enormous media coverage, including live images captured by eyewitnesses on mobile phones, which spread swiftly around the world. This event was a record in terms of the international response: six months after it happened some $12 billion of aid had been pledged.[2] Six years on, people were responding generously to the devastating earthquake that hit Haiti, which is believed to have killed 230,000 and left more than 1.5 million people homeless, and which received intense media coverage over multiple platforms, and attracted pledges of $9.9 billion worth of relief.[3]

The live twenty-four-hour coverage of disasters by the global media plays an important role in turning such events into constitutive moments in the global imagination – moments that evoke a global 'cosmopolitan outlook', a sense of 'humanity' as a universal identity. But this is not an entirely new phenomenon: contemporary representations of distant others in contexts of suffering are rooted in earlier modes of representation and currents of thought. Therefore, to engage critically with how, in the global age, media representations invite us to imagine others, a historical perspective might be beneficial. This chapter takes a historical perspective, not to systematically compare past and present representations or to suggest that there is necessarily a clear, coherent trajectory towards certain representational practices and narratives of the distant other. Rather, the discussion of representations of the 1755 Lisbon earthquake is intended to provide a backdrop to a critical reflection on representations of current natural disasters and distant others more generally. I hope that the account of representations of the 1755 earthquake will evoke images and narratives of more recent natural disasters in the modern media and, in particular, that consideration of the characteristics of those historical representations of distant others, will advance understanding of the ways in which contemporary representations invite us to imagine distant others.

We step backwards in time to the mid-eighteenth century when an earthquake devastated Lisbon – arguably, the first global media disaster event.

Lisbon Earthquake, 1755

On Saturday 1 November 1755, at approximately 09.30, one of the most powerful earthquakes in recorded European history occurred in Lisbon, Portugal, then a city of 275,000 inhabitants and the fourth largest in Europe. The activity lasted ten minutes and is estimated to have measured between 8.5 and 8.8 on the Richter scale. Destruction in the city was widespread. Fire destroyed much property, and estimates of the dead vary from 30,000 to 100,000. Many took to boats moored in the River Tagus, but these were wrecked by a 25 foot tsunami. Two more waves followed – in Tangier along the Portuguese coast, and in Spain affecting Huelva and Cádiz – causing further deaths and destruction (Braun and Radner, 2005).

News of the 1755 Lisbon earthquake and the tens of thousands of people who had perished spread throughout Europe and the New World and provoked a hitherto unheard of reaction (Illouz, 2003b). For example, fifty years earlier, an earthquake had destroyed Port Royal in Jamaica, but, to use Kofi Annan's metaphor, was an 'orphaned disaster';[4] it was ignored by public discourse outside Jamaica, which was constructed as 'a place full of pirates and half-breeds' (Neiman, 2002: 241), and framed as deserving the destruction it suffered. By contrast, the Lisbon disaster affected a major trade centre and one of the world's wealthier cities, and provoked an unprecedented flow of compassionate reactions that mobilized charitable actions and material aid from the main European powers.[5]

The Lisbon earthquake, whose aftershocks continued to send panic throughout the region long after its occurrence,

> marks one of the first times subjects were faced with a barrage of representations of distant suffering, 'snapshots' that elicited an imaginative and affective engagement with strangers at great distance . . . one of the first instances in which subjects became spectators faced with the ethical and political implications of regarding distant suffering. (Sliwinski, 2009: 31)

Representing the Lisbon earthquake

Representations of the Lisbon earthquake, both textual accounts and images, were produced and circulated throughout Europe and the New World. Textual representations were mostly low quality, printed on cheap paper, folded into small news pamphlets called *relaçiónes de sucessos*. *Relaçiónes de sucessos* encompassed several genres, including prose, romance (a kind of verse popular in Spanish poetry), letters based on anonymous and informative accounts of survivors' experiences, lyrical pieces, prayers and theological and moral essays. The pamphlets were published and sold quickly and presumably cheaply, often through the use of blind sellers. They were read in public and were the main sources of information for the illiterate throughout Europe (Araújo, 2006; Espejo Cala, 2005).

Visual representations were predominantly engravings,[6] available in alehouses and at fairgrounds. Some images provided a bystander's view of the destruction wrought on the city and its inhabitants. Notably, fresh descriptions of the quake continued to emerge for up to almost a century, demonstrating the public's insatiable desire for news of this disaster (Sliwinski, 2009).

Many visual representations were religious responses, which depicted the earthquake as God's punishment for the sins of the people. They focused on

Figure 2.1 Santa Catarina Square; 1760, painting by João Glama Stroberle; courtesy of the Earthquake Engineering Online Archive, University of California, Berkeley

people's suffering, showing injured and dying masses alongside heroic ecclesiastical and angelic figures, suggesting the earthquake was part of some providential order. For example, in an oil painting from 1760 (figure 2.1), angels are depicted rising above the injured and dying masses congregating in front of a severely damaged church. These images depict the catastrophe and the suffering of ordinary citizens and portray the disaster in exaggerated terms. The focus in the engravings and paintings is not an accurate portrayal of the effects, but a representation of the large-scale destruction of human lives. Those 'dramatically rendered portraits of human existence that has been seized and displaced' are 'specifically designed to elicit fascination, to portray the devastation suffered by the imagination – indeed, to visually conjure up the idea of a shared *humanity*' (Sliwinski, 2009: 30, emphasis in original).

Religious textual accounts place similar emphasis on the collective experience of suffering, and give a sense of its universality. In *Het Verheerlykte en Vernederde Portugal* (*Portugal Glorified and Humiliated*), a long poem in rhyming Alexandrines, published in 1758, the Dutch poet De Haes prays for Portugal's restoration, by conjuring up an obligation to help distant sufferers as if they were us (cited in D'Haen, 2006: 352–3, emphasis added):

> Banish that hellish vapour, that thick darkness,
> So that they may recognize how beautifully shines the Savior Sun,
> Whose fire of love teaches us to love you first, with our soul and our senses,
> *And next our neighbours, like as ourselves.*

Although the poet invokes compassion for distant sufferers, through the call to imagine them as oneself, at the same time he blames the victims for their agony, citing the disaster as retribution and punishment for the sins of Lisbon's citizens. The message of the earthquake as God's punishment of sinners was repeated in many of the reactions around Europe (D'Haen, 2006; Georgi, 2005; Neiman, 2002). The earthquake was held up as a warning to Europe to mend its sinful ways and regain a righteous path, or else experience a similar fate.

Thus, while religious accounts call for compassion and care for Lisbon's sufferers, and emphasize a sense of a common fate and shared humanity, the people of Lisbon are clearly framed as morally sinful others, deserving of the apocalypse.[7] And while these accounts of the quake talk about distant others, they ultimately focus on 'us' – the meaning of the catastrophe for 'us', for the lives of their readers. This dialectic conception of others, and the ways in which representations of distant others serve to achieve self-understanding, resonate with how we imagine others today – a theme that I develop later.

Alongside religious explanations of the quake, the disaster sparked fundamental doubts about God's influence over earthly affairs. The event is seen by many as a watershed marking the beginning of modern thought, which shook the foundations of faith and challenged the theological view of Providence (Braun and Radner, 2005; Neiman, 2002).[8] In particular, the disaster stimulated scientific and philosophical debate over the nature and causes of earthquakes.

The most famous response was from the French philosopher Voltaire, who questioned the role of Providence in human suffering. In *Poème sur le dèsastre de Lisbonne*, Voltaire (1911 [1756]) calls on his fellow philosophers to contemplate the disaster and the destruction and misery it wrought, and questions religious interpretations of it as God's punishment:

> What crime, what sin, had those young hearts conceived
> That lie, bleeding and torn, on mother's breast?
> Did fallen Lisbon deeper drink of vice
> Than London, Paris, or sunlit Madrid?
> In these men dance; at Lisbon yawns the abyss.

Voltaire's poem focuses on the sufferers' welfare and constructs a moral problem based on the incongruity between his audience (who continues to dance in London and Paris) and the distant sufferers (Illouz, 2003a). Voltaire refuses to view suffering as either proof of a providential order (punishment for a sin) or 'the incomprehensible but just decree of an unfathomable God' (Illouz, 2003a: 159), and is explicit about the unacceptability of suffering.

Figure 2.2 Lisbon, 1755; courtesy of the Earthquake Engineering Online Archive, University of California, Berkeley

Illouz (2003a) argues that Voltaire confronts us 'head on' with distant suffering: innocent others are suffering meaninglessly while we are merry and happy. His poem invites the reader simultaneously to engage in rational deliberation over the absurdity of the world and to experience emotion, to feel compassion for the distant sufferers (Illouz, 2003a).

Rational discourse on the events was perpetuated by the personal accounts of survivors, written in a very realistic, but somehow detached, almost forensic style (Espejo Cala, 2005). These representations refute the religious narrative of a clear causal relation between people's sins and God's punishment. Rather, they underline the arbitrariness of suffering, its incomprehensibility and unacceptability. The sufferers in these accounts are innocent victims, with no responsibility for or control over the misfortune that had befallen them. Many visual representations of the earthquake convey similar messages and the incapacity of the human mind to grasp the disaster. In a copper engraving from the late eighteenth century (figure 2.2), for example, ordinary citizens are seen helplessly running for their lives, and sinking in the water.

The potent sense of shared humanity in non-religious representations is based on a recognition of the sufferers as 'innocent victims, unfortunates who were dealt an unfair hand in the cruel game of chance that is human life' (Sliwinski, 2009: 30). These representations call their audiences to relate to the Lisbon sufferers on the basis of a 'politics of pity' (Boltanski, 1999, drawing on Arendt): they invoke a generalized concern for the suffering other, not abstract rules of right and wrong (politics of justice). The politics of pity is predicated on the spectacle of suffering, of morally arousing depictions of suffering, which position the observer of suffering as a spectator in a radically different situation from that of the sufferers (Boltanski, 1999). In this context, Voltaire (1911 [1756]) deliberately invokes the theatrical metaphor and positions his readers as spectators:

> Tranquil spectators of your brothers' wreck,
> Unmoved by this repellent dance of death,
> Who calmly seek the reason of such storms,
> Let them but lash your own security;
> Your tears will mingle freely with the flood.

Voltaire seeks to evoke compassion, while urging disavowal of the voyeurs' passivity and an acknowledgement of the distant sufferers' misfortune and its unacceptability. Importantly, Voltaire's poem evokes *guilt*: you citizens of European capitals sit in your comfort zones, spectators of the theatre of horror and agony in Lisbon (the 'dance of death'). He follows this with a call for the reader to imagine the disaster happening to them:

> Are ye so sure the great eternal cause,
> That knows all things, and for itself creates,
> Could not have placed us in this dreary clime
> Without volcanoes seething 'neath our feet?

Further, Voltaire demands that his readers reflect on the unfairness of the Lisbon disaster and the incommensurable conditions in other parts of the world: 'What happens in Lisbon is scandalous from the standpoint of what happens in London and Paris and vice versa; we should feel uncomfortable dancing in Paris when thousands are buried alive in Lisbon' (Illouz, 2003a: 159). Thus, the basis for engaging with distant others is neither geographical proximity to Lisbon nor national or religious ties. Rather, we see here the modern notion of relations among strangers (Warner, 2002) and 'global consciousness' (Robertson, 2009) – a reflexive sense of the world as one whole – starting to consolidate in public discourse and thought. This consciousness is evoked in Voltaire's poem to mobilize the politics of justice: it moves beyond the dramatic plight of the sufferers, that is, the politics of pity, to contemplate systematic suffering: the incongruence between people on a global scale (in relation to the concept of the globe at that time).

In sum, both religious and non-religious representations of the Lisbon earthquake, although predicated upon fundamentally different premises, present a meaningful call to readers and viewers to identify with another's distant suffering. Since the Lisbon earthquake, the religious narrative has been largely overtaken by the modern view of disasters, and even relatively conservative western cultures are no longer willing to contemplate God's hand in their daily affairs (Neiman, 2002). However, elements of both the religious and non-religious aesthetics and discourses of distant suffering continue to shape current representations, and how we imagine distant others and conceive our relations to them, in quite significant ways.

From Quill Pen to the Recording Studio – Voltaire with a Twist

'We Are The World', 1985 – the African famine

In the 1980s, a devastating famine in the Horn of Africa claimed the lives of nearly a million people. This famine is a classic story of denial: despite warnings and statements from aid agencies and international bodies, which began in 1981 when drought wiped out the harvest in Ethiopia, western governments were reluctant to become involved, and the Ethiopian government was keen to cover up the disaster and its scale. Pressure from aid agencies and horrifying footage of starving people broadcast on television across the world from 1984, finally forced western governments to pledge money, and public donations from the west increased.[9]

The footage accompanying the breaking story of the Ethiopian famine, filmed by BBC journalists Mohamed Amin and Michael Buerk, consisted of intensely moving portrayals of feeding centres in northern Ethiopia. They inspired Bob Geldof to record Band Aid's 1984 charity single 'Do They Know It's Christmas?', which became number one in the charts and raised $8 million for charity. It was followed by Live Aid, a concert in July 1985, held simultaneously in London and Philadelphia. The concert, which involved many superstars and was billed as the 'global jukebox', was viewed on television via satellite by 1.5 billion people, and raised over $80 million (Benthall, 1993).[10]

Following 'Do They Know It's Christmas?', which originated in the UK and achieved considerable visibility in the west, a single called 'We Are The World' was recorded in the US, by United Support of Artists for Africa. The song was produced by Quincy Jones and co-written by Michael Jackson and Lionel Richie. Forty-five (mainly American) singers participated, including some of the most famous artists in the music industry at the time. The single was released on 7 March 1985, and quickly topped music charts throughout the west[11] and became the fastest-selling American pop music single in history. By 2009, the song and the merchandise related to its promotion had raised over $63 million for humanitarian aid.[12]

'We Are The World', which mobilized the pop music industry to focus on a humanitarian cause, became one of the most memorable cultural responses to the African famine, and has left a lasting imprint on the public imagination, evidenced by its continuous popularity and commercial success, and various remakes more than two decades on. This makes the song and its video a productive site to explore how distant others are imagined today, and to question what makes this representation of them so widely acceptable and enduring. In view of the features of representations of the Lisbon earthquake discussed above, and Voltaire's poem in particular, the analysis that follows highlights how the moral scripts that orient our relations to distant others today are rooted in old modes of thought and representation, and how, in other respects, the ways in which we are called to imagine distant others today have changed.

Performing care: Distant others as deserving of pity

The lyrics, video and tune of 'We Are The World' generate strong emotional commitment to and investment in a project of care and giving to distant others. The lyrics call on western publics 'to lend a helping hand' to dying people in Africa, by evoking an emotional response to distant sufferers and invoking global interconnectedness, interdependence and compassion. This is conveyed explicitly in lines such as 'the world must come together as one' and 'we stand together as one'. The focus is on *our* obligation and responsibility in the west, to help *them*, the far-away strangers. Helping is presented not as an option, but as an obligation: we all '*must* lend a helping hand'. The formulation of the third line in the chorus drives home a sense of urgency for a concrete action: 'we are the ones who make a brighter day, *so let's start giving*'.

The emotional dimension is generated through the use of metaphors and symbols that resonate with the genre of romance (recall the Lisbon romance pamphlets), such as 'Send them your heart/ So they know that someone cares'. Religious references, for example, 'We're all part of God's great family' and 'As God has shown us, turning stone to bread', capitalize on religious belief – a deeply engrained component of American culture (Silverstone, 2007); they boost emotionality and inject the song with an explicit spirituality.

The video clip shows the forty-five artists singing in a recording studio – a visual composition that is resonant of a church choir and generates a sense of an impassioned, collective commitment to a common cause. Many of the artists sing with closed eyes, have fitting facial expressions, and hold hands with one another. The song and its performance have a gospel element, resembling soulful and passionate hymn singing.

In musical terms, 'We Are The World' is an anthemic pop tune: it is a classic, formulaic pop song with a strong 'hook', which is very accessible, and has a catchy melody allowing one to 'sing along' – a type of music that appeals to the majority, thereby promoting a feeling of inclusiveness. The formulaic chorus reinforces this: it carries a simple but powerful message that we are all part of a global community, and we can make a change to help suffering strangers.

Annihilation of the other and the hyper-presence of 'us'

At the same time, the construction of the other as deserving of pity and care, and the celebration of global connectedness and 'common humanity', are at odds with the absence of actual sufferers from the video. We do not see the African sufferers (textually or visually); nor do we hear their voices. They are imagined in the abstract and receive only three extremely vague mentions in the lyrics:

1 'There are people dying' (fourth line): the sufferers, whose misfortune the song seeks to alleviate, are completely disembedded from their particular identities and contexts – there is no mention of who these people are, where they are, how many are suffering, or the context of their suffering (famine) and its causes.

2 Later the song refers to the sufferers in the third person: 'Send *them* your heart / So *they* know that someone cares / And *their* lives will be stronger and free'. Since all we know about 'them' is that – to put it somewhat crudely – they are dying, somewhere, from something, the use of third-person pronouns renders them even less real: as invisible, far-away, vague, unknown others. 'We Are The World' consigns to its audience the task of imagining – constructing pictures in their heads, on the basis of the resources in their imagination 'archive'. Thus, the song calls its audience to imagine the distant sufferers on the basis of its intertextual relations with other texts and images, primarily the devastating images of starving Africans, especially children, which were circulating in the media when the song was first recorded and distributed globally.

3 The third mention of sufferers is in the phrase: 'it's time to lend a hand to life'. The construction of sufferers as 'bare life' or 'humanity', characteristic of modern discourse on humanitarian emergencies (Calhoun, 2008), evokes a universalist ethics: the obligation to help is grounded in the fact that they are human. However, as Chouliaraki (2006: 105–6) argues in

relation to the representation of distant sufferers in the news, aggregating sufferers into abstract groups and stripping them of their personal identities as individuals 'deprives the encounter between spectators and sufferers of any sense of humanness . . . the sufferers . . . remain irrevocably "Other" – distant, inactive, devoid of feelings and thoughts'.

The visual, vocal and textual absence of sufferers from the song is even more striking when contrasted with the hyper-presence of celebrity artists in the recording studio: the camera's focus on their gestures, their looks, and the passion and emotion they display. Musically, the integration of such a large range of distinct voices into a single tune foregrounds the presence of the celebrity artists. Against the overwhelming presence of western celebrities in the studio, the distant others are left to be imagined.

The collapse of the innocent other into 'us'

The second line of the chorus, 'We are the children', implies that many of the distant sufferers are children. This identity connotes innocence and lack of responsibility for the disaster, and is rooted in Enlightenment's rejection of the religious narrative, which sees the victims as responsible for their misfortune. The message of the innocence of the victims, the arbitrariness of their suffering and the use of children are common tropes in contemporary representations of sufferers (e.g., Cohen, 2001; Höijer, 2004; Moeller, 1999). Children (and women) constitute 'suitable' and 'ideal' victims (Höijer, 2004), commonly conceived as those most likely to stimulate an empathetic response (Moeller, 1999).

What is particularly noteworthy in the song's use of children is that these actual sufferers – the victims of the famine – have no identity or agency in their own right. Rather than saying 'they are the children, and we are obliged to help them', 'We are the children' incorporates them totally into us: they exist (in the song) only insofar as they are part of 'us'. Thus, not only are the distant others absent and faceless; they are collapsed into the collective 'we'. The other exists only by virtue of being incorporated into 'us' and 'our' (western neo-liberal democratic) values: love ('you know love is all we need'), freedom ('And their lives will be stronger and free'), choice and agency ('there's a choice we're making'), individualism ('just you and me'), and uniformity ('we stand together as one').

Voltaire asks his readers to contemplate the pain and suffering of 'those' far-away others and to feel compassion, precisely on the basis of recognizing that we are *here,* and they are *there* experiencing a radically *different* situation. By contrast, 'We Are The World', and many other representations today, promote collusion between 'us' and the other. Viewers are called on to embody the other, to relate to the other through complicity and 'the elision of the different to the same' (Silverstone, 2007: 47). A vivid current example is an online simulation game, *Darfur Is Dying*, which invites users to get a 'faint glimpse of what it's like for the more than 2.5 million who have been internally displaced by the crisis in Sudan',[13] by assuming the role of a displaced Darfurian who faces the obstacles and threats to survival in a refugee camp. This kind of extreme proximity and collusion is constructed as educational and morally desirable – an observation I return to in chapter 6.

'We Are The World' is also self-congratulatory. Nowhere in the song is this more explicit than in the line 'There's a choice we're making / We're saving our own lives'. Helping those 'dying people' is ultimately about saving ourselves. Through becoming the western saviours 'who make a brighter day', we proclaim our own salvation.[14] This echoes a broader critique of news coverage of distant suffering and the regime of 'Consumer Aid' (Lidchi, 1993) or 'Brand Aid' (Richey and Ponte, 2011), in which compassion is elicited and expressed through consumption (e.g., Live Aid concerts, the RED campaign): the relation to distant others is constructed through and on the basis of western spectators' self-congratulation for their generosity (Cohen, 2001; see also Nash, 2008). Thus, as Said (2003 [1978]) argues, the other is of concern only insofar as it helps to generate knowledge about 'us' (the west) and to establish our superiority.

Comfort, denial and the absence of denunciation of suffering

The second verse directly states that denial can no longer be sustained: 'We can't go on / Pretending day by the day / That someone somewhere will make a change'. These lines have a disruptive element; recall Voltaire's call to spectators to 'shake off' their tranquillity. However, this call is subsumed by an overwhelmingly sentimental construction that encourages disavowal rather than disruption, comfort rather than disturbance. The tune can be described as 'safe music': it is over-produced, with no dissonance or tension. The melody is very accessible; there is nothing challenging or uncomfortable about it. This musical 'safety' converges with the lyrics which, rather than disturbing, reassure listeners. The text is geared towards making 'we', who listen to the song – primarily in the west – feel virtuous, not angry or guilty: 'It's true we'll make a better day/Just you and me'. The guilt evoked by Voltaire's underscoring of the incommensurable conditions around the globe and the incomprehensibility of suffering is absent, as is any denunciation of its unfairness. Death is mentioned only once ('there are people dying'), and rather distantly and abstractly. There is nothing that clouds the 'feel good' spirit of the song.

The very limited and vague references to death and suffering are partly explained by the genre of a pop song: it is meant as entertainment, intended to have wide rather than particular or ideological appeal. It mobilizes people to donate money to starving Africans by allowing the listeners and viewers to feel good about doing so. However, this rationale for not showing death and for avoiding negative accounts and imagery of suffering is not reserved to pop music; it is characteristic of the broader realm of representations of others' suffering, as I discuss later in this chapter.

What I hope is becoming clear is that media representations of distant others cannot be understood within polarized paradigms as *either* distancing, excluding and annihilating the other, *or* humanizing the other, evoking care, compassion and aid towards distant others. Media representations are often more diverse and complex, and these contradictions and tensions in many cases play out simultaneously. 'We Are The World' illustrates this: it symbolically annihilates the sufferers whose misfortune it professes to alleviate. Despite mobilizing thousands to donate money to help alleviate the suffering of African people affected by famine, the song does not mention or denounce this suffering.

These paradoxes endure, and are further complicated in current media representations. To explore how these tensions continue to play out and are transformed in the twenty-first century, we fast-forward twenty-five years to 2010 . . .

'We Are The World', 2010 – the Haiti earthquake

At 16.53 local time on 12 January 2010, an earthquake measuring 7 on the Richter scale, struck the Caribbean island of Haiti. The earthquake hit the most densely populated area of the country, killing some 230,000 people, injuring 300,000 and leaving 1.5 million homeless. Major damage was caused in the cities of Port-au-Prince and Jacmel, and large areas of the surrounding countryside were devastated. Rescue efforts began immediately with survivors fighting to extricate the living and the dead from the rubble of collapsed buildings. However, treatment of the injured was hampered because hospitals in the capital, transport facilities and communication systems were severely damaged, making it very difficult to provide emergency assistance. Appeals for humanitarian aid were launched swiftly by various international aid organizations and the international community pledged a total of $9.9 billion in immediate and long-term aid to earthquake-hit Haiti. However, the planned reconstruction has suffered severe delays.[15] Six months after the earthquake, much of the devastation was still evident, and over a million Haitians were living in relief camps, mostly without electricity, running water or sewerage, and crime in the camps was widespread.[16]

On 1 February 2010, in the same studio in which the original was recorded twenty-five years earlier, more than eighty-five performers (almost double the number involved in the original recording) gathered to record a new version of the iconic charity single 'We Are The World', to help earthquake relief efforts and the rebuilding of Haiti. Jones and Richie were the executive producers alongside several co-producers, including Haitian-American musician Wyclef Jean, the nephew of Raymond Joseph, Haiti's Ambassador to the United States. Oscar-winning director Paul Haggis directed a seven-minute long 'We Are The World 25 For Haiti' music video. A short version of the video made its debut on 13 February 2010, during coverage of the opening ceremony for the Winter Olympics in Vancouver. It was used as part of a unique 'roadblock simulcast' on fifty-three United States broadcast and cable networks and on over 100 international broadcast and cable networks. Multinational corporations, such as AEG Live, Group M Entertainment, Fremantle Media Enterprises, iTunes Store, YouTube, Visa and Coca-Cola, signed up to promoting awareness of 'We Are The World 25 For Haiti', and encouraged people to donate by downloading the song.

The new incarnation of the 1985 song is largely faithful to the original song and its video. However, there are some differences that shed light on broader changes in the imagining of others in the current media space.

The other brought closer

The lyrics of the 2010 song reproduce a similarly universalist message to the one conveyed by the original text, of a 'world connected by a common bond' working towards a common cause. But a whole new segment added to the end of the song, with rhymes written by American rapper Will.i.am, introduces important differences. The new text refers directly to the sufferers and the context of their suffering (an earthquake). The Haitian people are referred to as 'you' (the second rather than the third person) – a linguistic choice that generates a sense of directness, proximity and intimacy with the other. We note an interesting discursive move from eighteenth-century Voltaire's '*those* young hearts', through 1985's 'We Are The World' 'there are *people* dying', to 2010's 'We Are The World 25 For Haiti' 'we'll help *you* make it through the storm'. The far-away 'they' who were 'there' have become 'you', here and now.

This transformation in the way in which the other is referred to is emblematic of a key mode of relation through which distant others are imagined today: 'intimacy at a distance' (Thompson, 1995: 219). This is manifest in the reception of the musical elements in the 2010 version by the press and in the online sphere. Three musical additions in the 2010 version are noteworthy in this context: (1) the inclusion of hip-hop at the end of the song, rapped by contemporary artists, including Lil Wayne, Will.i.am, Kanye West, LL Cool J, Swizz Beatz, Snoop Dogg and Busta; (2) the use of Auto-Tune – a proprietary audio processor used to correct pitch in vocal and instrumental performances; and (3) a verse sung in Haitian Creole by Wyclef Jean.

The incorporation of the musical genres of rap and hip-hop into the song and the use of Auto-Tune on some of the vocals, were criticized widely in the press and the blogsphere. They were seen as alienating, detaching and desensitizing. Wyclef Jean's Creole verse, on the other hand, was praised for its authentic connection to the scene of suffering, its harking back to Afro-Haitian roots (e.g., Pareles, 14 February 2010). A typical comment, posted on the entertainment-related website Entertainium, reads:

> When Wyclef Jean sings in Creole, you can hear the pain in his voice as he laments the utter destruction of his homeland. When T-Pain then auto-tunes some nonsense, the emotion is gone and the personal connection to the devastation in Haiti vanishes. (Lamagna, 13 February 2010)[17]

This interpretation of the musical elements in the song is extremely telling about how we imagine others in contemporary mediated space and what modes of representation and imagination are seen as desirable and accept-able as opposed to those considered to be inappropriate and unwelcome. The presence of the Haitian-American singing passionately in his homeland language – acting as the Orient, in Said's (2003 [1978]) terms – is regarded as providing a 'truthful' access to the other. As an American-Haitian, a celebrity and nephew of Haiti's Ambassador to the United States, Wyclef Jean is the ideal mediator who can provide 'authentic' connection to the victims, give viewers an (illusionary) sense of unmediated access to the 'real' experience of the people (the victims) in Haiti, and link between spectator and victims.

By contrast, musical genres and styles such as Auto-Tune, which high-light the presence of technology rather than the human, and emphasize the mediation of voice, are associated with distance and detachment, and thus are denigrated. They kill 'the personal connection to the devastation in Haiti' in the words of the web poster cited above. Ironically, it is probably the inclusion of these contemporary genres and artists that made so many young people 'connect' with the song and donate money to Haiti relief. However, in mainstream public discourse, these genres are associated with distance and 'coldness' rather than intimacy and proximity, and are seen as disconnecting, desensitizing viewers, and as inappropriate for relating and imagining suffering.

The other made visible

While the 1985 'We Are The World' was characterized by the visual and textual absence of others, the 2010 version is marked by their presence – primarily in the video. The 2010 version includes images of ruin and destruction in Haiti, relief workers, and smiling, hopeful Haitian children dancing amid the destruction. The opening chords of the tune are accompanied by footage of Haiti after the earthquake and the image of a man engaged in rebuilding; the camera then moves to a panoramic view of the rubble, after which it zooms in on a child standing in front of the rubble with the ocean behind him, waving to the camera. Crucially, we see these images *before* we see the celebrities in the studio: this is the context to their performance. From the opening onwards, the video moves seamlessly back and forth, between the recording studio in Los Angeles and Haiti. The clip ends with the studio choir belting out the chorus, images of Haiti, the sound of the traditional long trumpets and drums used in Haitian carnivals, and Wyclef Jean ululating 'Haiti, Haiti' in a Haitian Creole pronunciation (which is strikingly different from the Anglo-American pronunciation that dominated coverage of the earthquake in the English-speaking media).

While there seems to be agreement among commentators in the press and the online sphere that the 2010 version fails to live up to the 1985 song, the inclusion of images of Haitians (mainly children) in the video was hailed unanimously as an improvement on the original.[18] The inclusion of Haitian faces was seen as both providing context for the song, something that was missing from the 1985 original, and evoking the 'right' emotional response. A post on the Comments section of MTV's website neatly captures this idea:

> Paul Haggis is did an excellent job with the video. I'm so glad that he also wanted the haitian people apart of it. if they weren't I would just think its very cheesy like but the video truly touched me and brought tears to my eyes yet happy tears. =)[19]

What is it that arguably renders the visibility of distant others in the 2010 'We Are The World' so very acceptable in the eyes of some western spectators? In addressing this question, three aspects of how Haitian sufferers are constructed merit attention: the focus on positive imagery and the sublimation of suffering; the focus on agency and the individual; and the presentation of the other as spectacle. These elements are manifest in this particular clip, but are suggestive of the ways in which distant others are imagined in contemporary representations more generally, and what in the construction of others renders them legitimate, desirable and acceptable.

1 Positive imagery and the sublimation of suffering

The images of Haitians in the clip are positive and upbeat: smiling children are seen playing, dancing and singing, portraying joyousness and optimism. People are shown amid scenes of wreckage, but rejoicing, hopeful and, seemingly, happy. In contrast to the images of the Lisbon earthquake, depicting the large-scale destruction of human lives and the environment, and people dying in their masses, wounded and running for their lives (figure 2.2), in this clip, and in today's media more generally, we are frequently shown positive imagery of active, independent and empowered individuals (Benthall, 1993; Dogra, 2006, 2012; Rajaram, 2002; Smith and Yanacopulos, 2004).

This pattern of representation is indicative of a broader shift in the representation of distant suffering that began in the mid-1970s in response to criticisms levelled against the patronizing, Orientalizing, ethnocentric discourse used by NGOs and the media. Sufferers need to be given visibility and a voice, argue the critics; they should be represented as dignified, as knowing subjects, not passive objects. Negative images showing helpless, weak and vulnerable victims are damaging to their dignity, de-contextualize the sufferers' misery and perpetuate misleading views of the developing world as a theatre of tragedy and disasters (Cohen, 2001). These images, some critics contend, must be replaced by positive images signifying empowerment, agency and resilience.

However, there are also critics (e.g., Andén-Papadopoulos, 2009; Petley, 2003; Sontag, 2003) of the shift towards upbeat images on the grounds that they are sanitizing, distort reality and deny the vulnerability of the victims. The inclusion of negative imagery in accounts of suffering, they argue, is pivotal to its denunciation:

> Surely the point is to represent the problem at its worst. To be sure, this should be done with dignity – but why suppress the fact that the predicament of these millions of people arises entirely from their vulnerability? Without patterns of vulnerability and dependency, there is no need for political altruism or social justice. (Cohen, 2001: 183)

The close-ups of Haiti inhabitants in the clip create a feeling of intimacy between the viewer and the Haitian people, but the viewer is allowed highly restricted access to their lives – the pain they are experiencing is almost completely removed. Haitians' suffering is aestheticized through the use of a range of cinematic techniques, for example, the backdrop of pale, grey-coloured rubble contrasts with the colourfully clad people in the foreground and the colourful festival van, shown at the end of the clip; shots of wreckage are shown against exotic scenes of a Haitian beach.

The visual representations of the Lisbon quake are expressive of extreme devastation and helplessness: the viewer is confronted by the suffering of the people, the terrified citizens, arms raised above their heads as they drown. By contrast, the suffering of the Haitian earthquake victims in the 2010 'We Are The World' clip, as in other media representations of distant others today, are rendered 'beautiful' (Reinhardt, Edwards and Duganne, 2007; Stallabrass, 2010) and 'sublime'. Boltanski (1999: 127, citing Froidevaux, 1989: 121) argues that 'the beauty extracted from the horrific through this process of sublimation of the gaze, which is "able to transform any object whatever into a work of art", owes nothing therefore to the object'. A close-up of a child in a wheelchair neatly illustrates this effect: the child is looking up at the sky and smiling – a pose that signifies hope, to the words of 'love is all we need' being sung in the background. The boy's suffering is reified, transformed into a sublime spectacle, representing a universalized sense of human pain and suffering rather than concern for his and other sufferers' disability and pain, their causes or ways to alleviate them.

2 The focus on the individual and agency

Haiti's residents are shown standing in groups, in the context of their community, but the simultaneous use of close-ups, especially of children's faces against a backdrop of ruin – as in the opening scene of a child standing in rubble, waving to the camera – emphasizes the individual. Rather than being vulnerable, passive victims, the Haitian people are shown as active – dancing, singing, running, playing. The new lyrics amplify the message of sufferers' action and agency, enabled by the benefactors' acts of giving: 'lean on', 'wake up', 'look around', 'make it', 'stand on', 'hear', 'walk', 'find the dreams', 'move the obstacles', 'rebuild'. Representations of the 1755 Lisbon earthquake, on the other hand, are predicated on a view of suffering as a collective experience of vulnerability – with no room for either individual or agency. The Lisbon depictions convey a strong sense of human beings' lack of agency and their marginality and helplessness in the face of cosmic forces and Providence.

The 2010 'We Are The World' clip is characteristic of other contemporary representations that reflect a radical shift in the direction of depicting sufferers as individual active agents, and a focus on the self (an aspect that is developed in chapter 6). From survivors of environmental disasters, wars and terrorism, to victims of domestic violence and sexual abuse, cancer and torture, stories of suffering feeding the contemporary global imagination are largely of individual struggle and empowerment achieved through self-responsibility and self-management. These stories emphasize 'the individual's emergence from suffering, rather than the cause of the pain: I'm a survivor, in spite and because of the misfortune that befell me' (Orgad, 2009a: 152).

Some argue that presenting sufferers as sovereign agents acting in relation to adversity, is instrumental in humanizing the sufferers and engaging spectators with this misfortune (Boltanski, 1999; Chouliaraki, 2006; Tester, 2001). At the same time, this emphasis on sufferers as active agents may deflect concern for their vulnerability, their dependence on others and on the larger societal structures. It may work to reinforce rather than challenge denial of their suffering: their pain is presented as tolerable and with a solution (Cohen, 2001; Ignatieff, 1998; Moeller, 1999). Here, Nash's (2008: 173) observation on the Making Poverty History campaign applies: the 2010 'We Are The World' clip's depiction of Haitians, and of aid workers shown unloading supplies from helicopters and delivering food to the victims, elicits pride and joy rather than shame and guilt. The message to the western viewer is that 'you are part of the solution, not part of the problem'.

3 The spectacle of the other

The Haitians shown in the video are reduced to two main characteristics: (1) they are mostly children – corresponding to the line in the song 'We are the children', and capitalizing on connotations of children (discussed earlier) as lacking responsibility and as innocent; (2) they are frequently shown dancing, a depiction that invokes the racial stereotype of black people as having 'natural rhythm' and an allusion to exotic tribal rituals performed through collective dancing.

The way that footage from Haiti is incorporated into the clip and juxtaposed with the singers in the studio makes the dancing Haitians appear to be accompanying the celebrities: they seem to move and clap synchronously with the beat of the song. They are part of the performance, the spectacle being enjoyed by the viewer, which is compounded by connotations of their dance as 'primitive' and exotic. Blackness, to echo Dyer (1986: 89, cited in Hall, 1997: 255), is presented as 'avatism' – a return to 'what black people were supposed to be like deep down' and 'a guarantee of the authentic wildness within of the people who had come from there'.

However, although the Haitians appear to be dancing to the beat of the song and we see their lips mouthing the words of the song, their voices are

Figure 2.3 'We Are The World 25 for Haiti' © Kevin Mazur/Wire Image

muted. We hear only the voices of the 'approved' legitimate singers: the famous, desirable celebrities, in the safe, 'civilized', 'normal' zone of order – the west. 'You can join the chorus' – a small caption appearing on the screen invites the viewers to upload their own version of the song, but the Haitians cannot: their voices, literally and symbolically, are unheard. Thus, while the 2010 'We Are The World' pretends to celebrate global solidarity, it fails to incorporate Haitians' voices, from outside the studio.[20] These distant others are a spectacle to be gazed at, not voices to be heard.

In addition to the footage of Haiti edited into the clip, in the shots of the celebrity singers' chorus we can see big screens behind them on the studio walls, which show similar continuous footage of Haiti (figure 2.3). The camera is focused on the singers, but behind them we can see parts of the bodies of Haitian people: a waving hand, a dancing leg, a smile.

The meaning of these images of Haitians projected on the studio walls behind the singers is ambivalent. On the one hand, the sufferers constitute a background to the song: they are the context for this charity production – an aspect that was missing from the 1985 production, and that continues to be absent in many media representations of distant suffering. The images of the Haitian people shown on the studio walls can be seen as a symbolic reminder of the constant presence of sufferers in contemporary life. Distant others are the backdrop to our lives in a global age; visible in images, text and sound, they constitute an integral part of our imagination, which orients our thoughts, feelings and behaviour. At the same time, these distant others are *only* a backdrop: the viewer's eye is drawn to the celebrities, the Haitians' bodies are 'fragmented' and 'cropped', visually disassembled into relevant parts, fetishized, turned into objects (Hall, 1997). A symbolic frontier is erected between 'us', here, in the safe zone of modern western 'normality' and 'them', there, in the zone of chaos.

Ultimately, the Haiti earthquake victims are packaged as part of a commodity – a song led by celebrities, to be downloaded and consumed. A post responding to a blogger's cynical analysis of the song neatly summarizes the critique of the clip's symbolic commodification and reduction of Haitian sufferers:

> it [the song] ALMOST make me want to take my last donation back.
> luckily I realize that Haiti themselves are the biggest victims here. not only have they lost hundreds of thousands of lives in a tragedy of a mind-bogging proportions, but now they are forever tied to the lamest celebrity fundraiser-ego-boost of all times.[21]

The representational practices of stereotyping, objectification, fragmentation, fetishization and commodification converge to make the distant others a spectacle – an aesthetic regime deeply rooted in a racialized system of representation (Hall, 1997). However, these practices apply also to other dimensions of difference that are represented in contemporary media, as I show in subsequent chapters.

Urgency and action to help the distant other

The 1985 song appealed directly to the consciousness of its audience, by evoking an emotional commitment based on ethical universalism: no longer can we pretend that somebody else will do something; we share in a common fate and must all 'lend a hand'. It implies that people should donate money, although the song calls metaphorically on viewers to 'send their hearts' (rather than their money), to an invisible distant other.

The 2010 song rehearses a similar discourse, but includes a direct and specific call to help, linked to concrete action: 'to help you rebuild after the rubble's gone'. The change to the lyrics of the third verse demonstrates this: the religious metaphor of the miracle of turning stone to bread is replaced by an almost explicit call to the audience to help, and urgently: 'We can't let them suffer / No we cannot turn away / Right now they need a helping hand'. Further, the song reinforces the message of the urgency of aiding victims, by locating it intertextually, in the context of the massive scale of humanitarian disasters and their visibility in the contemporary global public sphere: 'Like Katrina, Africa, Indonesia/ And now Haiti needs us, they need us, they need us'.

This sense of urgency and directness is compounded by the guilt invoked – do it so that the victims' cries 'will not be in vain'. American television star Jamie Foxx reinforces this in his appeal to the viewers in the introduction to the video on the official website, 'to please, do more than just watch. Reach deep into your hearts and give anything you can, as we have, for Haiti'. Foxx's plea – albeit in much softer and far less critical tone – echoes Voltaire's call to readers to disavow the spectator's passivity. Similar calls for viewers to renounce their passivity are evident to varying degrees in other types of representation, such as NGO campaigns (Cohen, 2001) and news reports. *New York Times* columnist Nicholas Kristof's (23 February 2005) piece on the conflict in Darfur is a renowned example of direct confrontation of the western public's passivity. Juxtaposed with pictures of dead and mutilated bodies, Kristof reprimands his readers, writing that 'the real obscenity isn't in printing pictures of dead babies – it's in our passivity, which allows these people to be slaughtered.'

How can we explain the stronger and more explicit emphasis on the urgency for action to alleviate suffering in the 2010 version of the song? The Haiti earthquake was a milestone in the unprecedented immediacy and liveness with which news about suffering is disseminated. Some describe it as a tipping point for citizen journalism: tweets, blogs, photo sites and citizen video websites such as LiveLeak, photos taken by citizen journalists posted on free images sites such as TwitPic and PicFog, and special online forums for citizens' postings launched by main news organizations such as CNN, BBC and *The Times* – all became central means for gathering live news from Haiti, for documenting the scale and devastation of the disaster, and for later expressions of public outrage at the ongoing situation.

This new media environment allows different kinds of claims for audiences' moral responses and actions: these people suffer *now* and *you* can do something to alleviate their misery in *real* and *immediate* ways. 'Doing something' has never been easier or more user-friendly: simply click to donate now. In contrast to the immediacy that characterizes the production and consumption of the 2010 song, representations of the Lisbon earthquake continued to be produced decades after the event. Their meaning was less about a concrete call for immediate help – this was directed at institutions, such as monarchies, rather than individuals. Rather, the Lisbon quake representations focused largely on the moral lesson: the religious narrative of a testimony of God's hand intervening in daily affairs and a warning to people to reject their sinful ways; the Enlightenment narrative of a universalist humanitarian ethics. In the twenty-four-hour, consumer-oriented media environment of the twenty-first century, the broader moral agenda seems to be giving way to a 'petite' ethics. It privileges short-term and low-intensity relation to the suffering other, over engagement through large intellectual agenda informing a humanitarian sensibility (Chouliaraki, 2010). It privileges privatized action rather than grand ethical and political changes that seek to undermine and dismantle global structures of injustice.[22] It is an ethics of click, donate, and (possibly) forget it. This form of mediated intimacy at a distance 'allows individuals a great deal of scope in defining the terms of engagement and in fashioning the characters of intimate others' (Thompson, 1995: 220) – an observation we explore further in subsequent chapters, and to which I return in the book's conclusion.

Conclusion

Analysis of the representations of three historical natural disasters which became global events of distant suffering, namely, the 1755 Lisbon earthquake, the African famine in the 1980s and the 2010 Haiti earthquake, illustrates some of the ways in which distant others are constructed in the global media. Of course, these are particular examples; their analysis does not seek to and cannot capture the entire range of practices and patterns of representation of distant others and the ways they have been transformed. However, as I hope this discussion has shown, these examples illustrate ways of imagining that are central in today's media space, in particular, the simultaneous construction of distant others as strangers and intimates. I conclude by highlighting three issues which emerge from the analysis (which are developed in later chapters) and help to shed further light on the imagining of distant others in contemporary media representations.

Mediated proximity and intimacy

In today's global age, media and communication technologies bring the other closer than ever before. The immediacy and simultaneity enabled by these technologies 'compress' time and distance, enabling a distinctive kind of mediated proximity and 'intimacy at a distance' (Thompson, 1995). Voltaire appeals to his readers to contemplate the pain and suffering of 'those' far-away others and to feel compassion on the basis that we are *here*, while they are *there*, experiencing a radically *different* situation. Current representations of suffering seem to perpetuate the call to relate to distant others and their misfortunes based on the reverse premise: obliteration of distance and, concomitantly, of difference. The other is (or could be) you, here and now. These messages and images call us to collude with the other; they promote 'the elision of the different to the same' and a 'refusal to recognize the irreducibility in otherness' (Silverstone, 2007: 47).

This promotion of mediated proximity to and intimacy and collusion with the other as the desirable mode of relations, applies not only to distant others of the kind discussed in the analysis, but often also to others constructed as morally distant, social pariahs, for example, migrants, or sometimes the 'enemy' in time of war, as the discussion in chapters 4 and 6 reveals. 'The distant others whom one comes to know' through such mediated intimacy 'are others who can be slotted into the time-space niches of one's life . . . They are regular and dependable companions who can provide entertainment, offer advice, recount events in distant locales, serve as a topic of conversation and so on' (Thompson, 1995: 219–20).

The individual other

In the contemporary global media environment the other is often an individual: the famous 'National Geographic Afghan Girl', the faces of the 9/11 hijackers, the image of Pakistani baby Reza Khan, covered in flies, having his first bottle of milk after the August 2010 floods,[23] and so on. This representational regime poses the individual and the self as the primary frameworks for making sense of and experiencing the world, particularly in relation to suffering and trauma (Illouz, 2003a; Orgad 2009a; Rose, 1990). It is a regime embedded in the culture of the global north (but increasingly goes beyond it), conjoined with and supported by the reign of consumerism, neo-liberal ideology and therapeutic discourse.

Our relation as spectators to those individual others is formulated in current representations in mostly individualized and privatized terms, captured by the lines in the 1985 'We Are The World' that say: 'It's true we'll make a better day / *Just you and me*'. Alongside representations that retain an orientation towards a collective relation to the other and towards a denunciation of broader global structures of inequality and injustice, an increasingly central message carried by many representations is that in order to relate to distant others we need individualized affective and political responses. The interactive feature of online communication is particularly fitting for the enactment and exercise of this private and individualized relation to the other: show that you care by clicking and donating. The increasing visibility of humanitarian celebrities at the centre of the public communication of distant suffering – as illustrated by the 1985 and 2010 recordings of 'We

Are The World' – further embodies and endorses this idea. These celebrities offer viewers a model for engaging and acting as private individuals in relation to distant others, rather than relying on collective political action (Narine, 2010).

Symbolic space of contestation

The current media environment is a complex space of information flows in which words, images and symbolic content compete for attention, 'as individuals and organizations seek to make themselves seen and heard (or to make others be seen and heard)' (Thompson, 2005: 49). In this environment, while certain moral scripts about the other may be prevalent, they are neither fixed nor static, and potentially are being contested continually by competing messages. In the succeeding chapters of this book, I highlight and discuss more of these contestations and contradictions.

It would seem unhelpful, therefore, to explain how distant others are imagined in the contemporary media, using binary paradigms – the symbolic annihilation of distant others (how representations demonize, stereotype, exclude and symbolically annihilate others) versus the symbolic inclusion of others (how representations humanize, or should humanize, recognize and symbolically encompass others). A binary framework fails not only to recognize the inherent complexity of media representations and the ambivalence inherent in difference (Hall, 1997), but also to account for the empirical reality, the diverse and competing accounts of distant others in the contemporary media space, which may exist within a single text or image and within audiences' diverse interpretations of them.

To recall Danielle Rousseau's warning to the survivors in *Lost*, which is cited at the beginning of this chapter, the others are not coming – they are already here. A critical question is how they are imagined in the contemporary media space, and how this imagining informs and orients our thinking, feelings and actions towards the other and, inextricably, towards ourselves.

3   Imagining Ourselves
Representations of the Nation

Introduction

> [M]ostly we [educated and comfortable citizens of stable societies] gaze at
> distant others in poor, unstable and violent places, which are in the news
> because of more cruelty and suffering, or in places where juntas, refugees,
> death squads and famine are never more than a memory away.
> Cohen, 2001: xiv; reprinted by permission of Polity

Increasingly, however, 'we' are also the object of the world's gaze. The
greater transparency of societies to global scrutiny, enabled largely by the
rise of global media, has made 'us', especially in western societies, a central
object of the global imagination. This chapter focuses on the imagining
of 'ourselves' and asks what today's mediated images and stories tell us
about ourselves as national societies. How do media representations call us
to imagine ourselves as national communities in an age that is characterized by rapid processes of globalization and a 'new visibility' (Thompson,
2005)?

Of course, there are many identities and subjectivities that are relevant
and central to our lives in a global world, and to which the discussion
of imagining ourselves could be applicable. Some of these identities and
subjectivities, for example, ethnicity, religion and race are touched on in
this and other chapters. However, the focus of this chapter is on how contemporary media representations construct, deconstruct and reconstruct
the nation as a symbolic category of belonging, and the consequences of
the ways in which the global media invite us to imagine ourselves as the
nation.

The discussion inevitably refers to aspects of representation of the other,
since these are implicated in and interdependent with the imagining of
ourselves. We need the other in order to establish and maintain a sense of
who we are. Therefore, some of the questions raised in chapter 2 resurface
in this chapter in relation to the concern over how we imagine ourselves as
a nation. Ultimately, chapters 2 and 3 provide complementary accounts
that advance our understanding of the ways in which contemporary representations concurrently inform, guide and orient us to the other and to
ourselves.

The chapter starts by discussing some of the key questions and concepts concerning the symbolic construction of national belonging and, specifically, the role played by media representations in the constitution of national imagination. It moves on to examine the case of the representation of the 2005 urban riots in France as illustrative of this issue. Like all case studies, that of the French riots has some particularities; however, it is used here to demonstrate and develop a broader argument on the role of media representations in shaping how we imagine our national belonging in the context of globalizing forces. Media representations, especially in national media, play a key role in reproducing and reinforcing nationhood and invoking nationalism and patriotism. But these representations are produced, disseminated and consumed in a changing context of 'the new visibility' (Thompson, 2005), which introduces fundamental challenges to the work of imagining the nation, and expands and complicates cultural representations of ourselves as a nation.

Imagining the Nation: Between Identification and Symbolic Distancing, Attachment and Estrangement

In the 1990s, following the end of the Cold War and the ensuing rapid globalization, some (e.g., Ōmae, 1995) suggested that sovereign states were obsolete. By the dawn of the twenty-first century, this view had lost much purchase, and 'there were not many left for whom the fantasy of overcoming the state was not tinged with anxiety' (Calhoun, 2007: 6). However, many would still wish away nationalist accounts, arguing that we are witnessing a deepening erosion and, consequently, decreasing relevance of national identity. In particular, most cosmopolitan visions (some perpetuating a 'We Are The World'-type view) oppose themselves to nationalism (Calhoun, 2007). But, as Calhoun (2007: 9) observes, nations, and particularly the social imaginary of national peoples, still matter a great deal:

> Globalization challenges nation-states and intensifies flows across their borders, but it doesn't automatically make them matter less. Because nations matter in varied ways for different actors, it is important to think carefully about how they are produced and reproduced, how they work and how they can be changed . . .
>
> Nationalism matters not least because it has offered such a deeply influential and compelling account of large-scale identities and structures in the world – helping people to imagine the world as composed of sovereign nation-states. The world has never matched this imagining, but that does not deprive the nationalist imaginary of influence.

However multi-faceted, complex, unstable and contested the nation's imaginary in today's global age, it continues to be a central construct that is produced and reproduced through media representations, and is imbricated in our conceptual frameworks. It is precisely because the nation-state is undergoing significant transformations and is subject to growing contestations and struggles over its meanings, that it constitutes an important site in the global imagination. Thus, the work of national identities in organizing human life as well as politics in the contemporary world should not be underestimated. In tandem with the centrality of a narrative of 'We Are The World' in the media (discussed in chapter 2), a narrative – albeit far from coherent or stable – of 'We Are The Nation' is told and negotiated, and continuously redefined and retold.

In the global media space we are invited constantly to think of and relate to ourselves as a nation. But how? One way that has been discussed extensively in the literature concerns the *symbolic construction and reinforcement of national identity* – a sense of unity and belonging to a socio-spatial entity demarcated as the 'nation'. It relies on a discursive production of national people as an 'imagined community' (Anderson, 1983) through the ongoing perpetuation of shared symbols, construction and reproduction of dominant narratives and a collective national 'we', and the creation of a temporal framework (e.g., through the broadcast television schedule) that organizes people's everyday lives (Scannell, 1996).

Much of this symbolic 'building of the nation' and sustaining of attachment to the nation is continual, daily and mundane, what Billig (1995: 8) calls 'banal nationalism':

> In so many little ways, the citizenry are daily reminded of their national place in a world of nations. However, this reminding is so familiar, so continual, that it is not consciously registered as reminding. The metonymic image of banal nationalism is not a flag which is consciously waved with fervent passion; it is the flag hanging unnoticed on the public building.

The 'flagging' done by media images and stories goes largely unnoticed because these representations are embedded in how we see things; they appear 'normal' and familiar and, largely, are taken for granted. References made in the news to 'we' and 'us' (the implied national people), advertising's appropriation of national symbols, satirical use of jokes that rely on knowledge of national common wisdoms, names of media programmes and outlets that draw on national images and symbols – these and many other genres and practices participate in the unnoticed mundane 'flagging' in which the media are key players.

The engagement of the media in the production and reproduction of banal nationalism and symbolic flagging does not imply that they deliberately promote nationalism, or that they are in collusion with national political interests (at least in liberal democracies). Rather, as Scannell (1996: 145) observes, the media are underpinned by certain 'care-structures' that inform the representations they produce. National media make programmes for *their* national audiences and for what those audiences care about (or what media producers believe they care about). The care-structures within which they operate determine what they report, remark on, attend to, observe, pick out and foreground. They 'mark out the boundaries of our concerns' (Scannell, 1996: 144) – what matters and the extent to which it matters, to us, the nation.

In times of crisis, 'banal' nationalism and flagging often give way to flag-waving and overt patriotism, manifest in expressions of nationalist fervour. In his influential study of media coverage of the Vietnam War, Hallin (1986) shows how journalists tended in their reporting to move towards a 'sphere of consensus' and report events as members of a national community. Studies of news reporting of other crises, in other contexts (e.g., other wars, terrorist attacks) and in other countries, corroborate Hallin's observation. They show that journalism in times of crisis is characterized by an assumption of shared values, invoking patriotism and perpetuation of a generalized consensual 'we', and that national news frequently exhibits an adoption of unquestioned binary categories of 'us' and 'them' and reassertion of the dominant national narratives (Peri, 1999; Schudson, 2002; Waisbord, 2002; Zandberg and Neiger, 2005).

However, Frosh and Wolfsfeld (2007) argue for a more complex understanding of the work of media representations during political and military crises. Analysing news reports of a terrorist attack in Israel, the authors show how, in circumstances of protracted political and often military conflict, media representations lead to an affirmation of nationhood by turning the resilience of everyday interpersonal relationships into a conspicuous national value and, ultimately, into a national myth. This form of banal nationalism, which Frosh and Wolfsfeld (2007: 107) describe as 'mediated civil nationhood', emerges from and through representations that focus on citizens' everyday social interactions and personal stories. For example, the personal stories of bereaved families and survivors of disasters are frequently framed in news reporting as 'standing for' the nation, and are linked to nationhood rather than to the discourse of the state or organized politics. This was manifest vividly, for instance, in the global and national coverage of the prisoner exchange between the Israeli government and the Palestinian Islamist group Hamas in October 2011. On being released from more than five years of captivity, the Israeli soldier Gilad Shalit was described by both Israeli and international media as Israel's 'lost son' (e.g., *Independent*, 19 October 2001), returning to his national family. In the Israeli media Shalit's admirable survival of imprisonment was constructed as the resilience of his entire nation.

Thus, media representations do not engage in *either* 'banal nationalism' *or* flag-waving patriotism. Rather, identification with and attachment to the nation are produced and enacted in multiple ways, through a focus on personal, seemingly apolitical narratives, which do the work of 'flagging' in latent and implicit ways, and simultaneous reassertions of the grand political narratives of the nation in overt and explicitly patriotic fashion, for example, in the form of favourable accounts of the activities and discourse of national leaders.

In today's intensive, extensive and less controllable media environment, the imagining of the nation, especially during times of conflict, is even more complex than the majority of analyses of national media representations would allow. The symbolic production of nationhood takes place in a media environment characterized by the rise of digital technologies, where the field of vision is no longer constrained by the spatial and temporal proper-ties of the here and now, but by forms of simultaneous and de-spatialized communication. This has made it much more difficult to control the flow of symbolic content and, as a consequence, more difficult for any party completely to control the words and images that circulate in the public domain (Thompson, 2005). Accounts, words, images and symbolic content circulate through transnational flows on the Internet, mobile phones and satellite cross-border channels, and permeate national boundaries, render-ing visible many issues, activities and events that may have been invisible or marginalized in the national public domain.

The Internet and satellite cross-border channels, for example, CNN International, BBC World and Al Jazeera, become significant storytellers that compete over the symbolic construction of the nation with other local, national, regional, transnational and global players. Consequently, national media, historically the main, if not the sole, storytellers producing and dis-tributing accounts of the world and the nation, are no longer the exclusive or even the primary storytellers about the nation. Hence, while national (especially broadcast) news presumably is still 'the most central to the pro-duction of national social imaginaries' (Frosh and Wolfsfeld, 2007: 109), other sources, genres and narratives increasingly serve to nourish the imag-ining of the nation. Crucially, these representations may provide visions of the nation that are quite different from those presented by national media. They may be uncomfortable, disturbing and at odds with how nations see or would like to see themselves, notwithstanding that national media in liberal democracies do not constitute a monolithic force and the representations they produce are never totally synonymous.

Among the most arresting examples of the new visibility enabled by contemporary media technologies, and its consequences for the imagination of the nation, are the Abu Ghraib photos. These images of the practices of US military personnel in the hidden world of Iraqi jails, most famously the iconic photo of the 'hooded man', leaked into the public domain in 2004 via the Internet, swiftly circulating in newspapers and on television screens across the world. They were extremely disturbing and unsettling to western, and particularly US, imagination. 'Suddenly we (at least in the West, at least those in the US) are being asked to see ourselves both as other and as vulnerable' (Silverstone, 2007: 58). The photographs invited, perhaps forced, American viewers to see the familiar and commonsensical, upstanding and humane American soldiers, as alien and strange, 'our boys' as capable of evil. The photos called viewers to question generally taken-for-granted assumptions about American moral values and conduct.

Admittedly, Internet use and viewing of cross-border channels is still low in many countries relative to the consumption of mainstream national media. So one might question how meaningful are the opening up of the media space and the increasing porosity of the media environment that allow accounts to circulate and permeate national boundaries. In this chapter, I argue that the images and accounts on the Internet and international channels increasingly influence, in significant ways, how 'we' imagine our national belonging, though this influence may often be indirect. International news coverage and discussions on the Internet commonly are considered in national public discourse to reflect 'what the world says about us' – an issue that typically preoccupies national discussions during and after conflict (Orgad, 2008, 2009b). In this context, national media often appropriate and replay material shown on international media, exposing national audiences to international coverage 'through the back door'. Furthermore, global flows of images and accounts can challenge national media to broadcast stories and images they might otherwise ignore. Thus, 'the collage of images we have of the social totality [of the 'nation'] and our relationship with it' (Frosh and Wolfsfeld, 2007: 109), is becoming increasingly permeable and brittle and, consequently, potentially less coherent, consistent and homogeneous than in the past.

This points to a second way in which media representations circulating in today's global media invite us to imagine ourselves as a nation: through *symbolic distancing and estrangement*. Symbolic distancing refers to the ability to adopt some distance from the conditions of our daily lives and to think critically about our own lives and conditions. Symbolic distancing is a broad feature of the global flow of symbolic content and its appropriation locally by individuals (Thompson, 1995). In the discussion below, symbolic distancing is used specifically to consider how media representations allow us, as national audiences, to distance ourselves from 'the nation', how they invite us to exercise different kinds of relations to ourselves, gain a critical view of our lives and our country, and develop alternative understandings of ourselves as members of a national community.

Symbolic distancing is a continuum; it has different degrees. Thompson (1995) uses Lull's (1991) study, to show how, even in a strictly controlled broadcasting system such as China's, some symbolic distancing is enabled. By watching television programmes imported from Japan, Taiwan, Europe and the US, Chinese viewers gain glimpses of life elsewhere, allowing them to distance themselves from their own life conditions and gain critical purchase on official interpretations of social and political reality in their own and other countries. A study of media representations of the 2008 Beijing Olympics (Latham, 2009) shows that in the rapidly transforming media environment in China, symbolic distancing is substantially amplified. The Internet and mobile phones, in particular, are agents of the 'new visibility', encouraging Chinese audiences to question and contest notions of the 'real China', and to voice discontent and scepticism about official authoritative narratives (see also Meng, 2011).

Further along the continuum of symbolic distancing is what I call *estrangement*. This representational practice centres on a more overt form of de-familiarization, in which texts and images cast critical doubt on commonsensical and taken-for-granted understandings and explanatory frameworks. In the context of our discussion, estrangement refers to the ways in which media representations act as invitations to audiences to detach themselves from commonsensical conceptions of their lives in the national context. More specifically, I am referring to self-estrangement, or the way that media representations make the nation a stranger to itself, and remove nationhood 'from the automatism of perception', to use Russian formalist Shklovsky's (1991[1929]) words. Estrangement is a symbolic process of distancing national audiences from their own narratives, culture, politics and history.

Estrangement is an aesthetic technique commonly associated with art and literature, for example, the literary works of writers such as Tolstoy and Brecht, and the work of movements and artists such as Dada, Magritte and Duchamp (notwithstanding the huge differences in their approaches and traditions). Similarly, contemporary intellectuals often act as estrangers. For example, in the reflections of the twentieth-century modern intellectuals who were refugees from Nazism, who were dissatisfied with patriotism and nationalism (Gilroy, 2004), the nation emerges as a central object of estrangement. However, as argued by Gilroy (2004) and Orgad (2008, 2009b), and as I show in this chapter, estrangement extends beyond its traditional cultural spaces of art and intellectual writings, and increasingly is central also in the media and popular culture.

Satire is a genre strongly associated with estrangement. Satirical shows on national media frequently use wit and ridicule to disrupt familiar and commonsensical conceptions of nation and nationhood. For example, Gilroy (2004) discusses how, in the satirical *Da Ali G Show* (first a television show, later a film), the employment of artistic techniques construct the character Ali G as a stranger. He is constructed as a non-black, suburban male who revels in a mixture of American Gangsta Rap and Jamaican culture, whose 'strangeness' distances viewers from entrenched notions of Britishness and offers them different ways to imagine their identities and culture. Another example is the Canadian television show, *This Hour Has 22 Minutes*, which follows in the footsteps of its predecessor *CODCO* and 'revels in making fun of the lofty ideals of Canadian unity and dignified patriotism' (Rukszto, 2006: 80). The show satirizes a variety of national institutions and personalities and consistently promotes suspicions about authoritative dogmas, including nationalism and federalism. Similarly, Israel's *Eretz Nehederet* (*A Wonderful Country*), inspired by the American NBC *Saturday Night Live*, questions social, cultural and racial stereotypes in Israeli society and, through the use of classic satirical strategies, disrupts dominant nationalistic narratives and rhetoric.[1] In a memorable episode, shown at the height of the 2008/9 Gaza War, the show lampoons one of Israel's oldest military correspondents, Roni Daniel, depicting him bare-chested, with a machine-gun belt across his chest and wearing a Rambo-style headband. It mocks his eagerness for battle and, more generally, the tide of national sentiment and patriotic fervour that characterized public opinion in Israel during the war.

Estrangement generates a sense of the nation as a stranger to itself. It opens a space for critical reflection on common wisdoms, and for questioning of the nation as a stable, coherent and taken-for-granted collective entity of belonging. In so doing, estrangement engenders opacity of the self to itself, of seeing ourselves as another. Following Sennett (1994) and Gilroy (2004), I argue that the capacity to see ourselves as another is an important requirement for recognizing social differences and for developing an interest in the other, and a sense of compassion and care for others' vulnerability and suffering. Estrangement is thus an ethical project: it embodies a commitment to recognize not just the stranger as other, but also the other in oneself (Silverstone, 2007).

But while estrangement has a strong progressive moral dimension, it can have negative consequences, and even explosive potential. Think of a friend who tells you something about yourself or makes an observation that leaves you feeling uncomfortable, strange about and/or alienated from yourself.

These observations may be difficult to accept. The discomfort and disturbance created by the friend's comments can transform into denial: rather than opening up self-reflection, we may block the comment and the new vision it suggests of ourselves. Estranging observations may also produce the experience of a dangerous split: the role of the self reverses from observer of others to looker on to the self – pathologically, a potentially very alienating experience (Laing (1990 [1967]).

The discussion that follows explores how the media can act as the friend,[2] offering disturbing reflections on national belonging and the consequences of the estrangement that their representations can produce. It shows how the work of symbolic distancing and estrangement done by media representations is in constant tension with and dialectic relation to the work of identification, attachment, flagging and symbolic reinforcement of the nation as a stable, unified and consistent, imagined community. I explore this tension by examining the example of representation of the 2005 French riots in the French and international media, particularly cross-border television channels and the Internet. National conflicts are times that typically give rise to intensified ideological attachment to and identification with the nation. Thus, representations of national conflict, such as those related to the French riots which are analysed here, constitute a particularly fruitful site to explore the work of imagining the nation in a global age, and to gain an insight into the contesting scripts that inform this imagining.

Notwithstanding some idiosyncratic aspects, I use the case of the French riots for the broader examples that it offers of ways that representations circulating in the media environment compete over definitions and visions of ourselves as the nation. I hope that the analysis will invite comparisons with other events and contemporary contexts that received global visibility, for example, the 2011 riots in London, or the 2011 wave of uprisings across the Arab world. Of course, each case has significant particularities, such as the political context of the country, which should be carefully accounted for. However, there are also important similarities in terms of what these cases demonstrate about the role played by images, narratives and voices – on Twitter and Facebook, in the blogsphere and national and international media outlets – in disrupting and puncturing notions of nationhood and national identities. It is this disruptive work of media representation, and its consequences for national and global imaginations, that the analysis in this chapter aims to throw into relief. In particular, I focus on news and emerging new media genres such as blogs and citizens' online videos. These mediated forms and platforms, I suggest, present an interesting and important space where estrangement emerges and can be cultivated productively, beyond genres such as satire, which are 'designated' for and commonly associated with disruption of the common sense. I begin with a brief background to the French riots and their representation in the national and international media. This provides the context for a discussion of the role played by media representations in articulating and feeding, while simultaneously containing and diffusing, tensions and contradictions in the imagining of national belonging.

The French riots

The 2005 riots in France were triggered by the death of two teenagers of Maghrebi descent, Zyed Benna and Bouna Traore, who were electrocuted at a power sub-station in the suburbs of Paris. On the night of 27 October 2005, youths in Clichy-sous-Bois began torching cars and stoning police to express their anger at the boys' deaths. The riots escalated rapidly, fuelled by calls from Nicolas Sarkozy, then Minister of the Interior, to rid the *cité* of the 'racailles' (translated, rather controversially, in the international media as 'scum') (Auffray, 8 February, 2007). Curfews were put in place in the suburbs of Paris and some forty other French towns and cities. After twenty-two days of rioting, involving the destruction of 9,000 vehicles, 2,921 people taken in for questioning and 126 gendarmes injured, the police announced a 'return to normality across France'. The curfews were lifted on 4 January 2006 (Smith, 5 February, 2006).

As commonly occurs in the case of violent riots and protests, especially when they happen in global cities such as Paris that are normally constructed as and associated with being politically stable, ordered, safe and successful, the international media honed in. International daily newspapers and news channels, including CNN International, BBC World, Bloomberg and Fox News, provided twenty-four-hour coverage with special correspondents reporting live from the *banlieues*, France's impoverished suburbs inhabited mainly by minority ethnic groups, where the rioting had begun. Images of burnt-out vehicles were transmitted under headlines such as CNN's 'Paris in Flames', and the Fox News headline banner 'Paris Burning'. Concurrently, the online sphere played a key role in reporting the events, with bloggers reporting from the scenes of the uprisings, and citizens posting videos and images of the events on blogs and sites such as YouTube.

The mainstream French media, for example, France's leading commercial TV station LCI, and the state-run channel France 3, were more restrained in the images they broadcast. As a response to what they saw as the international media's exaggeration and sensationalism, the majority of the French media reduced their broadcasting of images of flaming vehicles, saying it was to avoid playing into 'the hands of rampaging youths seeking coverage of what they see as their exploits' (Ganley, 12 November 2005) and to contribute – in the words of the Director General of LCI – to 'maintaining law and order' (News Xchange, 2005).

The French media may have been quite extreme in their approach to events, especially in exercising self-censorship to supposedly help maintain order and control. Nevertheless, the tensions that emerged between the images and accounts projected by the French media and those that were disseminated by non-national actors – from international news networks to citizen journalists – are far from unique. They illustrate how in the current media environment, it has become impossible to control, contain and ignore images of national violence and conflict such as those of the riots in the *banlieues*. Nations' 'dirty laundry' more often than not is exposed to a global audience. Consequently, the encounter between national media accounts and images and stories from international news channels and the Internet becomes a symbolic space of contestation over definitions and visions of the nation and nationhood.

In the case of the French riots, France – a European society mostly used to gazing at distant others – had become the object of the world's gaze. On the one hand, media representations (primarily international news and the Internet) invited French viewers to understand the riots through a different lens from that usually used by the French media to present violent unrest. They invited French viewers to take symbolic distance from their national belonging, a distance from a sense of 'ourselves' as the French nation. At the same time, other media representations reinforced attachment and identification: nationalist accounts of France as a stable, unproblematized construct, 'our' democratic sovereign nation-state. This tension between attachment and symbolic distancing was manifested in four aspects of the media representations of the events: (1) temporality, exposure and placement; (2) competing frames; (3) particularity and generalizability; and (4) visibility of the other. In what follows, these dimensions are exemplified by the French case; however, they are not particular to it: they constitute areas in which contestation over the imagining of the nation occurs in the contemporary global media space.

Temporality, exposure and placement

One element that helps symbolically to establish issues and events as 'normal' and 'familiar' is their regular coverage within similar thematic categories and regular sections, and their being given similar amounts of air time or space in the media. News, as noted by Fiske (1987), produces highly conventionalized versions of reality, by (among other representational and editorial techniques) classifying events into compartments such as 'health', 'economy', 'education', 'world', and considering their treatment and solutions only within these categories. Events and issues are constructed within formulaic, often quite rigid, temporal (amount of time given to discussion of issues and when they are being discussed) and spatial (amount of coverage and placement of issues) structures.

The continual reproduction of temporal and spatial structures is one way that attachment and 'banal nationalism' are constituted and reconstituted: it marks the 'normality' of everyday life, a sense of the nation's 'business as usual'. Scannell (1996) argues that the temporality of broadcasting plays a central role in the symbolic building of the nation, in terms of the production for the national audience community of a patterned temporal regularity, at a calendrical level (e.g., by marking regular festivals and occasions) and at a daily level, where the construction of temporal 'dailiness' orients viewers' everyday lives (e.g., breakfast news as the 'time to get up').

The coverage of the riots in French media operated in this context at the daily level: although not about a straightforward marking of daily or weekly routines (time to wake up, time to go to sleep), its temporal and structural regularity produced a coherence with French life. 'This violence occupies a specific media category, a field of knowledge, called *Les Violences Urbaines* (urban violence), which constitutes a routinized, institutionalized segment of the *faits-divers* (news-in-brief)' (Ludwig, 2006: 11–12). This repeated and similar amount of coverage within specific categories works to normalize the events. They fix the violent unrest in a particular rhythm and temporality (e.g., the 8 o'clock news) and present it in a regular degree of exposure and a certain classification, rendering it familiar, 'normal' and taken-for-granted in the national imagination. As sociologist Erwan Lecouer argues, French viewers 'have long become accustomed to sporadic outbreaks of vandalism and violence in suburban housing projects across the country' (cited in Bennhold, 30 March 2006: 3). Such coverage marks out the boundaries to 'our' concerns – what matters and when, and significantly, *the extent to which it matters*, to us, the nation.[3]

Against the familiarization and routinization of events and issues in national media, global media may offer a (sometimes radically) different temporal and structural framework for explaining the same topics. Events that traditionally receive limited coverage at home are seen around the world, covered extensively and disseminated with a sense of urgency engendered by the twenty-four-hour rhythm, the immediacy and liveness of global news networks and the Internet. The sheer volume and immediacy of global coverage undermine the 'normality' and taken-for-grantedness assigned to events in national discussions, and may generate a sense of de-familiarization among national viewers. For example, what the French media treated as ordinary (violent outbreaks were regularly covered in 'designated' news-in-brief sections) was presented by the international media as extraordinary (breaking news continuously updated by live reporting from the scene of the events). The discrepancy between the temporality, exposure and placement of the same events in the national and international news contributed to widespread 'incomprehension and outrage' among the French public (Bennhold, 30 March 2006: 3).

This is not to suggest that the temporality and exposure of representations on national media are totally different from or are always polarized against those in international media. Neither national nor international news coverage follows a singular pattern; for example, there was live, breaking-news coverage of the events on French television, especially as the riots escalated. What is significant, however, is how in a media environment where multiple sources can produce and disseminate stories about national societies, different and disparate degrees of exposure, temporality and placement of representations contribute to generating contested meanings about and understandings of the nation. In presenting significantly different temporality and reporting structures, the international media invite viewers, even if momentarily, to rethink events and their severity and scale.

A broader point that this example spotlights is that how we imagine our national belonging (and the work of imagining more broadly) rests and feeds not only on the symbolic *content* of representations (i.e., what they select to present and how it is presented), but also on the *quantity, temporality* and *placement* of that content. The rhythm, temporality, placement and amount of exposure of the representations can be seen as part of their *connotative* level. Recall Barthes's (1977: 15) example of how the meaning (connotation) of the same photograph can change completely through its placement in a very conservative newspaper and a communist paper. The newspaper titles, Barthes (1977: 15) argues, represent 'a knowledge that can heavily orientate the reading of the message'. By the same token, as the analysis of coverage of the French riots demonstrates, the temporal structure, amount of exposure and placement of representations constitute important factors of connotation. Albeit not explicitly ideological, these elements significantly orientate the reading of the message, and may produce conflicting understandings of events and their implications for national identity. Depending on the context, they can connote normality, regularity, ordinariness and the limited significance of the issue, or urgency, extreme importance, severity and out-of-the-ordinariness.

Competing frames

A second area of tension between attachment and national identification and symbolic distancing and estrangement from the nation, centres on the framing of national matters. The concept of framing refers to the ordering processes through which media texts convey meaning in relation to reported events (Frosh, 2011a): 'To frame is to *select some aspects of a perceived reality and make them more salient in communicating text, in such a way as to promote a particular problem definition, causal interpretation, moral evaluation and/or treatment recommendation*' (Entman, 1993: 52, emphasis in original). The process of framing events, issues and experiences is increasingly complex and contradictory in the current media space. Research has consistently documented how national and foreign journalists and editors employ distinctively different frames when reporting on events (e.g., Nossek, 2004; Roeh and Cohen, 1992; Zandberg and Neiger, 2005). In the case of the French riots, two significant frames that the media employed in their representation of the riots are law and order, and war. Each promotes not only a different explanation of the problem and offers different solutions, but also offers fundamentally competing visions of the national community.

Law and order

Setting events of unrest and violence within the frame of law and order works to support the foundational myth of modern society: the idea that the state is capable of providing security, law and order, and crime control (Cohen, 1996). The death of the two youths, the event that triggered the riots, was described initially by French national television within the frame of juvenile crime. Examining the 8 p.m. news programmes broadcast on the private TF1 and the public France 2 channels between 18 October and 17 November 2005, Mattelart (2006: 245) notes how 'France was described as prey to "violence and damage", [and] the forces of law and order and the government were continuously presented as in control, locally and nationally, of the situation'.

A strategy frequently used by state discourses to reinforce the frame of law and order and, specifically, the message that the authorities have violence under control, is the citation of statistics. In the French media 'the statistics of the police presence and those of the numbers charged, both also organized in crescendo format, rang the same law-and-order bell' (Mattelart, 2006: 245). For example, twelve days into the riots, an article on the LCI's (8 November 2005) website ends with the information that Nicolas Sarkozy had met with police and firemen to tell them to keep cool and calm, and cites Ministry of Justice statistics that emphasize the enforcement of law and order: 93 people imprisoned, 599 arrested and 192 brought to court since the start of the riots. In an interview with CNN (29 November 2005), the then French Prime Minister, Dominique de Villepin, quoted numbers for police injured, cars burnt and buildings damaged. Unlike the figures cited in the LCI article, these statistics emphasize disorder and violence rather than law enforcement and police control. However, the discursive act of quantifying a social problem, that is, explaining violent unrest motivated by complex historical social factors in numbers, especially numbers provided by the head of state, works largely to support a message of containment, order and control. A complex political and social conflict is simplified and reduced to a set of numbers; the reality of destruction and chaos on the ground, underpinned by political rage, is compressed into clear-cut figures, and delivered in the detached form of statistics.

The repetition of certain vocabulary to describe and define unrest is another discursive strategy that works to reduce a complex political and social problem to a familiar, simplified and normalized event. As illustrated by the French media coverage of the riots:

> The burning of cars, buses and schools; the outbreak of fighting with police; the fear promulgated over rioting jeunes gens d'origine immigrée (young people of immigrant origin), France had seen them all before, on smaller quotidian scales, as well as larger ... Such events also occupy a topos in the French media, discussed from radio, talk-shows to sociological articles, with symptomatic titles and summaries: 'La Génération Malaise', 'L'Islamisme'. These topos function to normalise and homogenise the situation, to fix the signifier of émeute or violence into something familiar and knowable, though they recount different scenarios. (Ludwig, 2006: 11–12)

Further, the use of such terms as *La Génération Malaise* and *L'Islamisme* generalizes the rioting people in the *banlieues* as a singular, unified group, and attributes to this group responsibility for the problem. It is a classic discursive practice of stereotyping: the blame is displaced on to the rioters, who are reduced to one, big, religious and ethnic group.

Fundamentally, frames are defined not only by what they include, but also by what they leave out: 'the omissions of potential problem definitions, explanations, evaluations, and recommendations, may be as critical as the inclusions in guiding the audience' (Entman, 1993: 54). Omissions can be implicit and unintentional, and/or, as in the French riots example, deliberate: the majority of French media, including the state-run France 3 and France's leading commercial television station LCI, admitted to limiting their coverage of the riots and, specifically, refraining from including images of burning cars, for fear of engendering support for the rioters (Ganley, 12 November 2005; Russell, 2007). The French media saw their role as helping to maintain law and order by endorsing its symbolic frame and avoiding what might dramatically disrupt the coherence and consistency of this construction.

The rhetoric of crime and law and order reallocates political acts into criminal categories, for example, through terminology such as 'delinquents', 'destructives' (France 2, cited in Mattelart, 2006: 243), 'gangs' and 'rioters' (based on Cohen, 1996), rather than, for instance, 'victims', 'rebels' or 'protesters' (frequent terms in accounts of the 2011 uprisings in the Middle East, for example – telling of the radically different framing of the two events). Employing the vocabulary of crime and its enforcement de-politicizes the unrest. It is presented as a violent expression of a minority rather than a political struggle, which, in turn, de-politicizes the solution to the problem: as a France 2 report broadcast on 3 November 2005 stated, it is 'in the hands of the firemen and the police' (cited in Mattelart, 2006: 244). Ultimately, the frame of law and order reproduces the authority and legitimacy of the nation-state.

War

However, the law and order frame, although central, is not exclusive in explaining collective acts of violent protest and, increasingly in today's media space, it competes with alternative frames. One frame that challenges the representation of events within the law and order frame is that of war. Framing violence as war *politicizes* it; it presents the motives of the actors involved as political. While wars typically involve rallying around the national flag, and the war frame often supports identification with the nation and arousal of patriotic and nationalistic sentiments, framing events as war also locates them in the realm of politics, which can challenge and expose cracks in taken-for-granted national and patriotic narratives. Describing events as 'war' can question the legitimacy of the acts of the nation involved in these events and may invite symbolic distancing from, rather than identification with, that nation.

In the French riots case, the law and order framing and the attachment to the nation that it espoused, were substantially contradicted by depictions, disseminated mainly on international news channels and the Internet, that framed the riots in terms of war. Almost a third of the American, British and French press coverage of the riots uses the rhetoric and imagery of war (Ludwig, 2006). Direct references to war were frequent: for example, on CBS, Elizabeth Palmer (2 November 2005) described the Paris *banlieues* as 'combat zones', and the UK *Daily Telegraph* described the area as a 'war zone' (Randall, 8 November 2005). French networks, such as TF1 and France 2, despite condemning the descriptions in the foreign media, used similar vocabulary. For example, a woman interviewed by a TF1 journalist commented, 'You'd have thought there was a war on', and the Aulnay-sous-Bois hotel where world emissaries were staying was described as 'a little bit like the equivalent of the Palestine Hotel in Baghdad' (cited in Mattelart, 2006: 243, 249).

In a media space where information flows across time and space with increasing speed and ease, comparison with the experiences of other nations and other cultures becomes a regular discursive feature. In addition to evoking general rhetorical and visual references to war and employing conventions of war reporting, comparisons are made to specific wars. For example, on Al Jazeera, Hitham Manah, a spokesman from the Arab Committee for Human Rights, compared the French riots to the first Palestinian Intifada: 'While young Palestinians used stones against Israeli tanks, Arabs and Africans living in ghettoes are burning cars in wealthy neighborhoods to get the world's attention' (Ghazi, 9 November 2005). A *Washington Post* article made a comparison with the Palestinian Intifada (Pégard, 16 November 2005), TV 5[4] used the term 'L'Euro-Intifada' (Dajani, 11 November 2005) and a *Newsweek* article described the riots as 'a sort of chronic intifada' (Dickey, 21 November 2005). Faisal al-Qasem, a talk-show host on Al Jazeera, compared the riots to apartheid in South Africa (Nordbruch, 2005), and broadcast news, such as CNN and Fox News, made analogies to the Iraq War. In addition, the format of the reporting, especially in the American media, was reminiscent of the format of reporting on the Iraq War, and employed detailed maps, reporters on the scene in the most sensitive places, and experts in the studio providing comment (Leser, 15 November 2005).

The discourse of war and analogies to specific wars and political conflicts, carry an ideological and politicized baggage of racism and political oppression. Use of these comparisons removes the riots from a crime and law and order framing, and re-contextualizes them within a political-ideological frame. The war vocabulary, imagery and presentation format radically reframes events – from local violence expressed by a minority group, to a political struggle against the oppression and racism exercised by the national political powers, whose significance is international.

In the context of the French riots, the frame of war, used mostly but not exclusively by the international media, challenged that of law and order and opened the door to *symbolic distancing* and *estrangement*. From the perspectives of French viewers, the images and information which are a 'normal', taken-for-granted aspect of 'our' lives, appear removed, appear to be happening elsewhere, far away, and charged with a different scale of severity and significance. The de-familiarization and symbolic distancing engendered by reframing the riots as war is captured neatly in de Beer's (14 November 2005) description of the impact of a CNN war correspondent reporting from the *banlieues*: 'French citizens, used to CNN's emblematic war reporter Christiane Amanpour reporting from battlefields all over the world, have been shocked to see her standing in front of burned cars in the *banlieues*.'

Of course, what impact the contestation of frames over the interpretation of events has on how we come to imagine our national belonging can only be examined and understood in relation to specific contexts. In France, the use of the war frame and references to a 'French Intifada', alongside comparisons with the Iraq War, prompted critical reflection among the French public on the political roots and consequences of the riots. It questioned the French model of integration and presentation of the riots as an Arab issue (Russell, 2007). Some, however, argued that comparing the riots to the Palestinian Intifada, and framing them as war, linked the rioters and their motivations to terrorism and Islam, reinforcing rather than challenging racist views.

The more general point that this discussion illustrates is that the same frame can work in potentially opposing directions: on the one hand encouraging distancing from nationhood, self-introspection and recognition of social differences and of the other, and on the other hand reinforcing nationalism and, particularly, racial stereotypes that reduce the other to a singular religious group, constructed as violent and dangerous.

Particularity and generalizability

Allied to the contestation between frames is a tension, evoked by the global circulation of representations in an age of 'new visibility' (Thompson, 2005), between particularity and generalizability. A sentiment commonly propagated in national political and public discourse, especially in small- to medium-sized countries at times of crisis, is that of particularism. It rejects understanding of national matters and conflicts as affecting more than the national sphere, and emphasizes, often explicitly, that the problem should be confined nationally (see Cohen, 2001). On the other hand, in the international and global sphere, the emphasis tends to be the opposite: the generalizability and comparability of national issues and happenings. The notion is that the conflict or event that a particular nation is experiencing *can* be compared to other similar experiences, lessons from elsewhere *can* be drawn and applied, and the issue *can* and *must* be understood through an international prism.

Manifesting this tendency, the French media, in covering the 2005 riots, largely promoted a view of these events as a domestic problem, with idiosyncratic characteristics. Jean-Claude Dassier, Director General of France's twenty-four-hour news channel LCI, tellingly insisted that the riots were a 'local problem' (News Xchange, 2005) requiring action at the national level, both practical (police enforcement of order) and symbolic (national media reporting – Dassier saw the international media coverage as 'excessive').

Criminalization of the riots, which was embraced by most French media, supports the emphasis on particularity in fixing the events in the domestic sphere: the riots were classified as national crime, whose solution, eventually, was the responsibility of the state. Reports on French television of the violence and damage across France often concluded with a message about the government's actions to re-establish order (Mattelart, 2006). The construction of the conflict as a particular domestic issue was further endorsed by fierce criticism of international media by French media and politicians: 'From Italy to South Africa, Poland to China, from CNN to Al Jazeera, the newspaper headlines and television commentaries set against a background of blazing cars are really hyping it up,' wrote *Le Parisien* newspaper (Reuters, 9 November 2005). The French politician Alain Juppé[5] in his blog, accused the American press of 'unleashing its fury against France' in 'revenge for Katrina and our [the French] ironic condescension towards the American authorities' (Pégard, 16 November 2005, my translation). Underlying these criticisms (typical of official state rejections of international criticism) is the belief that outsiders cannot understand what 'we' are facing and experiencing; normal standards of judgement cannot apply because our country's circumstances are unique.[6] It follows then that practices of representation employed by the international media are seen as inapplicable and inappropriate. Outside knowledge is cast as irrelevant, lacking credibility and, ultimately, unhelpful for handling 'our' national affairs.

However, this 'outside knowledge' has become an inevitable and integral feature that feeds the imagination. It has become increasingly difficult to sustain arguments claiming the particularity, uniqueness and exceptionalism of 'our' circumstances as a basis for defending national narratives. Images are juxtaposed, accounts are compared, interpretations clash, and comparisons among and contestations over meanings are visible to all, in the national and international spheres.

A particularly interesting comparison in the French context, and one made by several international media outlets, was between the French riots and the 1992 riots in Los Angeles. On the one hand, it reinforces the law and order frame because it promotes an understanding of the unrest in the context of urban crime. On the other hand, and more significantly, comparison with the 1992 Los Angeles riots, which had a clear racial context (they were triggered by a controversial jury verdict which acquitted four policemen who beat up a black motorist following a high-speed chase), provoked critical questions about discrimination and racism in France. Unsurprisingly, the comparison was rejected by French Prime Minister Villepin, who, in a CNN interview (29 November 2005), refused to describe events in France as riots, stressing that, unlike the violence in Los Angeles, nobody had died in France.

Comparisons between a specific country's experiences and those of other countries are a common feature in discussions of national conflicts. While the official state discourse (and some national media narratives) tend to emphasize particularity and uniqueness, and insist that events are a local problem, the view largely embraced by the international media is of their generalizability. Thus, in the current global media space, such comparisons become a central site for contestation. They may trigger symbolic distancing and estrangement by inviting viewers to see the events as if they were happening in a country other than their own, and to judge them critically. At the same time, comparing one nation to others in similar contexts acts as a reminder of one's 'national place in a world of nations' (Billig, 1995: 8) and thus reproduces and reaffirms nationhood as a pertinent and stable construct. It confirms the nation as the ultimate framework for explaining and understanding our experiences and the world we live in.

Invisibility and visibility of the other, what they mean for the vision of ourselves

Another area where tension emerges over the definition of nation, and the imagining of national belonging in a global context, is presentation of the other. I argued in chapter 2 that how we imagine the other is inextricably implicated in and constitutive of how we imagine ourselves. Thus, examination of how 'others' are represented in specific contexts, and the struggles over their symbolic appearance and recognition in the media, sheds important light on the imagining of national belonging.

In France, the people from the *banlieues*, mostly migrants, historically have been excluded from the national media and public sphere (Bourdais, 2004; Harding, 2006; Hargreaves and Perotti, 1993). In the French media, Morley (2004: 423–4) observes that 'there are limits to how strange a stranger can be'. For example, migrants are excluded from 'spaces or genres of conviviality', such as game and quiz shows, and relegated to genres associated with problems and conflict, such as news (Hargreaves and Perotti, 1993).

The endemic invisibility of migrants and non-white French citizens, and the failure of French television to 'give a real sense of France's multiethnic composition' (Harding, 2006), were well established when the riots broke out:

> Neither France Télévisions, the public broadcaster, nor TF1, the major private channel, gives a real sense of France's multiethnic composition. When you consider the figure of four million to five million people of 'Muslim origin', add in sub-Saharan Africans (not all of them Muslim) and citizens of Asian extraction, then switch on your TV and surf the available dramas, soaps, news, or documentaries, you could be forgiven for thinking that France was lost in a timeless monoethnic fantasy based on the landscapes of the Barbizon School and the movies of Eric Rohmer. (Harding, 2006: n.p.)

The invisibility of the *banlieues* people in most French media coverage of the riots was particularly striking given that the rioters were *banlieues* residents and the riots were taking place in their neighbourhoods. A French blogger (Blog TV, 6 November 2005, my translation) comments cynically on this symbolic exclusion in TF1 news coverage of the riots:

> We note that, oddly, the principal actors in these events are not invited: the ordinary residents, the shop owners who have suffered damage, the owners of the burnt cars, and of course the youth themselves, or at least their representatives. Clearly, dialogue with these actors is not the order of the day; on the contrary, as we know, the interior minister, Nicolas Sarkozy, is convinced that with the 'racaille', one doesn't 'discuss': we 'get rid of', we 'clean out', we 'power-hose' (*karcher*).

However, in the contemporary media sphere, the invisibility, silencing and 'symbolic annihilation' (Silverstone, 2007) of the other, are increasingly challenged and transformed. Global news is one important site where 'others' and marginalized groups gain visibility and voice, challenging their invisibility and silencing in the national sphere. In the French riots example, international news channels, such as BBC News and CNN International, provided a stage for people from the *banlieues* and allowed their voices to be heard. 'There is a hint of pride', argued Richebois (24 November 2005, my translation), 'the satisfaction of a late, but real recognition, with the microphones beginning to be pointed more or less everywhere towards the youth of the *cités* to gather, analyse and dissect their frustrations and anger.'

But the challenge to the invisibility and silence of others, which many regard as the most significant in today's media space, comes from Internet representations, specifically the blogsphere and social media. For example, in contrast to the largely homogeneous descriptions of the *banlieues* residents in the mainstream French media and in some international media, their representation online was substantially more diverse. A heated exchange on Wikipedia revolved around how the young people at the heart of the event should be referred to, and more than fifty pages of deliberations appeared during the weeks of the unrest under its entry '2005 Civil Unrest in France' (Russell, 2007). Examination of the 'Talk' and 'View History' sections of the Wikipedia entry reveals contestations and numerous revisions and edits made to descriptions of the rioters, such as 'predominantly of French Muslim background', 'North African Arabs', 'anarchists', 'French Muslims' and 'immigrants' (to mention only a few). Similar contestations can be seen in other contexts where marginalized groups and individuals gain visibility and recognition in online spaces. However, how often and to what extent the explosion of online opportunities for giving voice to marginalized groups and individuals provides important forms of public recognition and exchange is a critical question that is yet to be seriously answered (Cottle, 2006; Couldry, 2010).

French blogs[7] and some user-generated video online sites, such as YouTube and Dailymotion, played a particularly interesting role during and after the riots by providing a stage for the *banlieues* residents to represent themselves.[8] Bloggers in France and other countries in Europe and North America published reports and contributed unedited opinions, hearsay, photos and information (Russell, 2007). Blogs were used also by some mainstream media outlets, such as the French daily newspapers *Libération* and *Le Monde*, and the Swiss magazine *L'Hebdo*, to provide the *banlieues* residents with a voice.

Representations in the blogsphere can take different forms and promote different, sometimes competing, frameworks for understanding events or issues and their implications. In the context of the French riots, one strand of blog representations focused on expressions of sympathy, homage and solidarity. The Bouna93 blog,[9] for instance, was set up as a memorial to the two teenagers, Bouna and Zyed, who had been electrocuted. Rap clips posted on YouTube (e.g., *Hommage Bouna et Zied*), and images circulated on blogs of a vigil with participants wearing T-shirts bearing the slogan *Mort Pour Rien* ('Dead for Nothing'), conveyed similar messages (figure 3.1).[10] The use of hip-hop to promote tolerance and pay homage is particularly interesting, in that it challenges the association of this musical genre, in much of the mainstream coverage of the riots, with incitement to violence (several French MPs had urged the prosecution of certain rap groups for 'provocative lyrics', and the police had threatened hip-hop artists over provocative and downloadable soundtracks).[11]

Figure 3.1 'Mort Pour Rien' vigil; photograph by Brian Holmes <http://www. brianholmes.wordpress.com/2006/03/26/images-of-fire/>

In contrast, there was a strand of blogs that made outright – sometimes very aggressive – calls for collective resistance. These postings were characterized by their use of slang and expressions of hatred of police (referred to as *keufs*, the French slang equivalent of cops), at whom the violence was targeted, and sometimes by direct calls for participation in the riots. For instance: 'People in every housing project, show your hatred' (cited in Schwarz, 9 November 2005, my translation), or 'Unite, Ile-de-France, and burn the cops. Go to the nearest police station and burn it' (cited in Jarvis, 14 November 2005).[12]

Calls for visibility and voice through resistance were manifested also in representations that did not incite violence. They highlighted the discrimination and racism experienced by the people of the *banlieues*, and emphasized French society's imposition of otherness on them. One fascinating example of this is a short user-generated animation film called *The French Democracy*,[13] which was circulated widely on the web (e.g., YouTube, Dailymotion, blogs and websites) and received attention from the mainstream press (Russell, 2007). The film was made by twenty-seven-year-old Alex Chan as a computer game, and used Machinima, a computer games software enabling the creation of low-cost, easily distributable films. Alex Chan's film starts with the electrocution of the boys, but goes on to uncover deeper reasons underlying the riots. It highlights the racist abuse suffered by three young men, and the discrimination that triggered their participation in the riots; it shows arrests of black people not carrying their identity papers, the disparity in wealth between black and white people in France, police brutality towards black people, the difficulty for people with African-sounding names to find jobs and accommodation. The film ends with images of Bouna and Zyed, and is dedicated to them, and to 'all other

103

coloured youth in the world'. The voices of the characters in the film are muted, mimicking the silent films of the 1920s, and their words appear in subtitles, accompanied by background music. This technique requires the viewer to rely on visual prompts to make sense of the story, an allusion, perhaps, to what the film critiques: that appearance signifies racial and ethnic identity and difference, determines how individuals are treated, and establishes their inclusion or exclusion in French society.

Alex Chan's objective was to counter depictions in the mainstream media of the rioters as Muslim and to challenge the links made to terrorism, especially in US media (*China Daily*, 16 December 2005). Ironically, several pieces in online sources and the press described the characters in the film as Muslim, and later had to apologize for and correct this, following complaints from the film's creator (Russell, 2007). Similarly, many blogs challenged depictions of the *banlieues* and their housing estates as dangerous places, emphasizing the sense of belonging and pride felt by their residents.

The proliferation of online representations during and after the riots presented a different take, often with a starkly contrasting style, form and content to representations of the riots, the *banlieues* and their residents to those that appeared in much of the mainstream French and international media. Blogs and other online representations, alongside international news, contributed to the construction of a multi-faceted other; they offered a more complex understanding of the *banlieues* people, their motivations and reactions to the riots. The blogsphere played a particularly important role in legitimizing the inhabitants of the *banlieues* and showing that these minorities, who were absent from French television screens, could no longer be kept invisible. Once they achieved some visibility on international news channels and on the Internet, the French television channels began to include them in their reporting.

Allowing victims a voice and visibility, enabling them to speak for themselves, begins to challenge the deep-seated truism that 'if the Orient could represent itself, it would; since it cannot, the representation does the job, for the West, and *faute de mieux*, for the poor Orient' (Said, 2003 [1978]: 21). Cottle (2006: 168) observes that 'in such a way, former Others can be rehabilitated, past stereotypes can be fractured and identities begin to be fleshed out and repositioned as active subjects'. The emergence of the experiences and voices of 'others' in the national and global mediated space offers viewers critical purchase on their own societies. These accounts endow with strangeness commonsensical (and therefore largely unquestioned) conceptions of 'us' and 'them'. The faceless others, for years symbolically excluded, stereotyped, generalized and homogenized, acquire face and voice in the symbolic space of the media. Their representation calls for the imagination to open up to other perceptions: their visibility in the media acts as a catalyst for reflection on and rethinking of not only the immediate issues, but also the national community and its relationship to these marginalized groups, the processes and mechanisms of this marginalization, and the urgent need to challenge them.

The Consequences of Estrangement

An article published in the French daily, *Les Échos,* describes France after the riots as 'a France that doubts herself' (Hubert-Rodier, 25 November 2005: 30, my translation). This neatly captures that sense of a nation's opacity to itself, which nations increasingly experience today, where information that is exposed on the global stage becomes harder if not impossible to control. International criticism levelled at national societies and their governments, growing discrepancy between the amount and the temporal structuring of coverage of certain issues in the national and international media, the contesting framings of events, tensions between particularity and generalizability, and the emergent visibility of marginalized groups in the media, contribute to generating estrangement. Feelings of self-doubt, disturbance, incomprehension and shock are the consequence of the familiar becoming strange.

Of course, whether the various invitations issued by media representations are accepted by their viewers, that is, whether viewers feel estranged from, attached to the nation or deny the information they receive from images and news, remains to be investigated. Examination of the blogsphere and readers' comments on websites provides a glimpse of the ways in which citizens relate to media coverage of their country and how they exercise (or not) symbolic distancing from taken-for-granted accounts of their nation. Whether and how this symbolic distancing translates into positive changes also remains to be investigated. In France, this process contributed to de-legitimizing 'visions of the social world put forth by the media' (Russell, 2007: 293, citing Bourdieu, 2005: 37), and gave a push towards media policy changes to 'dewhiten' the screens, acknowledge diversity and increase the representation of minorities (European Broadcasting Union, 2006; Harding, 2006). In 2009, President Nicolas Sarkozy announced new measures designed to introduce diversity into elitist institutions such as the civil service, politics and the media (Poggioli, 2009).

At the same time, estrangement can have opposite consequences, that is, it can amplify and reinforce attachment. It also can have negative and even dangerous potential. Nationalist narratives may become more stubborn and defensive when confronted by the threat posed by estrangement. In response to the de-familiarization and doubt engendered by global representations, expressions may surface of defensiveness, entrenchment in 'our' truth and 'our' moral superiority, and denial (Orgad 2008, 2009b). These responses are translated sometimes into hostility and arrogance towards the international media, and towards other countries, and accompanied sometimes by nationalist sentiments and xenophobic discourses (see Orgad, 2011). Thus, estrangement may reinforce its conceptual opposite, namely, attachment and entrenchment; encouraging the emergence of a nation more confident than doubtful about its (re)actions.

The 'new visibility' and the threat it represents to nations push nation-states (at the institutional level) and citizens to try to reclaim their 'old visibility' and regain control over the management of their image on the global stage. As a result in part of the international scrutiny during the 2005 riots, in 2006 France launched its own twenty-four-hour transnational satellite news channel, *France 24*, to offer a different interpretation from those made by CNN and the BBC (*The Economist*, 30 November 2006; BBC News, 2007), and to give France more weight in the 'battle of images and airwaves' as President Chirac described it in a speech made during the build-up to the Iraq War (*The Economist*, 30 November 2006). Similarly, nations such as China (Xinhua's twenty-four-hours global news channel in English, CCTV's Arabic television channel), Japan (NHK World) and Iran (Press TV) have launched their own global networks in an attempt to enhance their capacity to manage and improve their image in what is an intensely competitive and porous media environment.

Conclusion

The global imagination is established through concurrent articulations of the nation through attachment and estrangement, identification and symbolic distancing. Both positions are necessary for making sense of the reality in which 'we', the national people, live, especially during times of conflict and perceived risk. On the one hand, media representations play a significant role in reassuring communities and societies, providing ontological security and helping consolidate a sense of coherence, control and belonging, especially in a world of global uncertainties and fears (Billig, 1995; Calhoun, 2007; Dayan and Katz, 1992; Scannell and Cardiff, 1991; Silverstone, 1994, 1999). Communication is directed towards the maintenance of society over time and the representation of shared beliefs – the 'presentation of reality that gives life an overall form, order, and tone' (Carey, 1992: 21).

Simultaneously, media representations, especially in times of conflict, can play a crucial role in evoking distance, disturbing order, making the nation a stranger to itself. Community is claimed as much through refraction and moments of symbolic reversal, as through activities and representations that present values, ideas and beliefs as unproblematically shared (Cohen, 1985, cited in Silverstone, 1999). A degree of de-familiarization from the commonsensical national narrative of 'us' is vital to enable understanding of others and ourselves in more complex, inclusive and moral ways. As Sennett (1994: 374) observes, 'without a disturbed sense of ourselves, what will prompt most of us . . . to turn outward toward each other, to experience the Other?'

While cultural representations have always been a site of struggle over the symbolic imagination of the nation, a struggle that is amplified and highlighted during times of conflict, the changing environment in which they are produced, circulated and consumed presents significant new opportunities and challenges for this work of imagination. As my analysis of the French case illustrates, and corroborated by studies of other national cases (e.g., Latham, 2009; Orgad, 2008, 2009b), contestation over the symbolic construction, reconstruction and deconstruction of the nation takes place across multiple channels, media and levels including the global, international, transnational and national. They include individuals (e.g., citizen bloggers, wiki commentators) and institutions (national daily newspapers, television channels, politicians' commentary); 'old' media (e.g., newspapers) and 'new' media (e.g., blogs), mainstream and 'alternative', commercial and public. This contested space of symbolic representations opens up, expands and potentially diversifies the collage of images and accounts we have of 'ourselves' as a nation. It makes the work of imagining the nation more difficult and more troubling, but also richer, more complex and more inclusive. As students of media, nationalism and globalization, we are assigned the crucial task of investigating the consequences of contestation over the imagination of the nation, and whether and how it translates, or could be translated, into dialogue, interaction, social action and progressive political change.

4   Imagining Possible Lives
Representations of Migration

Today's global culture is one of ongoing circulation of and exposure to an ever-changing store of possible lives. We are called on, especially in the global north, continuously to reinvent ourselves, to seek new, alternative, improved lives. Consumer culture and the centrality of self-help and self-improvement play a particularly influential role in feeding imaginings of possible lives (Illouz, 2007; McGee, 2005; Wood and Skeggs, 2004), by cultivating a 'makeover morality' (Redden, 2007), calling on people to transform their lives, identities and bodies through rigorous discipline and a consumer lifestyle.

However, for millions of people around the world, an alternative life means something quite different. For them, to imagine possible lives or a 'makeover' would imply the possibility that they or their children might live a different kind of life and in a different place; in short, to migrate. Millions of people around the world are forced to leave their homes and countries; others migrate willingly. There are immense differences between forced and voluntary migrations in particular contexts, and the subject positions that they produce, such as 'asylum seekers', 'refugees', 'economic migrants', and 'illegal migrants'. There are important variations between these discursive categories and their use in contemporary public discourse. They are charged with very different connotations of legal status, which shape vastly different experiences for the individuals involved. Nonetheless, despite significant variations among people who leave their homes, communities and cultures and move to a new place, often very different from what they know, for all of them imagination constitutes a central force in their experience. Migrants engage continuously in imagining. They imagine how life *might* be, an imagining inevitably and inherently juxtaposed to their imagining of how life *is*, or how and what it *used to be*.

While the phenomenon of mass migration is hardly new in human history, its juxtaposition with the rapid flow of mass mediated images and narratives impels the imagination (Appadurai, 1996). The imagination has broken out of the designated expressive spaces in which it was sequestrated, such as art, myth and ritual, and has entered everyday life. The migration of populations and the intermingling of people from different cultures and traditions form a source of enormous cultural creativity and symbolic activity. At the same time, they are also sources of conflict, tension and instability (Appadurai, 1996; Thompson, 1995). Representations circulating in our media-saturated globalized culture are the product of this cultural creativity, and an expression and negotiation of the conflicts and tensions that accompany migration: from news accounts of migration, to video games simulating migrants' experiences of fleeing and entering a new country, to refugees' blogs. In turn, these representations constitute symbolic resources upon which people draw to make sense of, and judgements about, migration, migrants and people's possible lives.

Building on Appadurai's (1996) account of imagination as a key force in the new global order, this chapter explores some of the central scripts that propel the imagination of migrants' possible lives today. Specifically, it investigates the symbolic resources in the media space available for people to draw on, to imagine how they or their children might live and work in places other than their place of birth. I examine what this store of possible lives consists of and what frames of understanding it offers about migration and the pursuit of different lives. The analysis draws on the literature on media representation of migration and on original analysis of contemporary representations. The first section explores the largely polarized accounts in media representations of migration, which I describe as 'dreams' and 'nightmares'. My analysis shows that even within these binary constructions there is ambivalence, although in many cases this is suppressed or swallowed up. The second section examines an example of a mediated site that allows ambivalent, more complex and incomplete imagining of possible (and impossible) lives. I conclude by reflecting on the value of binary oppositions and ambivalence in representations.

A note to the reader: this chapter draws on a rather large number of examples of representations of migration in different contexts and countries. The breadth of the discussion is constrained by the need to maintain a clear focus and to contain the length of the chapter. I therefore do not provide detailed background to the examples that I discuss. This is not to deny the significance of the specific contexts of particular representations, for example, national debates on migration, within which representations are situated and to which they respond. Rather, following Foucault (see chapter 1), I aim to highlight the links and similarities between representations across different national and political contexts, genres, media and modes of address, to show how certain scripts about migration and the pursuit of alternative lives are constructed in today's global age. These scripts circulate at the interpersonal, local, national and global levels, and feed personal and collective imaginations of migration. I hope that the discussion in this chapter is sufficient to make sense of the examples and the aspects they illustrate;

for those interested in more detail in relation to the examples provided and/or their context, the references I cite provide useful resources.

Possible Lives: Dreams and Nightmares

Representations of migrants' possible lives are commonly polarized between utopian constructions of 'dream' lives and dystopian accounts of 'nightmare' existences. The representations within each type of script vary in terms of their sources, contexts, goals, ideological and political interests, genre, audience (addressees), form and temporal point in the experience of migration.[1] However, all support a similar moral script. *Dreams* are narratives of a desire for lives that are different and fundamentally better than people's (implied) existing lives. They construct migrants' possible lives in the new place as positive experiences to aspire to. This construction is often presented as congruent with the host society's interests. Both migrants and host societies are constructed as collaborating in the enterprise of building and realizing the dream. By contrast, in dystopian scripts, the dreams become nightmares in which two narratives prevail. One constructs the pursuit of a new life as resulting in worse, often radically worse, life conditions, or even death. The host society is presented as implicated in causing the nightmare, and benefiting from it. The second sees the host society as the victim of the nightmare, by being forced to endure the consequences of migration. This construction is frequently intertwined with discourses of danger, risk and xenophobia, nationalist sentiments, and the symbolic othering of migrants based on stereotyping, demonization and symbolic annihilation. The migrants are 'aliens', 'invaders' or 'parasites', living off the host society.

Dreams

Utopian constructions of possible lives focus on the promise and benefits derived from migrants' moving to a new place. They may include reference to the problems of migration, for example, the types of obstacles that need to be overcome, but the overriding narrative is of a better life and has a happy ending. The new life is depicted as better, fairer and substantially happier; it evokes desire for a different experience in the future. The impetus behind this narrative is exploration of the 'what if' – the crux of imagination. Accounts sometimes have a fantastical dimension – projecting a future that appears somewhat divorced from reality, but deliver the message that another life is possible, the dream is achievable. The host country in this script is constructed as the 'land of opportunity', generally willing and open to migrants entering its society. The migrants' dreams are embraced by the host society, which seeks to realize the benefits of migration, on economic and/or moral grounds.

Humanitarian and human rights organizations are perhaps the most committed and vocal producers of the dream narrative of migration, typified by the UN Secretary General's account of the times we live in as 'the age of mobility'. Different versions of the piece appeared in different outlets; I quote here the Secretary General's concluding words in a piece published in the *Guardian*, which neatly capture the dream imaginary of migration: 'The keys to making this happen [fully realizing the benefits of migration and harnessing the power of migration to advance development] are fundamental to our shared global humanity: tolerance, social acceptance, education and mutual openness to cultural differences' (Ki-moon, 10 July 2007). This dream story is premised on humanitarianist discourse (Mummery and Rodan, 2007), an inclusive, cosmopolitan ethos that emphasizes a common identity of being human, and thus a moral obligation of hospitality towards migrants (similar to the 'common humanity' narrative of relations to distant others discussed in chapter 2).

The website of the UNHCR, the UN Refugee Agency,[2] is a good example. It presents the profiles of more than 130 refugees 'who have achieved special status within a community due to their achievements, or because they have overcome hardship to build a new life'.[3] The collection of photographs and brief biographies of refugees from different world regions, including writers, artists, political figures and activists, emphasizes the hopes and possibilities offered by migration, for the individual migrant and the host society.

Although the UNHCR website makes reference to some of the problems that the migrants have had to overcome, the overarching message is one of success and inspiration to others. It capitalizes on the celebrity status of many refugees – composer Frédéric Chopin, actress Marlene Dietrich, scientist Albert Einstein, former US Secretary of State Madeleine Albright, President of the Republic of South Africa Thabo Mbeki – to promote the humanitarian dream script of migration. The use of celebrities is characteristic of the broader media space, in which celebrity migrants are significant and highly visible symbolic carriers of the dream of migrants' possible lives. Examples include Hollywood star and later Governor of California Arnold Schwarzenegger, Hollywood actors Penélope Cruz, Djimon Hounsou, Nicole Kidman and Salma Hayek, and singers Ricky Martin, Kylie Minogue, Gloria Estefan, Katie Melua, and – a particularly interesting case

– Shakira, the Colombian singer widely acclaimed for her performance in both Latin American and mainstream North American pop music.

Shakira embodies the ideal transnational citizen, enacting and celebrating the experience of multiple citizenships and multiple identities: Lebanese-Colombian, Caribbean-Colombian, female, popular performer, and recent US migrant who 'made it' (Cepeda, 2003). A line in her highly popular song 'Hips Don't Lie' neatly encapsulates the sense of empowerment, success, achievement and mastery that her cultural persona of migrant popular singer embodies: 'Refugees run the seas 'cos we own our own boats'. At the same time, Shakira's popular representation is deeply confined within stereotypical paradigms of Latina identity and is highly sexualized (perpetuated by her and her management team) (Cepeda, 2003). This is illustrated by another line in the same song: 'Señorita, feel the conga, let me see you move like you come from Colombia'. This dialectic construction of Shakira – the migrant who transcends identity boundaries and at the same time reproduces those boundaries – contributes to her personification of the migration dream. Shakira is a cultural object of desire for both migrants and aspiring migrants who want to 'make it' and to 'own their own boats' (metaphorically speaking), and for the host society, which accepts her on the condition that she 'moves likes she comes from Colombia'. Thus, the dream narrative, which depicts migrants as empowered agents, is embraced by the host society, and emphasizes migration as a moral and economic joint venture involving the migrant and the host society, while at the same time relying on and reproducing clear frontiers between 'us' (the privileged host society) and 'them' (migrants), and re-enacting the fundamental power relation embedded in this distinction.

The dream narrative promoted and propelled by international, transnational and global actors, such as the UN or global celebrity figures, derives a considerable part of its meaning from its articulations in particular national contexts. The US, for example, was founded on migration, and the issue of migration maintains a place at the top of the political agenda, generating continuous heated debate and contestation in the national and extending to the international realm. In 2010, Shakira, capitalizing on the trend of celebrity figures mobilizing their symbolic power for humanitarian causes (e.g., the UN's 'goodwill ambassadors'), exploited her public persona to protest against the Governor of Arizona's enactment of a stringent immigration law aimed at identifying, prosecuting and deporting illegal migrants. In April of that year, Shakira gave an interview on CNN to draw attention to the inhumanity of this law and its contradiction of the values and spirit of the US Constitution. With the intention of placing herself on the same level as other American migrants and to highlight their vulnerability, Shakira confessed that she was not carrying with her the documentation required in Arizona and, therefore, technically was open to prosecution. However, this comment served only to highlight her privileged status as a celebrity migrant who, despite non-compliance with the law, was protected. Unlike migrants who lie about or conceal their national identities for fear of deportation and/or discrimination in basic employment and services, Shakira, as one of the transnational elite, 'is free to enjoy the "luxury" of declaring her Colombian identity in a public forum' (Cepeda, 2003: 215). Shakira's success in achieving a new life as a migrant to the US is practically impossible for the majority of migrants or would-be migrants; thus, paradoxically, she epitomizes the impossibility of the 'possible' life.

The case of Shakira is an example of how migration is imagined in the blurring space between politics and entertainment. However, a considerable part of the discussion on migration occurs within political discourse in its more 'traditional' sites and contexts, for instance, in mediated debates on migration laws. An interesting example, still in the US context, is the discussion of DREAM Act, a bill proposed in March 2009 for federal legislation to help illegal migrant youth in the US to get green cards. The name DREAM, abbreviation for Development, Relief, and Education for Alien Minors,[4] is revealing of the premise underpinning the proposal: the notion that creating the opportunity to become legally part of the American culture is a dream. The DREAM Act website (http://www.dreamact.com) offers *migrants*, whose transition to becoming American involves overcoming various rules and obstacles, a set of tools that will allow their children to access education resources, and rallies *Americans* – the host society – to support the Act (which, at the time of writing, had not passed into US legislation), for example, by signing a petition. The site's interactive features allow citizens to take part in debating the proposed Act. Though discussions on the Comments forum and on Twitter mention some of the problems experienced by the children of illegal migrants, and include criticisms of American society and its government's policies, the posts from both American citizens and migrants generally reproduce and enhance the construction of the 'dream'. The posts below were on the website's Comments forum in 2010: the first is from a Mexican-American migrant teenager and the second is from an American citizen (emphases added to highlight the use of 'dream vocabulary'):

Post 1
I *hope* and *desire* greatly for this legislation to come about. For the Dream Act will *enable* me to *pursue* a career and *achieve* what my parents brought me hear to do ... *TRIUMPH!* I am only 18 but have been living in the united states of america for 17 years and 6 months. I consider myself a mexican-american

deeply and are *proud* of the fact that i was raised in this *beautiful land*. I have *waited* and *hoped* for such an advocacy or movement to set in progress and now *anxiously hoping* for it to finalize that last step which is to be passed by our fellow congress and passed so that the millions of graduated students including myself can say to our parents ... *I've made it.*

Post 2

I think this ammendment would be *great* for our country. We have already spent money to educate these kids now lets keep our investment here instead of sending them out of the country. I have seen to many kids start out going to college only to be told they can't go anymore because of papers. We should give them the *chance*. If we are going to kick out anyone in this country we should kick out the lazy people not the ones *willing to work hard for a dream*.

The language of both posts has all the 'ingredients' of the dream narrative: 'hope' (repeated three times in Post 1), 'desire', 'anticipate', 'wait', 'chance' – all describing actions oriented towards a positive vision of the future – and 'deeply' and 'anxiously' giving them a strong emotional tone. The words 'enable', 'pursue', 'achieve', 'make' ('I've made it'), 'will' and 'work' signify agency, constructing migrants as active, determined and empowered agents.

The two posts (and many others on the site's forum and on Twitter) show a fit between migrants' wants and the host community's desires and interests. The migrant poster is explicit about seeing himself as belonging to the American society and country: 'I consider myself as mexican-american deeply', 'proud of the fact that i was raised in this beautiful land'. He refers to the US Congress as 'our' fellow congress. The US citizen (Post 2) embraces the dream as beneficial for 'our country'. Thus, their common point of reference for belonging is the American nation. In both posts, the hardships involved in the project of pursuing a new life are overridden by the possibility of the dream being realized, as illustrated by the euphemism 'willing to work hard for a dream' (as opposed to the reality of earning a pittance and being exploited), and by the migrant poster's 'shout': 'TRIUMPH!'

At the same time, the narratives that the two posts construct are premised on contesting ethics and employ different rhetorical styles. In Post 1, the migrant's dream is articulated as a highly *personal* and *emotional* account, and is linked to the poster's *moral* obligation to his parents. The American citizen's dream in Post 2 is constructed as a *collective* ('we' – American society) story, based on *rational reasoning*. The motivation to realize the dream of migration by giving migrants citizenship is *utilitarian* and *instrumental*; American society has already invested in educating 'these kids' and they are the ones 'willing to work hard for a dream'; thus, it will benefit American society.

Analysis of these posts illustrates how the wider dream narrative that is produced and disseminated via political and cultural discourses and representations, such as the DREAM Act bill, works its way into what Appadurai (1996) calls the 'local imagining' of individuals. These local imaginings do not simply mirror the meta-narrative; they give way to particular readings and articulations of the 'dream' and its meanings. The 'big' story of the possibilities opened up by migration, predicated on human rights and humanitarian ethos (manifest in the Dream Act vision expressed on its website and illustrated by the words of the UN Secretary General) is appropriated rather differently by individuals, generating new 'small' stories. Rather than 'big politics', the migrant child's story (Post 1) is one of a personal quest to tell his parents 'I've made it'. Rather than being human rights-driven, the American citizen's story (Post 2) is based on 'rational' logic of realizing the benefits of migration for the American society, curiously depicting migrants through dehumanizing practices: infantilizing them by describing college students as 'kids', and objectifying them through a rationalized quantification and commodification of their 'exchange value'. These contradictions resonate with the dual meaning discussed earlier in relation to Shakira: a simultaneous articulation of a genuine desire for illegal migrants to become citizens and be accepted by the host society, while at the same time objectifying them, in the case of Shakira through sexualization, and in the case of Post 2, on the DREAM Act website, through infantilization and commodification.

Another country where the media play a central role in the production, circulation and contestation of narratives of migration is Australia, where migration is a very politically sensitive issue. Since the beginning of the 1990s, Australia has experienced a rise in levels of migration. The state authorities have taken a tough stance on unauthorized arrivals; but have scrapped a controversial policy of holding asylum seekers in detention centres until their cases can be heard. One critical response in the Australian press to this harsh policy emphasizes the humanitarian values of the Australian nation and its shared humanity with the 'boat people' – asylum seekers arriving on Australia's shores having undertaken a dangerous journey by sea. The media depict these refugees as being denied a voice in their home countries, as fleeing from oppression and seeking a refuge, the implication being that their actions make sense and can be understood. It follows, then, that Australia, a humane and moral nation, is morally obliged to help them and to open its borders to asylum seekers (Gale, 2004; Mummery and Rodan, 2007).

This example captures an interesting dialectic, in which a cosmopolitan humanitarian discourse that celebrates the promise of an all-inclusive humanity shared by 'we', self and other, is appropriated to reinforce a national imagination. 'We', the Australian nation, endorse the dream of a 'shared global humanity' (Ki-moon, 10 July 2007); *we* are humane, hospitable, deeply morally committed. The Australian example is not unique: nations and their governments often embrace a humanitarian and cosmopolitan narrative of a 'common humanity' to explain their migration policies (although their acts may not match up to it). In so doing, they simultaneously construct their moral superiority and uniqueness, and celebrate their belonging to a humane, moral nation. In Israel, for instance, discussions about the state's and society's treatment of African refugees (mainly Sudanese) are framed by references to Israel's 'special sensitivity' to and 'unique awareness' of what it means to be a refugee and a migrant.[5] Thus, cosmopolitanism and nationalism and, by extension, the global and national imaginations, are mutually constitutive (Calhoun, 2007). They can exist in contention, as shown in chapter 3, but at the same time can be mutually reinforcing.

A third example of dream representations can be found in China. This country, like the US and Australia, has been experiencing high levels of migration, although in the case of China this consists mainly of the move to its cities of rural Chinese, not foreign nationals. The political system and closed media environment in China are profoundly different from the democratic regimes, cultures and media environments in the US and Australia. These extreme differences are obviously crucial in shaping very different migration narratives available in the Chinese public sphere. Nevertheless, these narratives have common tropes with the dream narratives in the US and Australia, and the dream version promoted by international humanitarian NGOs.

Since the start of the post-Mao economic reforms in the late 1970s, rapid commercialization, urban economic growth and privatization have induced increasing waves of labour migrants within China. In 2009, the national 'floating population' in China was estimated at 211 million.[6] These migrants are mainly peasants fleeing to China's cities in search of work and business opportunities. Their presence tends to exacerbate rural–urban differences and create tensions based on competition for limited urban space and resources (Zhang, 2002), similar to the tensions evoked between foreign migrants and national citizens in other countries. Migrant workers in China, mostly young, single men and women brought up in the countryside, perform various low-end, low-pay, sometimes dangerous manual or physical work, in urban economic sectors, such as construction, manufacturing, food services, street cleaning and domestic work, and struggle to make a living by selling their labour. They are very vulnerable, mainly because they do not have urban *hukou* (household registration or residence permit), which gives access to social services and employment protection. Most live in temporary living quarters provided by their employers and are unable to obtain permanent jobs and urban housing, making unemployment and homelessness ever-present threats (Chang, 2008; Fix, Papademetriou, Batalova, Terrazas, Lin, and Mittelstadt, 2009; Sun, 2008).

In denial of this bleak reality, in 2008, the official Chinese news international television channel, CCTV9, as part of its Spring Festival programme, which caters to foreigners living in China and Chinese people living abroad, broadcast a 'Song for the Rural Migrant Workers'.[7] The choir consisted of actors from the Art Troupe of Chongqing Representatives of the Rural Migrant Workers, dressed as cleaners, cooks, factory workers, nurses and construction workers – typical migrant jobs – singing:

> Grime on my clothes, sweat on my face
> I come to the city in pursuit of a dream
> Yesterday a farmer, today I'm a worker
> We're the new masters of the city
> Sisters and brothers, throw out your chests
> Undaunted by hardship and difficulty
> Trusting our truth and trusting our future
> Our lives will be just fine.
> We're all homesick working away from our families
> We do this for our parents and children
> And also to build more skyscrapers
> Let's sing, sisters and brothers
> With our sweat the neon lights will shine brighter
> Trusting our strength and trusting our future
> Our lives will be just fine.
> (CCTV International, 2008; words by Wang Xiaoling)

The song explicitly expresses the idea of a 'harmonious society', promoted by Chinese President Hu Jintao in response to rising social tensions and China's wealth gap. It is a dream representation par excellence. Its very stage-managed and over-produced style and utterly idealized lyrics, present migrant labourers as empowered, resilient agents of China's development ('we're the new masters of the city'), and emphasize liberation and triumph over hardship. The words of the song relate a singular, utopian story of migration as an experience of upward mobility ('Yesterday a farmer, today I'm a worker'), national advancement and unity and harmony ('Sisters and brothers').

This example, produced to convey the official government line, while clearly totalizing, highly orchestrated, controlled and one-dimensional in its depiction of migrants' possible lives, has some significant similarities with the dream scripts in liberal democratic countries explored earlier. It is, perhaps, an 'ideal type' of the dream script of possible migrant lives in an age of mobility. It is oriented strongly to the future ('trusting our future . . . our lives will be just fine'). It emphasizes individual agency, celebrates the migrant's experience as being in complete harmony with the host community, and casts endurance of hardship as satisfying and worthwhile, erasing any negative meanings. Migration is charged with personal and collective moral force ('we do this for our parents and children; And also to build more skyscrapers') that evokes the desire to pursue the possible lives it offers.

This discussion of examples of dream representations in international and national contexts demonstrates how tensions and complexities are overridden by a narrative of resolution (or a promise for resolution) and a happy ending: the Chinese rural migrants' lives 'will be just fine' despite the enormous hardships and lack of social protection; the illegal migrant youth in the US will 'triumph' and 'make it' 'in this beautiful land'; the refugees profiled on the UNHCR website have 'made a difference' and achieved acclaim and success despite the obstacles; Shakira 'rules her own boat', embodying the dream of becoming a transnational citizen able to transcend the barriers that migrants face.

The potential complexity and ambivalence within these representations is further negated by being juxtaposed in public discourse with scripts of migration as a 'nightmare'. Dreams and nightmares largely exist as two oppositional frameworks for understanding migration and for migrants' imagining of possible lives. This discursive relation, as I show next, further polarizes the narrative promoted by each of these scripts.

Nightmares

In the dream script, migrants and the host society share the 'dream' and are jointly committed to its realization. In the nightmare script, there is a split (although a minority of texts refer to migration as a nightmare engulfing both host and migrant): in Nightmare 1, the host society is the victim; in Nightmare 2, it is the migrant who suffers the horrors.

Nightmare 1
This narrative focuses almost exclusively on migration's negative consequences for and threat to the host society. Host society and state are the

victims, forced to bear the high price of migration in terms of the pressure on public services, jobs displaced by cheaper labour, etc., in a nightmare caused by the 'others', that is, migrants. Many studies of representations of migration focus on this script. They show how media discourses and representations in different national contexts construct migrants as 'others', 'criminals' and 'undesirables', by stereotyping and demonizing them and investing them with negative meanings (e.g., in the UK: Baker and McEnery, 2005, 2007; Buchanan, Grillo and Threadgold, 2003; Kaye, 2001; King and Wood, 2001; Philo and Beattie, 1999; Speers, 2001; Van Dijk, 2000; in France: Hargreaves, 2001; Rosello, 1998, 2001; in Germany: Brosius and Eps, 1995; in Italy: Campani, 2001; Forgacs, 2001; ter Wal, 1996; in Australia: Cottle, 2006; Gale, 2004; Mummery and Rodan, 2007; in the US: Berg, 2002; Davila, 2001; Gilbert and Bauder, 2005). These studies highlight the critical role of media representations in shaping the way migrants, asylum seekers and refugees are seen and received, and how their depictions in the press, films and television programmes impact on their experience.

Nightmare 1 script is produced, fuelled and sustained by various actors within the host society: from unofficial, unflinchingly protectionist, xenophobic, racist and extremist discourses, to official discourses premised on 'reasoned' accounts of migration as a threat to the host country. An example of this is a political ad put out by the ultra-conservative US National Republican Trust PAC (Political Action Committee), attacking President Obama for allowing illegal migrants to obtain a driver's licence:[8]

> 19 terrorists infiltrate the US. 13 get driver's licenses. The 9/11 plot depended on easy-to-get licenses. Obama's plan gives a license to any illegal who wants one. A license they can use to get government benefits, a mortgage, board a plane, even illegally vote. Barack Obama: too radical, too risky.

The nightmare is constructed by equating terrorism with illegal immigration. Its objective is to evoke fear of what migrants' possible lives entail, for both migrants and the host society. It thus builds on the prevalent discourse of terrorism and its intertwining with the discourse of fear, 'the pervasive communication, symbolic awareness, and expectation that danger and risk are a central feature of everyday life' (Altheide, 2007: 288; Furedi, 2005).

Similarly, following the terror attacks in London on 7 July 2005, nightmare narratives of fear, conflating migrants with terrorism, proliferated in the UK (see Tulloch, 2006). The UK right-wing organization, Migration Watch, has been an active promoter of this story, exemplified in a statement from its chairman, published in the *Daily Mail* in December 2005:

> Britain is a soft touch. A potential terrorist who claims asylum here can be sure of a year, perhaps two, at the British taxpayer's expense while his case

> and his appeals are heard. If he succeeds in bluffing the immigration courts he is in clover. He becomes entitled to the full benefits of our welfare state. If he fails, he can go underground and join the hundreds of thousands of failed asylum seekers whom the Government has still not removed from Britain. (Green, 23 December 2005)

Similar examples abound in other national discussions of migration. Use of hyperbolic rhetoric that emphasizes migrants as criminals and a threat, and use of metaphors such as invasion and flooding to describe migration, are discursive aspects typical of this narrative (Van Dijk, 2000). Because they are designed to induce fear, nightmare scripts often deploy the kinds of scare tactics familiar in political and social 'fear appeals' and horror films. A fear appeal is 'a persuasive message that attempts to arouse the emotion of fear by depicting a personally relevant and significant threat and then follows this description of the threat by outlining recommendations presented as effective and feasible in deterring the threat' (Witte, 1994: 114, cited in Walton, 1996: 302). It is oriented to the future and based on the warning of a bad or scary outcome if the receiver does not take a recommended action (ibid.).

The use of this type of appeal is vividly illustrated by a US Attorney's Office television ad against illegal immigration, put out in Maricopa County, Arizona. It shows a black-and-white shot of the blurred and cropped faces of a group of young, gun-toting men holding a roomful of people hostage. The voiceover, accompanied by dramatic music, relates that:

> Illegal immigration is fuelling Arizona's violent crime and drug problem. About 90 per cent of illegal drugs come from south of the border. Armed gangs involved in human smuggling have made Phoenix the kidnapping capital of America. Drop-houses full of illegal immigrants become centres of crime and violence. These drop-houses can appear in any neighbourhood. If you suspect a drop-house in your neighbourhood, contact the Sheriff's office or the County Attorney's office. Together we can stop illegal immigration in Maricopa County.[9]

A similar example is of a television ad which is part of a campaign by the Geneva-based International Organization for Migration, funded by Switzerland and the European Commission (Swissinfo, 30 November 2007). The advert directs its fear appeal to African migrants: 'Don't believe everything you hear. Leaving is not always living,' and tells them that the dream of migration will dissolve into horror and struggle upon arrival in Switzerland. Aired on prime-time television in Cameroon and Nigeria, it shows a newly arrived African migrant speaking to his father from a public phone somewhere in Europe in the pouring rain, assuring him that all is well. This clip of their conversation is constantly interrupted by flashes representing the reality of his living on the street, being pursued by the police and reduced to begging to survive. Ironically, the ad was broadcast on Nigerian state television, during the half-time in a friendly football match between Switzerland and Nigeria (Swissinfo, 30 November 2007).

States and political authorities are not the sole producers of nightmare representations; citizens of countries receiving migrants perpetuate similar narratives, especially online. For instance, the US online Coalition Against Illegal Immigration invites anyone who is 'fed-up with the illegal alien invasion and our government's refusal to do anything about it'[10] to blog about it on its site. One blogger posts a response to the launch of ICED (ICE is the US Immigration and Customs Enforcement department),[11] an educational video game developed by an international, non-profit, human rights organization, purporting to reflect the hardships suffered by illegal migrants and to put the players in the shoes of illegal migrants:[12]

> OH, YES – . . . in playing the game, five immigrant characters go through 'the regular hassles' of being an immigrant in the U.S., including being detained and departed.
> Folks – I have had ENOUGH of this ridiculousness. A video game called 'ICE'D'? If it's games they want, I have an idea for their next one:
> I'll call it: **'SCREWED'** – The plight of the American worker.
> **Synopsis:**
> – Be the first to play a low- to middle-class, American worker as they get screwed out of their jobs.
> – Combat the illegal immigrants as they steal your job by working lower wages. Experience what it's like to live in a community that is overrun with invaders as they infiltrate your country, your state, and your city.
> – Learn how the average American loses the ability to obtain work in their city, because they are not bilingual.
> – Watch how your children's education deteriorates as they are pushed out of their classrooms by non-english speaking students.
> – Attempt to maneuver through the streets of your city without getting shot in a drive-by; try dodging gangster drug dealers and prostitutes who clog the streets.
> – Watch out! Don't get hit by a drunk illegal alien driver!!!
> – As if that's not challenge enough, try to make it to retirement to collect social security or the Medicare you've worked so hard for! What!? You don't qualify? Oh, no! Your identity has been stolen!
> – Face your biggest challenge yet as you attempt to clean up your credit after multiple illegal immigrants have used your SSN numbers!!!

– Remember – no benefits for you until YOU can PROVE you are a VICTIM!
– If you can defeat all these challenges without being called a RACIST – YOU WIN!
GOOD LUCK!

The blogger rejects the narrative of the original game ('I have had ENOUGH of this ridiculousness') and invents a new game, giving what in his view is the true account, in which the American citizen is the sufferer. The new video game (corresponding to Nightmare 1) is predicated on reversal of the original game's (Nightmare 2) roles, plot and resolution, as shown in table 4.1. Americans rather than the illegal migrants are the victims; the powerful are the migrants, not the American citizen. Interestingly, the blogger chooses to deploy exactly the same symbolic structure as the one employed by the narrative that s/he rejects, that of a video game based on a narrative of struggle to overcome the hardships imposed by the 'others'. The new game, rather than departing from the terms, structures and rules of the discourse that it opposes, reproduces them in the construction of its own narrative.

This characteristic feature reveals the logic that underpins the broader discourse on migration and possible lives: a structure of binary opposition. The meaning of Nightmare 1 depends on its differences from its opposite, Nightmare 2.

Table 4.1 Comparison of SCREWED and ICED video games

	SCREWED (Nightmare 1)	*ICED (Nightmare 2)*
Player's character	Low–middle-class American citizen who was sacked	Migrant teenager
Character whom the player is fighting	Illegal migrants ('invaders', 'aliens', 'drunk', 'gangster' 'drug dealers', 'prostitutes')	US ICE officers
Game's goal (the meaning of 'winning')	To 'PROVE that you are a VICTIM' by defeating challenges posed by illegal migrants	'To become a citizen of the United States' by trying 'to avoid ICE officers by making correct moral choices in response to various scenarios'
The meaning of losing	Losing your job and the ability to obtain work; 'watch how your children's education deteriorates as they are pushed out of their classrooms by non-English-speaking students'; be in fear of death, experience identity theft and credit fraud.	Going to detention: you could be in jail for an unknown length of time, enduring unjust conditions, sent to . . . confinement, and possibly deported back to a country you may have never known.

In the ICED game, the user identifies with the illegal migrant whose role s/he adopts. The migrants are the 'goodies', innocent, vulnerable and morally right. The American officers are the 'baddies' against whom the player struggles. The migrant characters are active and are required to draw on their resources to exercise their agency and survive the challenges to becoming a US citizen. In the SCREWED game, the player identifies with the American citizen, passive and helpless in the face of the threats posed by illegal migrants. The player must compete with the illegal migrants in order to claim the title of victim and be awarded benefits.

The rhetorical power of both these narratives – exemplified by the juxtaposition of the two games – resides in their positioning in relation to each other. This underpinning logic throws into relief the simultaneous *interdependence* and divisiveness of the two narratives: Nightmare 1 relies on Nightmare 2 to construct its meaning (and vice versa – see discussion below of Nightmare 2), while at the same time each narrative is locked into and entrenched in its own claim to reflect the 'truth', and each dismisses the truthfulness of the claims made by the other. The result is a set of crude, rigid and reductionist antinomies, which depend on each other, but paradoxically cannot engage in dialogue.

The other element in the blogger's post, revealing of the broader discourse of the nightmare scripts of migration, is the end for which the narrative aims: claiming victimhood (in order to receive benefits). The player's triumph over the series of obstacles is cynically described as 'PROVE you are a VICTIM!' (competing with the migrant's claim to victimhood), conditioned by 'defeat(ing) all these challenges without being called a RACIST'. The language of 'proving' victimhood, and its association with claiming benefits and calculatedly avoiding accusations of racism, reduce the relations between the host society's citizens and the migrants to a cynical, legalistic competition, which on both sides is devoid of compassion for people's real pain. The genre of a video game, which the blogger appropriates, reinforces this message: it locates the real lives of both citizens and migrants in the realm of a game. The articulation of the blogger's views in the form of a video game where American citizen characters battle against the hurdles created by migrants, represses any recognition that the lives of *real* people are being affected in *real* ways. It carries the connotation that these lives are divorced from real material actions and consequences; they can be toyed with in a virtual computer game.

At the same time, to be able to express a personal view of migration using a video game could be regarded as a potent example of the de-sequestration of imagination enabled by new media technologies. The debate over migration is so politicized, and governed by sites seen traditionally as 'serious' and reserved for 'proper' political discourse and the formation of public opinion, that it may fail to enable meaningful connections to people's everyday lives. Thus, the ability to talk about migration through the imagined space provided by a video game enables the subject of migration to enter people's 'local imaginings' and 'localized structures of feeling' (Appadurai, 1996); it allows 'ordinary citizens' to try to make sense of the meanings of the macro-narratives of migrations that they encounter in the news and official political discourses for their own lives.

Nightmare 2

Nightmare 2 highlights the injustice, extreme hardship, discrimination and racism that migrants experience. It is often underpinned by an agenda of greater tolerance, inclusiveness and respect for human rights (thus, the same ideological discourse of humanitarianism, discussed earlier in relation to the dream script, supports and participates in the construction of migration as a nightmare).

The example of the ICED video game illustrates how Nightmare 2 constructs migrants' pursuit of possible lives as extremely challenging, scary and dangerous, almost a 'mission impossible', whose result is worse, often much worse, life conditions, or death. The host society is presented as the guilty party – both causing the nightmare and benefiting from it. Another example of this narrative is a television documentary called *Broken Promises* that was broadcast in two parts in 2005, on Canada's CTV channel.[13] The programme was constructed as a direct and explicit rebuttal of the dream script that feeds the imaginings of migrants and Canadians about Canada being a land of opportunity. The 'broken promise' refers to the experience related by migrants to Canada attracted by the promise of a better life, who met only obstacles and resistance. Their dreams were unfulfilled to the extent that they are unable to practise the professions for which they are trained.

To underline the truthfulness, authenticity and validity of migrants' nightmare, the programme uses migrants' voices – a strategy commonly used in news to amplify its reflective claim of representing the truth. For example, it features a statement from a migrant from India that (cited in Trotter, 21 November 2005):

> Far from being the El Dorado of repute, for many immigrants Canada has emerged as a land of unmitigated disaster. From rampant discrimination to hidden booby traps, Indians have been forced into an economic quagmire, having to settle for a dead end job.

The programme refers to a website (http://www.notcanada.com – which was shut down in 2009), which purports to have been created by former migrants to Canada who wanted to warn others who might be considering migrating there. As its name indicates, the site was underpinned by a narrative of rejection. It denies the binary narrative of the dream script of Canada as a migration 'heaven'. The site lists reasons for not emigrating to Canada, and quotes horror stories from people who went to Canada in search of prosperity only to have their 'dreams shattered'. Disillusioned migrants share their disconcerting accounts on this website's forum; some directly appropriate the binary language of 'dream' and 'nightmare' to describe their experience, for instance: 'My Canadian dream turned into a nightmare.'[14]

Table 4.2 Binary narratives of 'Not Canada' and 'Yes Canada'

	Nightmare script: *Not Canada*	Dream script: *Yes Canada*
Migrants' experience	Disillusion and disappointment	Inspiration and success
Narrative's goal	Discouraging people from migrating in order to pursue possible lives	Encouraging people to migrate in order to pursue possible lives

In structuralist terms, the website's narrative is predicated on binary opposition, as shown in table 4.2. There were doubts raised about whether the notcanada.com website was created and run with the genuine intention to help/forewarn those planning to migrate to Canada. The website had no genuine identifying information and had several oddities, and there was no clear explanation given for why it was shut down in 2009 – all evidence in the opinion of one blogger,[15] to suggest that the site might have been linked to conservative Canadian racist anti-immigration groups who wanted to scare off potential immigrants. Determining who was behind this site is clearly beyond the scope of this discussion. However, the lack of clarity about the website's goals and authors is useful for the light it sheds on how in the contemporary media space, not only is it impossible sometimes to identify and validate the source of narratives, but also those same narratives can derive from sources whose political agendas and motivations are not congruent.

Filmic representations are another important resource for the construction of migrants' worlds and lives. An interesting contribution to the production of nightmare scripts is the 2002 award-winning, independent film, *Dirty Pretty Things,* which offers a gritty depiction of the exploitation of illegal migrants living in London. The movie is centred on Okwe (Chiwetel Ejiofor), a Nigerian 'illegal' in London, who works as a hotel porter by night, and a mini-cab driver by day, and Senay

(Audrey Tautou), a young Turkish woman, also illegal, who earns a pittance working as a maid in the hotel where Okwe is night porter. One morning, Okwe is brusquely instructed to clean up the room of a guest who had been accompanied by a prostitute. He has to unblock a lavatory pan overflowing with blood, and finds that the obstruction is a human heart. This discovery leads Okwe and Senay to become embroiled in the underground, illegal trade in human organs. The film reveals the sinister network of control that relies on keeping asylum seekers and migrants, desperate to obtain EU passports, in a state of mendicant servility and fear (Bradshaw, 13 December 2002).

In a scene in an underground car park, Okwe delivers a box containing human organs to one of the native British men involved in the trade. 'How come I've never seen you before?' asks the man. In a calm, quiet, measured tone, Okwe replies, 'We are the people you don't see. We are the ones who drive your cabs, clean your homes and suck your cocks.' Okwe's poignant response captures the film's unsettling call to the British host society (and by extension to other western societies experiencing migration), to address and to redress migrants' invisibility and the discrimination and exploitation that they suffer: open your eyes, see the people that you do not see and their vulnerable, precarious lives.

Films depend on what Barthes (1977: 45) describes as 'the more projective, more "magical" fictional consciousness'. This fictional orientation makes films the quintessential imaginary spaces for exploration of the tentative, the 'what if'. They do not carry a commitment to reflect the truth as do factual genres such as news or documentaries. This gives them a special power and ability to disturb the imagination, to estrange audiences and unsettle the cultural order, in ways that reflectionist genres, such as news, for example, cannot (although, as argued in chapter 3, news participates in self-estrangement in other significant ways). At the same time, however realistic and moving the performance of Chiwetel Ejiofor, who plays Okwe (and those of other actors in similar movies), it is a fictive representation. The commonplace comment 'it's just a film' encapsulates this limit: the disturbance to perceptions can be denied or blocked by the audience with the reassurance that the representation is fictional, projective, fantastic, unreal.

That said, in today's environment of media representations, the lines between the factual and the fictional increasingly blur. This blurring is used to promote narratives of possible lives, as in the following example in which the boundaries between the real and the fictional are playfully violated by American comedian Stephen Colbert to promote the migrant's plight. Like Shakira, Colbert uses his celebrity status in a form of political activism in support of migrants' struggles for political and social recognition. But while the example of Shakira illustrates how the celebrity migrant figure embodies and promotes the dream script of migration's possible lives, Colbert's demonstrates how celebrity perpetuates the Nightmare 2 narrative.

Colbert is well known in the US as host of the satirical television show *The Colbert Report*, in which he appears as a caricature of a political, ultra-conservative pundit. In September 2010, he testified before the US Congress House Immigration Subcommittee about the day he spent picking vegetables on a farm in upstate New York as part of the 'Take Our Jobs' campaign organized by the United Farm Workers of America (UFW), in order to highlight the plight of migrant workers. Curiously, alongside witnesses such as Arturo S. Rodriguez, the President of UFW, Colbert testified in character:

> I don't want a tomato picked by a Mexican – I want it picked by an American, then sliced by a Guatemalan, and served by a Venezuelan in a spa where a Chilean gives me a Brazilian . . .
>
> After working with these men and women, picking beans, packing corn, for hours on end, side by side, in the unforgiving sun, I have to say and I do mean this sincerely: Please don't make me do this again, it is really, really hard . . .
>
> The point is, we have to do something because I am not going back out there. At this point, I break into a cold sweat at the sight of a salad bar.

Colbert's appearance in front of Congress oscillated between political activism and show business, a genuine eyewitness account and a disingenuous cynical celebrity act, the factual and the fictional, the serious and the absurd. It deliberately and reflexively confuses the boundaries within which the imagining of migration is cultivated in the contemporary media. This blurring of the boundaries, although unique in the way it was enacted by Colbert, has become increasingly characteristic of the work of media representation today.[16] Recall the discussion in chapter 2 of the growing symbiosis between humanitarian activism, celebrity and show business, the description earlier in this chapter of video games designed to reproduce the 'real' experiences of refugees and of migrants, and the example in chapter 3 of a computer-game film highlighting discrimination and racism towards young migrants. Contemporary representations invite us to construct imagined worlds in far less stable and clearly classified ways than in the past. The systems of rules and the codes by which texts are produced and understood are blurred: Colbert embodies the factual and the fictional, news and entertainment, the political and the personal.

To sum up, critical debates on media representations of migration largely and quite rightly stress the divisive and polarized nature of the symbolic resources that guide and discipline public imagination. These polarized discourses produce and sustain clear divisions not only between migrants and the host community, but also between proponents of each of the major discourses, thus tending to close down the debate and deny dialogue (Mummery and Rodan, 2007).

As the examples discussed demonstrate, the voices of authority, such as those of political leaders, official institutions, journalists or celebrities, who speak *for* and *on behalf of* migrants, centrally shape the debate on migration in public discourse. However, today's media environment allows migrants (and other marginalized groups) to talk about their nightmares and dreams and directly to address fellow migrants and host society citizens. They need no longer to appeal to the mainstream media to give them a voice. New media platforms, and especially participatory online sites, such as blogs, forums and social media, provide meaningful spaces for migrants' self-representations, and there has been an upsurge in migrants' voices in the public mediated realm (e.g., Elias and Lemish, 2009; Hiller, 2004; Langmia, 2008; Li, 20 May, 2009). These voices disrupt the 'exteriority of representations' (Said, 2003 [1978]) – the structure upon which traditional journalism relies, of *speaking for* and *speaking on behalf of*. New media allow migrants to speak for themselves about their experiences and hardships, and to voice their frustrations, rage and fears.

Some of these self-representations support and perpetuate the binary terms of the discussion. However, when these broader macro-narratives of dreams and nightmares work their way into people's 'localized structures of feeling' (Appadurai, 1996: 153, drawing on Williams), their rigidity and crude antinomies may be transformed in unpredictable ways. As Appadurai (1996: 4) notes, the work of imagination in a world marked by modernity and globalization 'is neither purely emancipatory nor entirely disciplined, but is a space of contestation in which individuals and groups seek to annex the global into their own practice of the modern'. The imagining of possible lives is far more ambivalent, indeterminate and open than most research on representations of migration to date allows.

Studies of diasporic and transnational communities' consumption of media have contributed substantially to highlighting the complex nature of this 'local imagining' and the role played by media, such as television and the Internet, in migrants' negotiation of their identities and everyday lives. These studies, which predominantly are grounded in ethnographic and phenomenological accounts of *reception* of media texts and *use* of media technologies, underline the centrality of the media as a space for migrants' representations of their lives, identities and experiences. Yet little attention has been paid to the mediated representations produced by migrants: texts expressing localized, individual imaginings of migration.

In the remainder of this chapter, I try to contribute to this project by discussing a blog written by an Iraqi refugee, as a site of 'local imagining' of possible lives of migration. Although representations of its kind are mostly at the margins of public debate on migration, I argue that they play an increasingly central and significant role in the production and reproduction of the store of possible lives on which people draw and which, over time, shape the global imagination. My analysis of this example, although not exhaustive, illustrates what such scripts, produced by migrants – often more complex than either dream or nightmare representations – consist of and where they can be found in the contemporary mediated space.

Beyond Dreams and Nightmares: Ambivalent and Incomplete Imaginings of Possible Lives

Riverbend is a blog (http://riverbendblog.blogspot.com/) that was written by an anonymous young Iraqi woman, who began posting in August 2003; her last post was dated 22 October 2007.[17] Riverbend is an excellent example of a war blog, a subgenre that has attracted much attention in discussions about the changing nature and conditions of journalism, and the transformations and challenges of war reporting in particular (Matheson and Allan, 2007; Wall, 2005). In the context of the discussion in this chapter, however, I use the blog as an example of a mediated representation of possible lives created by enforced migration. I focus especially on the final posts (but still within the context of the blog as a whole), which relate Riverbend's enforced departure from her home in Iraq (she is one of an estimated 1.8 million displaced persons)[18] and her flight to Syria, the country hosting the largest number of Iraqi refugees from the war in Iraq.

Riverbend describes life in Baghdad from the beginning of the war, her partings from more and more friends who left during the war, and her reflections about whether it 'is time to wash our hands of the country and try to find a stable life somewhere else' (5 August 2006). On 26 April 2007, Riverbend tells her readers that she and her family have finally decided to leave:

> I guess I've known we would be leaving for a while now. We discussed it as a family dozens of times. At first, someone would suggest it tentatively because, it was just a preposterous idea – leaving ones home and extended family – leaving ones country – and to what? To where?

Since last summer, we had been discussing it more and more. It was only a matter of time before what began as a suggestion – a last case scenario – soon took on solidity and developed into a plan. For the last couple of months, it has only been a matter of logistics. Plane or car? Jordan or Syria? Will we all leave together as a family? Or will it be only my brother and I at first?

After Jordan or Syria – where then? Obviously, either of those countries is going to be a transit to something else. They are both overflowing with Iraqi refugees, and every single Iraqi living in either country is complaining of the fact that work is difficult to come by, and getting a residency is even more difficult. There is also the little problem of being turned back at the border. Thousands of Iraqis aren't being let into Syria or Jordan – and there are no definite criteria for entry, the decision is based on the whim of the border patrol guard checking your passport. [. . .]

So we've been busy. Busy trying to decide what part of our lives to leave behind. Which memories are dispensable? We, like many Iraqis, are not the classic refugees – the ones with only the clothes on their backs and no choice. We are choosing to leave because the other option is simply a continuation of what has been one long nightmare – stay and wait and try to survive.

On the one hand, I know that leaving the country and starting a new life somewhere else – as yet unknown – is such a huge thing that it should dwarf every trivial concern. The funny thing is that it's the trivial that seems to occupy our lives. We discuss whether to take photo albums or leave them behind. Can I bring along a stuffed animal I've had since the age of four? Is there room for E.'s guitar? What clothes do we take? Summer clothes? The winter clothes too? What about my books? What about the CDs, the baby pictures?

The problem is that we don't even know if we'll ever see this stuff again. We don't know if whatever we leave, including the house, will be available when and if we come back. There are moments when the injustice of having to leave your country, simply because an imbecile got it into his head to invade it, is overwhelming. It is unfair that in order to survive and live normally, we have to leave our home and what remains of family and friends. . . And to what?

It's difficult to decide which is more frightening – car bombs and militias, or having to leave everything you know and love, to some unspecified place for a future where nothing is certain.

This lengthy quote clearly captures the ambivalence in imagining the new lives awaiting refugees. This imagining is governed by uncertainty and confusion, a mix of hope and anxiety, desire for a better, but unknown, future, and grief over the loss of soon-to-become former lives. Crucially, ambivalence is different from balance – the principle underpinning news reporting – as a means to achieving the gold standard of objectivity and neutrality. Riverbend's account is not (and does not try to be) balanced; it does not discuss the positive and negative aspects of migration. It is a mixed, confused account, full of question marks (thirteen just in the extract above) and expressions of uncertainty: 'I guess', 'someone would suggest', 'just a preposterous idea', 'we don't know', 'it's difficult to decide'. This and the posts that describe her experience of migrating dwell chiefly on *not* knowing rather than knowing what the new life will be like. This ambivalence is often lost in binary scripts of dreams and nightmares, which, unlike Riverbend's account, aim to provide 'true' knowledge of how and what a migrant's life *is*. The examples discussed earlier demonstrate this lack of ambivalence – from biographies of 'successful' refugees in the dream narrative, to fear appeals based on establishing 'facts' in the nightmare discourse.

Riverbend's post captures a moment in the temporal trajectory of migration that is rarely represented in the nightmare/dream constructions: the moment of deciding to leave the home country, without knowing the destination, or how and when the move will take place. Her post encapsulates the liminality of migration, the in-between experience of migration – between past and future, here and there, old and new, nightmare and dream. This liminal temporality stands in contrast to the temporal structure of the dream and nightmare narratives, which are predicated on a before/after binary. In the dream scenario, life before was a nightmare, the new life is a dream. In the Nightmare 1 scenario, the host country's life before the migrants arrive was a dream and after becomes a nightmare, and, in Nightmare 2, the migrants' lives before were bad, but after migrating become fundamentally worse. This discursive before/after formulation, so familiar in makeover discourse (e.g., 'makeovers' of one's body, one's house, one's life), not only reduces a complex experience into two oppositional moments, it fails also to account for the experience of migration as an ongoing process, which does not necessarily progress in a linear way. Migrants' lives, even after decades of living in a new place, are always, to varying degrees, liminal, ambivalent, fraught with contradictions and incomplete.

Riverbend juxtaposes her experience against the macro-narrative of migration as 'such a huge thing that it should dwarf every trivial concern'. Media representations such as official political and policy discourses, news and NGO communications, play a central role in feeding and sustaining this framing of migration as a 'big issue', a 'bigger-than-self',[19] large-scale national and international concern. But in her straightforward, direct account, Riverbend confesses that 'it's the trivial that seems to occupy our lives'; matters such as what to pack and what to leave behind. Of course, these concerns are far from trivial or insignificant, but Riverbend's reflections highlight the absence of these 'trivial', practical and material aspects of the experience of migration in the macro-story of migration that is produced and legitimated in mainstream public discourse.

In a post written on 22 October 2007 from Syria, the country to which Riverbend and her family fled, Riverbend situates her experience and identity against the broader identity category (or subject position) of 'refugee' constructed by public media representations:

> By the time we had reentered the Syrian border and were headed back to the cab ready to take us into Kameshli, I had resigned myself to the fact that we were refugees. I read about refugees on the Internet daily . . . in the newspapers . . . hear about them on TV. I hear about the estimated 1.5 million plus Iraqi refugees in Syria and shake my head, never really considering myself or my family as one of them. After all, refugees are people who sleep in tents and have no potable water or plumbing, right? Refugees carry their belongings in bags instead of suitcases and they don't have cell phones or Internet access, right? Grasping my passport in my hand like my life depended on it, with two extra months in Syria stamped inside, it hit me how wrong I was. We were all refugees. I was suddenly a number. No matter how wealthy or educated or comfortable, a refugee is a refugee. A refugee is someone who isn't really welcome in any country – including their own . . . especially their own.

The last post on the blog describes Riverbend's first days in Syria, and the warm welcome she and her family received from other Iraqi refugees in their building. It ends with the sentence 'I cried that night because for the first time in a long time, so far away from home, I felt the unity that had been stolen from us in 2003.' The ending is quite abrupt; there is no clear closure to the story. What happened to Riverbend? How did her new life in Syria or some other country work out? Did she, or does she, intend to return to Iraq? Online spaces and online communication allow a 'no ending', which goes against one of the fundamental principles of narrative: closure. The lack of ending allows, even forces, the imagination to accept incompleteness: that not only can we not get access to the 'facts' and the 'full picture' (the basis of the reflectionist approach that underpins traditional journalism), but we also cannot conclude or classify Riverbend and her experience with complete coherence and certainty.

Riverbend's blog is a vivid example of what Appadurai calls (1996) 'local imagining': the ways in which broader, macro-events and global issues work their way into highly localized structures of feeling. New media spaces, such as blogs and online discussion forums, become increasingly important sites where the work of local imagining occurs and becomes visible. These texts, some of which – such as the Riverbend blog – are adapted and transformed into other media, reach wider audiences beyond those they were originally intended for. Over time, they generate structures and narratives that become staples on which global imagination feeds.

Conclusion

The juxtaposition of migration with the rapid flow of mass-mediated images and scripts has brought 'a new order of instability in the production of modern subjectivities' (Appadurai, 1996: 4). In the face of this new instability and the 'liquid times' (Bauman, 2007) of today's globalized world, the imagination clings to stability and seeks to reclaim certainty, fixity and coherence by establishing comprehensive and clear scripts: dreams and nightmares. These scripts, which circulate in various forms, media and genres in the contemporary mediated space, are often constructed as binary oppositions. They are predicated on the logic of exclusion and divisiveness – between migrants and host society, between a protectivist and nationalist view, and a humanitarian and cosmopolitan perspective. They offer crude, and often oversimplified ways of imagining migration and its many possible lives. Ambivalence, uncertainty and complexity – which are the crux of everyday life and the experience of migration – tend to be swallowed up in many of these representations.

The dream/nightmare oppositions that dominate representation of migration on television and Internet screens, and in cinema films and newspapers, are important in terms of capturing the diversity of migration and its very different consequences within their 'either/or' extremes. What is 'TRIUMPH!' for one child of illegal migrants in the US is 'SCREWED' for an American citizen-blogger; what for one is a humanitarian moral obligation to accept migrants and give them refuge, is for another an act that makes life dangerous and violent.

Alongside these representations, and increasingly in response to them, more ambivalent and incomplete accounts are emerging in the mediated spaces of local imagining, such as online forums, blogs, Twitter and Facebook, as well as in more traditional mediated sites. These accounts may be very brief, for example, a short post on an online forum or a tweet on Twitter, and as such can be argued to lack depth. They also are often anonymous and lack closure, an issue I return to in the book's conclusion. However, they have a potential to expand and open up the imagination, to allow and accept ambivalence, instability and uncertainty of meaning. This is not to suggest that we should abandon the pursuit of clear, informative accounts. Rather, I argue that, as media consumers and producers, students of the media, and, above all, as citizens of the world, we might benefit from allowing more ambivalence, incompleteness and a degree of doubt and uncertainty in the landscape of contemporary representations that shape and are shaped by our imagination. How else can we imagine better possible lives for others and for ourselves?

5   Imagining the World

Representations of New Year Celebrations

> The world and its players appear in the media, and for most of us that is the only place they do appear. Appearance itself becomes, in both senses of the word, the world.
> Silverstone, 2007: 10; reprinted by permission of Polity

For many people, media representations are the main, if not the only, place that they come to know the world. In the ongoing flow of mediated images and stories, the world emerges as a common space that we inhabit and traverse, a space where we engage and exist with other agents. It is a space of commonality and sameness, a global village (McLuhan's famous term), a 'flat' place (a metaphor popularized by *New York Times'* columnist Thomas Freidman's account of globalization in *The World Is Flat*), where geographical, cultural, political, economic and religious distinctions are increasingly less well delineated. The growing presence and prominence of the discourse of humanitarianism in the public sphere, in which the media and NGOs play a considerable role, reinforce this narrative of the world. In this imaginary, as Calhoun (2008) observes, the world is pictured as united by common humanity, a social space inhabited by individuals who are equivalent, who are all deserving of moral recognition and are disembedded from kinship, religion, nationality and other identity and relationship webs. At the same time, contemporary representations reveal an image of 'the world' as a place divided by deep inequalities, moral and material hierarchies, violent conflicts, competition and illicit exploitation. In these constructions, the world is a place marked by and constituted upon division, difference, exclusion and marginalization.

This dual image of the world is enacted in the stories and imagery that we encounter in the media on a daily basis and that constitute the 'normal' way of seeing things. It provides a broader framework that enables a grasp of the space and place we inhabit, and how we 'fit' together in the carrying out of collective practices that constitute contemporary ways of life. In this sense, 'the world' is a construct, a social imaginary that confers legitimacy on certain common practices and thoughts, and embeds them in a normative scheme (based on Taylor, 2002).

How are this social imaginary of the world and its contradictory meanings conveyed in contemporary representations? The preceding chapters have to an extent already touched on this question, since imaginings of ourselves and others, and of possible lives, are inseparable from imaginings of the world. The world constitutes a sort of a background (following Heidegger and Wittgenstein); a complex, unstructured, and not fully articulated 'understanding of our whole situation, within which particular features of the world become evident' (Taylor, 2002: 107). In this chapter, we narrow the focus and examine a particular instance of the world appearing on our mediated screens: New Year celebrations.

New Year Celebrations: A Global Media Event

Beginning at midnight on 31 December each year, most of the major transnational news channels, such as CNN International, BBC World, and Bloomberg, and national channels and various websites, report the New Year celebrations taking place around the world. This is a vivid and regular example of a global media event (Dayan and Katz, 1992): a ritual of media communications, that articulates, reproduces and deepens certain understandings and beliefs (many of which are beyond the scope of this chapter) about the world. Specifically, New Year celebrations are an example of Dayan and Katz's (1992) third script of media event:[1] a 'recurrent media event, taking place based on traditions in public spaces, marked by the drama of "will the ritual succeed?" and presented in a reverent way to an audience renewing the contract with the center, confirming traditional authority, focused on the past' (Couldry, Hepp and Krotz, 2010: 2).

Drawing on Couldry, Hepp and Krotz's (2010: 12) instructive critique of media events as 'centering performances', and Harvey's (2001) account of the symbolic production of 'geographical knowledges', chapter 5 explores New Year celebrations as a media event in which geographical knowledges are produced – information is assembled, used, framed and presented in certain ways so as to construct a particular understanding of what the world is. I analyse the mediated ritual of the New Year celebrations, in terms of how it constructs the world in relation to a particular 'centre', deeply related to the production and maintenance of global power relations. I use this case to tease out broader reflections on some of the ways in which the world is constructed and imagined in the media today.

Dayan and Katz's (1992) influential study of media events argues for the relevance of 'single', 'outstanding' ritual ceremony in media and communication. Media events constitute a distinctive genre: pre-planned 'interruptions of routine', they exploit media communication across channels and programmes, and are broadcast live. They are staged as historic occasions enacted with ceremonial reverence and 'enthral very large audiences who view them in a festive style' (Couldry et al., 2010: 2).

Dayan and Katz (1992) highlight the significance and relevance of media events as a form of mediated ritual that becomes a force of social integration, making 'possible an extraordinary shared experience of watching events at society's "centre"' (Couldry, 2003: 61). Couldry et al. (2010) revisit the theory of media events, and this argument in particular, in an attempt to establish the basis for researching media events in a global age. They argue that the national framing in Dayan and Katz's original argument, and their understanding of societies as being marked by a shared set of values, are highly problematic as we move to an examination of media events within a global perspective.

In what follows, I draw on Couldry et al.'s (2010) critique and analyse the construction of 'the world' in international news broadcast reporting of Christian New Year celebrations. The analysis shows how this media event reinforces a celebratory account of the world as united around sameness, joined by the same ritual and by reverence of the spectacle, and occupied by similar people in similar spaces. At the same time, my analysis shows how this image of the world, which is constitutive of the global imagination, simultaneously contains and enacts that which it wants to exclude: it promotes competition as the primary relation through which people, cities and countries interact with each other, and constructs symbolic exclusions and emphasizes hierarchies. The second part of my analysis presents other cases of representations of the New Year, which offer a different 'cartographic consciousness' of the world.

International News Reporting of New Year Celebrations around the World

The following discussion is based on an analysis of ten broadcast reports on the international news channels CNN, Sky, Reuters, ABC, BBC, CN24 and CCTV International of the 2008, 2009, 2010 and 2011 New Year celebrations. Although New Year celebrations are represented through and across various media, channels and genres, arguably, it is the television news reports that are the most spectacular, visible and constitutive representations of this event. Their reporting follows fairly similar conventional formulas: a montage of clips of scenes from various cities around the world, organized into a narrative of people around the globe celebrating and welcoming in the New Year. Reporting commonly starts with Sydney, Australia (where

Figure 5.1 Fireworks over Sydney Harbour, © Courtney Keating/istock

New Year arrives first), followed by images of scenes of celebration from the world's largest capital and other cities, such as London, Paris, Berlin, Tokyo, Moscow, Beijing and New York.

There is a consistent set of specific visual tropes present in these broadcasts: outdoor scenes in central (often famous touristic) public spaces of cities, firework displays, showers of confetti, crowds, people embracing, dancing and laughing. The visual focus on individuals is limited and where it occurs, it is usually to show prominent figures, such as mayors or heads of states. When 'ordinary' individuals feature, it is usually to obtain sound bites expressing conventional hopes for the New Year, for peace, prosperity and love.

Although these reports are not synonymous, they exhibit similar patterns and employ similar strategies. In what follows, I focus on one news channel's reporting in order to examine in detail how a particular representation constructs a certain vision of the world. How does the world appear in this CNN news report? What do we learn about it from this report? Drawing on Foucault, in analysing this clip we focus on what ideas about the world are made legitimate or desirable, and attain the status of 'truth', and how, and what ideas are excluded, marginalized, rendered deviant, illegitimate, implausible and false. What remains invisible? What and who are excluded from this representation, and what 'truth effects' (Foucault) do such exclusions produce? Table 5.1 illustrates how the rhetoric and images of 'the world' are at play within a news report.

Table 5.1 CNN, *New Year 2008 Around the World*

Sequence	Audio	Visual
1	(*Correspondent voiceover*) At the stroke of midnight, Europe's largest city re-staked its claim as its most exciting, with the aid of 1.5 million pounds worth of fireworks. 700,000 revellers witnessed London's most lavish pyrotechnic display in years.	Distance shots of the London Eye and the Thames, skies filled with fireworks.
2	Elsewhere on the continent, meanwhile, both Paris and Berlin hosted more restrained festivities, with fireworks budgets perhaps a touch more modest.	Crowds celebrating and cheering outdoors, against a backdrop of the Arc de Triomphe in Paris, and the Brandenburg Gate in Berlin. All faces in the crowd are white. Close-ups of white men in the crowd, toasting the New Year with champagne. Close-up of younger white man, waving a sparkler.
3	Whilst Slovenia's celebrations taking over the EU presidency belie potentially tough diplomatic months ahead.	Slovenian skies lit by fireworks. Some buildings (possibly in the capital city, Ljubljana) are covered in Christmas lights. Close-up of a white couple in Santa Claus hats, kissing in the midst of the crowd.
4	Malta along with Cyprus joins the Euro at the stroke of midnight, a misfiring publicity stunt dispensing no ill will.	Fireworks in Malta (possibly in the capital, Valletta). Indoor scene: close-up of Maltese Prime Minister unsuccessfully trying to get money from an ATM.
5	(*Lawrence Gonzi: Maltese Prime Minister*) We are the smallest member state of the European Union, but we are as proud as the largest country, and we have achieved what perhaps other countries have not yet done.	Close-up of Maltese Prime Minister's face, smiling as he speaks. A crowd is assembled behind him, composed of elderly white men, who smile and nod in agreement as he speaks.
6	(*Correspondent voiceover*) Russia meanwhile underlined its newfound economic confidence with a robust display of firepower.	Close-up of two Russian girls dancing. A large crowd is assembled behind them, people are wearing brown, fur-trimmed parkas; one person is wearing a Santa Claus hat. Distant shot of a church in St Petersburg. Skies lit with fireworks.

Sequence	Audio	Visual
7	Whilst across the Atlantic one million Americans packed into Times Square: Mayor Mike Bloomberg triggering the traditional ball drop. This midnight marriage proposal, leaving one New Yorker untypically speechless.	Panning over the cheering crowds in Times Square, New York. Streets are packed. Angle and distance is such that the crowd appears faceless. Close-up of Mayor Bloomberg and a New York policewoman initiating the Ball Drop. Quick switch to the Ball Drop. Switch to a close-up of a man proposing marriage, beginning by showing the man on one knee, then moving to show the woman's reaction: she covers her mouth in disbelief. The couple is white, dressed in warm coats and festive red hats. The crowd behind them is white – a blonde woman in a fur coat is shown, smiling at the marriage proposal.
8	In Rio de Janeiro, two million Brazilians hosted the world's biggest beach party.	Fireworks in the sky over the beach. Crowd on the beach is faceless. Close-up of groups in the crowd. A group of dark-skinned males wearing T-shirts and festive necklaces dancing energetically. One of the men is shaking a champagne bottle.
9	Whilst in Australia, the self-styled world firework display kings put down a typically flamboyant marker of the Sydney Harbour.	Distant shot of the firework display over the Sydney Harbour. Orchestral music playing in the background. No crowds in the shot.
10	In Beijing, huge crowds braved the cold weather to see the famous 274-year-old bell toll in the New Year.	Distance shot of the crowds in Beijing, waving multicoloured flags. Close-up of Chinese men wearing suits, hitting the bell. Close-up of the large bell, surrounded by crowds of Chinese people, waving coloured flags.
11	And finally, to Iraq, where the appetite for explosions is understandably low. Instead, a friendly football match between British and Iraqi soldiers, the glint of a peaceful rivalry many will be hoping for more of this year.	Close-up of the legs of soldiers playing football. Individual faces are not shown. The camera follows the ball as it moves back and forth across the dirt surface. Close-up of cheering, clapping and smiling Iraqi and British soldiers on the sidelines. One man is white, the others are dark-skinned.

The world as a space of sameness

The CNN report centres on the same social event (celebration) being enjoyed simultaneously by people in geographically remote places and from different cultural contexts (understood largely on the basis of their national affiliation), around a common object: the calendrical transition to a new Christian year. This story is created visually through the editorial technique of montage: juxtaposition of similar images of the same event in different places – mostly large capital cities in the global north. Discursively, the visual montage is organized by the reporter's voiceover (although some reports show a reporter at the scene), which links the different events and places temporally, through the use of connectives such as 'while' and 'whilst'.

At the most immediate and overt level, the message is of *global similarity and sameness*: cities and countries around the world (albeit, only specific parts of it) are joined together, visually and discursively, in a single story centred on a common event. The event of the New Year celebrations acts as 'symbolic glue' that enables the various cities and countries to be brought into a coherent narrative. The world is 'condensed' into this single report, constructed as a unified social space inhabited by people who take part in a common ritual.

Most explicitly, a sense of similarity is created between and among the places and people included in the report, through the construction of visual sameness. Scenes from eleven countries are broadcast, all except one displaying similar visual features: firework displays, and celebrating crowds in urban centres. This repetitive visual trope, even without the reporter's narration, conveys a clear message of similarity. The skies lit up by fireworks act as 'placeless' markers: their appearance is pretty much the same everywhere, which diffuses the specificities of the places beneath these skies, for example, historical, economic, cultural, national and ethnic differences marked by visual elements such as architecture, dress, facial features and skin colours. The crowds for the most part are faceless; specific individuals are largely rendered invisible. With the exception of the final scene of a football game in Iraq between British and Iraqi soldiers, all the representations are of highly organized scenes of public life, from which emerges a strong sense of national and global, spatial and social standardization, in which all the citizens of these countries take part. Not only does it appear that the citizens of these countries participate in these highly orchestrated celebrations, but the celebrations in the different countries are similar, as if there were some global standard against which they are all managed and produced.

A sense of global sameness and standardization is inextricably intertwined with the emphasis in the report on collectiveness. The visual focus on celebrating crowds is a central generator of this meaning. It generates nostalgia for embodied peaceful participation in public life: people gathering together in city squares to share and express similar emotions (excitement, hope, happiness) through a public ritual of celebration. This kind of image of celebrating crowds is fairly rare in contemporary western media, especially on television. Pictures of crowds or large collectives of people are often either enforced embodied collectives, for example, refugees fleeing their homes, victims of wars and political struggles, or members of an institutional collective, gathered in a crowd in pursuit of a common (often political) goal, for example, demonstrators in the streets or military forces on the battlefield. It is less common to see large crowds rejoicing, in a festive context, engaging in friendly physical and intimate contact (touching each other, kissing, hugging), and particularly crowds in different places and countries, celebrating the same event. The transitions from scene to scene and place to place are edited smoothly and because the pictures are so similar and 'placeless', it appears almost as if the separate crowds were one large crowd in a singular space – a space of sameness and standardization which is 'the world'.

The particular scenes of cities' celebrations act as instances and exemplars of a generalized mode of belonging to this spatial imaginary, which is constituted as urban and national. The majority of the images are decidedly urban, capitalizing on touristic imaginaries and the (manufactured) desirability of spaces; they include the London skyline, New York's Times Square, Russia's St Petersburg's cathedrals. There are no images of rural scenes, and even in the case of the less distinctively urban image of the Brazilian beach, the location is the capital Rio de Janeiro, rather than some other, non-urban part of the country's coast.

At a more implicit level, the underpinning spatial imaginary is of a national imagined community (Anderson, 1983) – images of celebrations in London are indexical representations of Britain, the fireworks display in Sydney Harbour represents Australia, and so on. This implicit spatial frame is constructed through the relations between the visuals and the commentator's voiceover. In some scenes we see images of a particular city, but the reporter refers to its country location rather than mentioning the name of the city. In other scenes, the reporter identifies the city rather than referring to the country name. This selective naming is closely tied to and reinforces power relations: the more prominent cities are identified by name, the less prominent ones by their country. Overall, this discursive operation of naming establishes the nation as the governing spatial mode. Each city acts as a metonym for its country; therefore, there is never mention of more than one city in one country. Alternative modes of celebration and belonging, for example, community neighbourhood rituals or transnational festivities, are absent. While migrants across the world celebrate the New Year as a ritual and an expression and negotiation of their transnational identities (as revealed for instance by various citizen clips on YouTube), this type of experience and mode of belonging is absent from the report.

Another visual trope that contributes to creating a sense of similarity between different cities and countries, and to constructing the world as a coherent spatial frame within which these events are situated, is enormity and grandeur. Not only are the celebrations spectacular and large scale, but very large and/or tall objects, usually historical and tourist attractions, are associated with the festivities. They act as identifiers for the particular places; they are recognizable to most viewers as a result of their history, or touristic image, and all reify the emphasis on size and scale. Examples include Beijing's enormous old bell, the London Eye, the Arc de Triomphe in Paris, Berlin's Brandenburg Gate, the huge digital billboard in New York's Times Square, and the distinctive outline of the Sydney Opera House. In 2011, most reports included a new building in Dubai – currently the world's tallest building – showing a mass of fireworks exploding from its base to its needle-like spire nearly half a mile above the ground. Underpinning the inclusion of Dubai, arguably, is its status as a global city and a business hub in the Persian Gulf.

This visual focus on a limited range and type of scenes, activities and objects – the repetitive displays of skies lit by fireworks, celebrating crowds, and well-known architecture and monuments – constructs a portrait of the world as a unified, standardized, singular space. This picture is endorsed by a narrative creating a sense of temporal and spatial unity through the use of connectives such as 'meanwhile', 'whilst', 'elsewhere on the continent' and 'along with'. These verbal cues work symbolically to glue together the happenings in eleven different places around the world, to construct a cohesive story. The use of these visual and discursive strategies binds these different events in different places and situates them within a coherent spatial frame of 'the world'.

The world as a competitive space marked by distinction

The logic that organizes the CNN report, at the same time, is fundamentally *comparative*: the montage of numerous images of the same event in different, far-flung places inherently foregrounds the *differences* between them, highlighting the idea that they are *not* the same. The reporter's voiceover organizes the comparison by identifying the objects – naming the cities and countries shown in the images, and establishing criteria against which they are compared. Crucially, these differences are evaluated and hierarchized by specific criteria; most explicitly, the expenditure on fireworks is cited as a measure of the overall success of each country's display. At the start of the transmission, the commentator's voiceover marks particular criteria for distinction: the spectacular character of the celebration, its scale and its grandeur. The scale and spectacle of the celebrations are directly associated in the narrative with economic prowess. Each country's celebrations act as a metaphor for its overall financial resilience entering the New Year.[2] A comparison is drawn between London, 'Europe's largest city', and its large, expensive fireworks display, and the more 'restrained' celebrations in Paris and Berlin. The distinction is quantitative: the modest budgets of Paris and Berlin are compared to the £1.5 million spent by London on fireworks. Expensive fireworks displays and large public groups of people are thus established as the conventions of New Year celebrations. By extension, size, spectacle and grandeur act as symbolic benchmarks for comparisons among the positions on the global map of cities and countries: for example, London 're-staked its claim as [Europe's] most exciting [city]' through its 'lavish pyrotechnic display'. Financial capitals are showcased as embodying each country's relative competitive strength. Thus, the same elements that work to unify the places and people – grandeur and size – are the basis also of competition, and a mark of superiority.

The binding, positioning and locating of the different countries and cities in the report play a central role in the production of the world as a place marked by difference, hierarchy and competition. The ordering of the celebrations shown in the report is not arbitrary; it is based on the dominant European cartographic identification (Harvey, 2001) of continents: starting with Europe (1 London; 2 Paris and Berlin; 3 Slovenia; 4 Malta and Cyprus; 5 Russia), followed by America (1 New York; 2 Rio de Janeiro), Australia (1 Sydney) and Asia (1 Beijing; 2 Iraq). By binding places within the categories of continents, the report establishes internal comparisons against which each place is evaluated in relation to its category. Thus, for example, within Europe London is presented first, endorsed by the commentator's voiceover as its 'largest' and 'most exciting' city, with the 'most lavish pyrotechnic display in years'. Paris and Berlin are in joint second place: they are bound together by the pronoun 'both' – they do not appear independently, which works to mark their inferiority to London. The text explicitly positions them as weaker than London: their festivities are 'more restrained' and their fireworks budgets 'a touch more modest'. Third in Europe is Slovenia. The voiceover does not make an explicit comparison with the previous European cities (as it did for Paris and Berlin compared to London), a discursive technique that implies it is not in the same league. What marks Slovenia's fundamentally weaker position is that it is identified only as a country, compared to the implied identification of the previous three countries through their capital cities. The reporter also does not refer to the size, character or budget of Slovenia's celebrations, but rather to its political importance (taking on the next EU presidency), reinforcing the sense that it cannot compete in terms of economic prowess (for which the firework displays are a metaphor).

The transition to Slovenia after London and Paris and Berlin creates an implicit subdivision within the category of Europe, between the economically powerful and the less prominent. It situates the places within a coherent frame based on an implicit descending order: from the most to the least economically powerful. Cyprus and Malta's positioning after Slovenia fits with this, and is corroborated by the Maltese prime minister's statement referring to the size of his country: 'We are the *smallest* member state in the European Union' (emphasis added). The inclusion of Cyprus and Malta in the represented 'world', places that could be considered outliers in the overarching trend towards prominent 'global destination' cities and countries, is connected to their accession to the European Union. However, at the same time that the report validates their inclusion into an implied category dominated by large, economically prosperous countries, it also reinforces their *relative* and inferior economic position with respect to established (superior) players such as the United Kingdom. This is implicit in the joke made by the commentator about the 'misfiring publicity stunt', and pictures showing the Maltese prime minister failing to get money from an ATM: the correspondent chooses to joke and make light of this event – and by extension, of the Maltese – rather than to emphasize its seriousness and significance.

The sound bite from Malta's prime minister in some ways runs counter to the implication of Malta's inferiority: he expresses pride in his nation's membership of the Union, and the value it will bring despite the country's being the smallest of the current members. He explicitly promotes competition as the mode of relations among member states, stating that Malta has 'achieved what perhaps other countries have not yet done'. At the same time, in highlighting Malta's small size as a distinction, the norm is reinforced: it is the size of a country and its related economic status that allow it to compete on the regional (European) stage and, by extension, on the wider, global stage. This trend is consistent throughout the report: in countries that are established internationally, the style of the New Year celebrations serves to reinforce this position. For example, while 'in Australia, the self-styled *world firework display kings* put down a *typically flamboyant* marker on the Sydney Harbour', in countries that are striving to achieve the global stage, the New Year celebrations operate to announce their debut, for example, 'Russia meanwhile underlined its *new-found economic confidence* with a robust display of firepower' (emphases added).

Thus, through the employment of discursive and visual strategies of binding, classifying, identifying and positioning, the report produces a symbolic map, what Harvey (2001: 221) calls a 'cartographic consciousness' of 'the world'. The underpinning principle that organizes and hierarchizes places on this map is economic success and prowess. The economic occupies a central place and it is implied that the collective goal of the world is a strong economy. Thus, the news report manifests the modern social imaginary by which 'things cohere, because they serve each other in their survival and flourishing. They form an ideal economy . . . the economic now defines a way in which we are linked together, a sphere of coexistence that could in principle suffice to itself' (Taylor, 2002: 104–5).

Capitalist logic frames this view of the world: it reduces the world which it describes to a single term: market (based on Couldry, 2010). Market competition, embodied by world cities' competition over their expenditure on celebrations and their spectacularity, constitutes the common practical and normative reference point. Places and peoples are evaluated by this single criterion, and it provides the organizing framework for understanding the world and its players. Accordingly, economic weakness, disorder, conflict and tension are suppressed. The spectacular qualities of the New Year media event and its positive connotations of excitement, festivity, collectiveness and hope, aestheticize and sublimate the less positive and rather aggressive meanings of economic competition, especially in the context of the financial crisis that had erupted just prior to the event analysed. To put it somewhat crudely, the story of countries' and cities' struggles for survival, let alone recognition and success, in extremely volatile financial times, is told through spectacular scenes of fireworks and rejoicing crowds celebrating in some of the world's famous venues. Clearly, this representation of the world, like many others circulating in the media, has no interest in highlighting 'the geography of social distress' (Harvey, 2001: 209).

The symbolic production of hierarchies between and among places is further highlighted if we look at what the report does *not* include: which places, people and practices are not shown and, therefore, are excluded symbolically from the world. By privileging economic competitiveness as a legitimizing category for participation and inclusion in the world, this report noticeably excludes developing countries. This key discriminating factor, along with the unspoken fact that not *all* of the world's people celebrate Christian New Year, explains (but should not validate) why, for example, the entire continent of Africa is excluded. It explains also why Beijing, where clearly Chinese New Year is of greater significance than the Christian New Year, is included in the picture of the world: China is represented, albeit in a typically Orientalizing fashion, by focusing on the '274-year-old Bell toll', as a rising global economic power.

In this context, the inclusion of Rio de Janeiro in the category of legitimate global players might appear somewhat curious. The celebrations in Rio de Janeiro simultaneously resonate with established conventions, such as fireworks displays, and depart from the largely western visions of New Year. Unlike the urban scenes of street celebrations and fireworks displays in the global north, the celebrations in Rio are set on a beach, men are shown dancing in a jerky, energetic way, and the faces shown are not white. In contrast to the close-up of a couple's marriage proposal in the New York scene, the crowd on the Brazilian beach is faceless. This representation subtly connotes 'primitiveness', invoking the racial stereotype that black people have 'natural rhythm', and alludes to exotic tribal rituals performed through collective dancing (as discussed in chapter 2 in relation to the 'We Are The World 25 For Haiti' clip). Specifically, it is in relation to other visual elements in the report, of crowds in urban spaces dressed in layers of warm clothing against the cold weather, which are implicitly established as the norm, that the Brazilians' partying is connoted the exception to the norm, as 'tribal' or 'primitive'.

If we follow the organizing principle underpinning this map of the world drawn by the report, the reason for including Brazil is its newfound economic prominence. As the most developed and competitive of the countries of South America, it serves as a safe representative for that part of the world. It adheres to and reinforces the frame established in the report: participation in the 'world' is defined exclusively by the logic of the market; inclusion in the 'world' and recognition and legitimacy of its members depend crucially on economic status and an aspiring country's relative willingness to 'play the game'. The inclusion of Brazil fits the doctrine of 'harmony of interests' (Taylor, 2002: 104), which underlies the economic-centred notion of a modern moral order. It is coherent with the overarching narrative of the economic as defining the way people across the world link together.

However, the representation of Brazil, as exemplifying a developing country and 'standing in' for other developing or less developed countries, is fleeting (lasting only a few seconds), not substantive, and lacks elaboration from the commentator. Rather than focusing on economic viability in this narrative, Rio de Janeiro boasts 'the largest beach party'. Thus, Brazil's representation produces what Harvey (2001: 211) calls 'empty geographical knowledges' which construct and maintain geographical ignorance. It re-enacts and reinforces racial and cultural stereotypes, but does not provide any specific information about the people, conditions and circumstances in Brazil. Arguably, within the constraints of the genre, formula and short length of this report, it would be impossible to provide much meaningful geographical specificity. However, in relation to the comments on the other places included in the report, the commentary on Brazil stands out as brief in the extreme, and its representation as superficial and 'empty'.

More broadly, any subtleties or contradictory realities are effectively effaced. The report clearly excludes religious or minority groups who do not celebrate the Christian New Year. Low-income people living in the cities represented, who are working over the period of the New Year, often doing extra work to make ends meet and to survive the impending global recession, are also absent. The selectivity entailed in the choice of the images and places included, constructs the globe generally as a fiercely competitive and prosperous playing field. It paints a positive picture of the world and does not address the negative implications of the economic successes that it privileges. This is glaringly obvious in the final scene, from Iraq, where there is admittedly 'less appetite for explosions'. The faces of Iraqi and British soldiers initially are not visible; we see only their legs entangled in a tackle over the ball in a friendly football match. The facelessness of the representation glosses over the complexity of the war, obfuscating the political tensions surrounding military intervention and silencing any uniquely Iraqi account of the conflict, and is geared to projecting an optimistic future for the region. Thus, the visual technique of 'cropping' the players' bodies into parts (see chapter 2) and the choice of a football match as the event represented, work to de-politicize, trivialize and sublimate a highly politicized, bloody and complex conflict. The sentence that concludes the report, 'the glint of a peaceful rivalry many will be hoping for more of, this year' affirms the 'mediated centre': the position of privilege occupied by Britain and the rest of the developed western world, in the pursuit of a 'world' that looks like the one in CNN's report, and where they have a favourable position and are bound to prosper.

The televised performance of New Year celebrations that is shown annually on international news channels, starting at midnight on 31 December, provides particular ways of describing and thinking about the world. It selects, arranges and prioritizes certain assumptions and ideas about the world; it foregrounds and idealizes some places and casts others as marginal or non-existent in the story that claims to reflect the world. At the same time as this media event constructs the world as a unified social space of similarity, it symbolically produces a world marked by difference, hierarchy and competition. This construction, I suggest, is characteristic of the broader way of imagining the world that prevails in media representations.

Commercial requirements go some way to explaining the bias towards the immediate, the spectacular and the aesthetically acceptable in these types of representations on international news channels (based on Harvey, 2001). More substantially, however, these representations of the world reveal the centrality of capitalism in framing how the world is imagined. They are examples of the embedding and banal reproduction of neo-liberalism as a 'hegemonic rationality' which 'presents the social world as made up of markets, and spaces of potential competition that need to be organized *as* markets, blocking other narratives from view' (Couldry, 2010: 6).

However, alternative narratives are never completely blocked. Notwithstanding their formulaic conventions and tropes, accounts and images shown on television can differ widely within and among channels, programmes and genres. Furthermore, international television news chan-nels constitute only one source of images and narratives of the world. The contemporary media space offers a wide variety of media representations, which are produced, disseminated and consumed at the local, national, regional, transnational and global levels, and allow people to access a view of the world and gain potentially more diverse geographical knowledges.

In particular, new media spaces, such as video-sharing sites and blogs, offer alternative, sometimes radically different, visions and accounts of the world. Thus, 'there are limits to understanding media events on a global scale as the genre of integrative ritual they were originally thought to be' (Couldry et al., 2010: 10); their character is potentially more contradictory than Dayan and Katz's original theory assumes. Studying media events in today's globalized media culture makes it clear that the performative aspect of media events cannot be related to a singular power centre; a variety of interest groups and discourses, exercised across multiple channels, are related to the performance of these events (Couldry et al., 2010: 11).

Alternative Cartographic Consciousnesses

In the remainder of this chapter we explore the potentially more contradic-tory character of the mediation of New Year festivities, by looking at three examples of representations which seem to offer different 'cartographic consciousnesses' of the world, and which may be seen to offer 'voice', in the sense that Couldry (2010) writes about voice, as counter to the capitalist market-driven logic that provides the organizing framework for describ-ing the world in many mainstream media accounts and in social life (at least in the west) more generally. There are many other examples; I chose some of those that illustrate the potential as well as the challenges of the contemporary landscape of media representations for expanding and reconstituting geographical knowledges of 'the world'.

A joyful New Year 2010 in Mankon-Cameroon, West Africa[3]

An amateur video, produced by a villager from Mankon in Cameroon in West Africa, captures the 2010 New Year celebrations of a group of local residents. It was published on YouTube in February 2010 and at that time had received just over 200 hits. The video, which is just short of six minutes in length, is amateurish and most likely meant for personal use and safekeeping of memories.

This New Year celebration takes place in a local house or apartment and focuses on the village children. In the first part of the piece, the camera focuses on individual children's faces, and it is their voices rather than that of a controlling voiceover, that accompany the images. The videographer's voice is only heard encouraging the children to announce their names and ages, describe their families and where they live, and what they are happy about and thankful for as a new year begins. The second part of the video shows the children and some of the adults in the room, dancing and singing Christian songs, thanking God for their togetherness. The lyrics of the songs are provided in subtitles, and emphasize the unitedness of man governed by God (e.g., 'Do you have reason to praise the Lord?/ I have a Father that will never ever fail me / Today I will lift up my voice to pray'). The clip ends with an image of the roomful of people at prayer.

This YouTube clip is unspectacular; it is intended for a very different audience and purpose from the CNN and similar international news reports. It focuses on ritual, displayed through dance and song, but not on spectacle. While in the news reports the spectacle privileges vision, here people's voices and the sound of their singing are as central, if not more so than their images; the video is a record of a local, low-key celebration, one that is small but appears inclusive and accessible.

A brief comparison of the basic elements in this video (table 5.2) and the CNN report (table 5.1) sheds light on how differently rituals of the same event are mediated, producing not only distinct understandings of the event itself (New Year celebrations), but also situating the event within a fundamentally different spatial frame and, thus, understanding of the world. The 'ceremonial centres' (Dayan and Katz, 1992) of the events in the two clips are constructed as fundamentally different: in the YouTube clip, it is the dancing children in the small space of a room in the home of one of the villagers that take centre-stage; in the CNN video, the viewers' eyes are drawn

Table 5.2 Comparison of CNN report and YouTube clip

	CNN Report	*YouTube Clip*
Space	Outdoors: large urban public spaces	Indoors: Small room in a local flat
Place	Eleven large, mainly Western, cities	Mankon Village in Cameroon
People	Caucasian mixed crowds (long-shots of big crowds)	African children and their families (camera focusing on their faces)
Key actions	Fireworks lighting the sky, crowds counting down, shouting and kissing	Kids and some adults talking, dancing and praying
Geographical knowledges	The production of 'the world', national and urban imaginary	The production of locality and community

to the fireworks displays in the skies over eleven cities. These centres construct fundamentally different spatial frames within which the events are situated: in the former, it is the local community of a particular village; in the latter, it is 'the world'. The focus on children's faces, the amateurish filming and editing, and children's stories about their families and hopes, construct 'cartographic identification' (Harvey, 2001) of a local community.

In contrast to the faceless crowds in the television broadcast, in the YouTube clip individual children tell their stories. In other representations these children would likely be relegated to the condensed category of 'the other' – the large mass of young Africans whose immediate priorities are very far removed from the global financial pecking order highlighted in mainstream coverage – but here they claim (and proclaim) their space and voice. In contrast to the conventional news representations of the kind examined before, which deny voice and affirm the primacy of economic prowess, competition and market logic, in this YouTube representation, children give an account of their experience and how the New Year affects their lives. In this sense, to follow Couldry's (2010) account of the value and power of voice, these children's self-narratives allow an alternative view of the world, which values different voices and recognizes the centrality of people's voices for their social lives.

The children's individual stories are articulated in the context of their community – the visual background to each child's narration is the other children and adults in the room of this village home. While in the CNN report belonging is constructed in relation to a national, urban and global imaginary, here the spatial frame is the local village community.

The strong specificity of the YouTube clip lies also in its explicit emphasis on the religious context of the celebration. Legitimization of the Christian calendar underlies, but is subsumed by, mainstream international news narratives; the Christian New Year is constructed as universally shared. By contrast, in the YouTube piece, the singing, the song's lyrics set out in the subtitles, and the ending with a prayer, explicitly frame the event as religious. On the one hand, this works to emphasize a collective and inclusive spirit of celebration: each of the participants shown is implicitly identified as the child of the 'Father that will never ever fail me' (a line appearing in the clip's subtitles). On the other hand, it places clear boundaries around the meaning of the event, of who belongs and who does not. In contrast to the high geographical specificity of the YouTube clip, the CNN video is marked by abstract, placeless and faceless representations through which it seeks to project a universalist vision of the world on behalf of an entire human race comprised of many different nations.

CCTV Chinese New Year gala[4]

On the eve of the Chinese Lunar New Year, the state-run Chinese Central TV (CCTV) and its satellite channels (including the international English-speaking channel) broadcast the Spring Festival gala: an elaborate, expensive, large-scale and highly produced televised show with singing and dancing (*ge wu*), mini-dramas (*xiaopin*) and 'cross-talks' (*xiangsheng* – comic two-person dialogues in the Beijing dialect). This media event has become institutionalized as an indispensable part of the ritual of Chinese New Year celebrations (Bin, 1998). In 2010, the gala attracted an audience share of around 75 per cent and viewer ratings of around 40 per cent (Pan, 2010). It addresses the people of China and Chinese immigrants all over the world and 'is a global media event in design and reach' (Pan, 2010: 252).

This media event reminds us of the obvious but important point that not all the world's people celebrate Christian New Year. Although CCTV carries reports of the Christian New Year, these pale in comparison to the Chinese New Year/Spring Festival celebrations. Examination of this global media event is a useful reminder that the depiction of the world in international news reports, such as the CNN piece and media representations encountered daily, is a very particular construction, underpinned by and in turn reproducing specific cartographic consciousnesses and geographical knowledges.

The Chinese New Year gala is a vivid instance of the televised production of national identity, which has assumed greater significance in post-Mao China. Analyses of the televised Spring Festival gala (Bin, 1998; Lu, 2009; Pan, 2010) stress the integrative and cohesive function of this media event and its function of articulating a nationalist ideology and party propaganda

(Pan, 2010). Central to this 'carefully orchestrated "happy gathering" on television' (Bin, 1998: 43) is the use of family and home as the 'master metaphor of the nation' (Pan, 2010: 247), a metaphor that is reiterated throughout the gala in the song lyrics and the hosts' scripts. For example, the classical Confucian notion of the state as a large family, and 'the Confucian dream of "great oneness" (*da yitong*) is brought to an atmospheric and symbolic realization on Spring Festival Eve' (Bin, 1998: 46. Home, the spatial anchor of the family, is co-opted in order to protect and project the common experience of the Chinese people, so as to induce 'an instant sense of national belonging that transcends both immediate families and narrow localities' and establish a 'united front' with Chinese people overseas (Bin, 1998: 48).

Since the gala has been beamed globally, via satellite and the Internet, this celebration has served not only to articulate and symbolically 'renew the "family ties" among all Chinese but also [to] reassert China's place in the world of nations' (Pan, 2010: 241). In constructing China's position in the world, the gala employs similar discursive strategies to those used by the CNN report – locating, positioning and binding. However, it produces radically different meanings and is mobilized for fundamentally different political purposes. For instance, the 2002 gala included a song-and-dance routine called 'Networking with the World':

> Want to decorate Fujiyama's midsummer with Mount Tai's rosy dawn,
> Want to splash Danube's water with oars from the Yellow River,
> Want to caress the Siberia with the tropical wind of Hainan Island,
> Want the camels of the Silk Road to carry my Hatha,
> Want to use the bricks of the Great Wall to connect to the iron Eiffel
>   Tower,
> Want to kiss the Sahara Desert with the waves of Yangtze River,
> Want to move Vienna with the music rock from Gulangyu,
> Want to use Niagara Falls to brew my fragrant tea.
> Networking with the world, the west has man-made tales,
> Networking with the world, the east has natural grace. (cited in Pan, 2010:
>   251)

The spatial relations and geographical hierarchies here are substantially different from the ones constructed by the CNN report. The narrative expresses the insatiable ambition of the Chinese cultural empire and is embedded with imaginings of China's cultural superiority (Pan, 2010). Sharp boundaries are drawn between 'us', the Chinese, and 'them', the rest of the world, and between east and west. China is the centre, the gravitation point that pulls all other places in the world towards it. This is reinforced through the use of 'Beijing time' (Bin, 1998; Pan, 2010) as the temporal ceremonial centre that calls viewers in China and around the world to join the ritual countdown to midnight. The same ritual countdown as in representations of the Christian New Year is enacted to establish a fundamentally different temporal and spatial order.

A significant difference between the Chinese New Year gala and the events reported on CNN (and other channels) is the event's location – a key component in the production of geographical knowledges. In the CNN report the celebrations take place in the streets, outdoor city centres and on a beach; they are public celebrations. This exclusive focus on 'public' life constructs the legitimate world and its players as democratic, although there is little, if any, overt expression of politics in these public gatherings, and the representations are highly orchestrated, regulated and contained, rather than spontaneous expressions of public life. The Chinese gala, by contrast, is staged in a large performance hall, and lasts for more than four hours: public life is conspicuously absent. The gala's location emphasizes festivity and harmony, while spontaneity and the potentially contentious political expressions of public life are invisible, thus rendered illegitimate. Democracy does not fit into this narrative in which the world, and the relationships between China and the world and the hopes and aspirations of the Chinese nation, are constituted symbolically (Pan, 2010).

Nevertheless, this enactment of a myth-filled narrative of the Chinese family-nation, in a spectacle consistent with the New Year spectaculars in international news broadcasts, makes the Chinese gala a display of an 'increasingly confident and assertive China as a rising economic powerhouse in the world' (Pan, 2010: 241). Thus, while the Chinese gala offers a very different view of the country and its position in the world and significantly different cartographic identifications from those presented by international representations of Christian New Year celebrations, it confirms the notion of participation in 'the world' as being defined by competition and economic status. It imposes a similar global order, in which places and spaces are ranked, legitimized, included, excluded or annihilated according to an overarching measure: economic prowess.[5]

Gaza diary: Welcoming the New Year[6]

Al Jazeera's representations of the dawn of a new year seem radically to diverge from those discussed so far, especially reports on western news channels such as CNN. The thematic core and tone of Al Jazeera's reporting are consistently anti-celebratory. At New Year 2010, for example, its reporting focused on the destitute state of Greece; in 2009, Al Jazeera focused on the

Gaza War and displayed on its English website *Gaza Diary: Welcoming the New Year* – a journal written by Mohammed Ali, an activist living in Gaza, attesting to the destruction of people and memories.

This online journal, from the outset, constructs a dramatically different cartographic consciousness from those promoted by the other representations examined in the chapter. At the top of the webpage is the image of a man holding a wounded Palestinian child. Beneath it appear Ali's daily entries, ordered in descending chronological order in a blog format. The first entry starts with:

> At around midnight, Israeli jets hit the Palestinian Legislative Council (PLC) building, 1km away from my home. Needless to say, we were not celebrating this entry into the New Year.
>
> I received calls from friends in Europe telling me that in solidarity with Gazans, they were not going to celebrate. I pleaded with them to go out, and to enjoy themselves because they could.
>
> A friend in France called to say that she was thinking about my family, in the background I could hear the sounds of fireworks exploding, people laughing and celebrating. At that same moment, the sounds of explosions shook my home and my children cried out.
>
> I felt both happy and sad. Happy because I knew that there were people outside of Gaza who had not forgotten about us, sad thinking of all the Gazans who would be spending this New Year shaking from fear in their homes, mourning their loved ones.
>
> I asked myself, do we not deserve to be happy and enjoy the New Year as much as any other human?
>
> I will let the international community answer this question.

The online diary explicitly positions events in Gaza against the world celebrations of the kind shown on CNN. It highlights the stark contrast between 'here' (Gaza) and 'there' (Europe), while presenting the two spatial imaginaries as intimately connected by human solidarity. Europe's fireworks explosions are signs of normality, safety and order; the explosions in Gaza represent the reality of destruction, suffering, chaos and abnormality.

On the one hand, the Al Jazeera's online journal brings to the fore the conflictual and unequal character of the world: the world is constructed as a space marked by dramatic inequalities and unfairnesses – resonant of Voltaire's contemplation of the unfairness of the disaster for Lisbon's citizens and the incommensurable conditions around the globe (chapter 2). In Mohammed Ali's account, the world is Europe; the US is conspicuously absent – a meaningful omission, consistent with the construction of the US as 'the other' in other images and discourses on Al Jazeera and in the Arab public sphere. This example illustrates how Al Jazeera, a central media player, highlights the need for a considerably augmented exchange of images, ideas and experiences from different vantage points around the globe (Cottle, 2006), and for substantially expanding, diversifying and reconstituting geographical knowledges.

On the other hand, the online journal implicitly reaffirms Europe as the centre of the world, a benchmark for evaluating and understanding life for the people of Gaza. The rhetorical question 'do we not deserve to be happy and enjoy the New Year as much as any other human?' subsumes the urgent concern for the lives and future of the more than 1.5 million people living in Gaza – almost all of them Muslim Palestinians – within the narrow frame of western Christian celebrations. The question implies that to be human is to 'be happy and enjoy the New Year', and it is in relation to this highly specific and, arguably, irrelevant definition, that Palestinian suffering, and the injustice inflicted upon them are explained and understood, rather than to the basic fact that they are human. It could be claimed that this construction derives from the account's being published on Al Jazeera English, and being aimed, therefore, at primarily western, English-speaking readers many of whom do celebrate Christian New Year, and that this makes the juxtaposition of suffering in Gaza and celebrations in Europe more meaningful and potentially effective. However, in using the New Year celebrations as its point of reference for explaining the lives of people in Gaza, Ali's account, implicitly and probably unintentionally, supports the hierarchies of places and human life that underpin and are continuously enacted in the western imagination.

Conclusion

This chapter is meant as a modest contribution to the larger project outlined by Harvey (2001): to develop explicit consideration and evaluation of the construction of geographical knowledges. Media representations are prolific sources of geographical knowledges that feed the way we, individually and collectively, imagine the world and our position in it. Through this examination of a range of examples representing the same event, related by different storytellers, we see how geographical knowledges and particular versions of 'the world' are produced – from the journalistic report of celebrations across the world, constructed as an 'objective' account of the world, to citizen-generated representations of their subjective personal and community experiences. The discussion was based on analysis of a particular media event, namely, New Year celebrations, but the argument deriving from it about the construction of the world, is suggestive of other representations circulating in the contemporary global media space.

Media events are extraordinary mediated rituals that produce and reproduce geographical knowledges. They capitalize on and reinforce 'ordinary' assumptions, values and explanatory frameworks about 'us' and 'them', and allow us to construct mental maps of our positions, as individuals and collectives, in society and in the world. Media events act as vital forces of social integration: situating events, processes and things within coherent spatial frames, they articulate, sustain and reassert the legitimacy and desirability of particular modes of belonging to certain spatial imaginaries (e.g., community, city, nation, world), and the undesirability of others.

At the same time, and especially in the contemporary fragmented, globalized, media culture, media events constitute sites for articulating and constructing contesting geographical knowledges and visions of the world.[7] In a world marked by strong geographical, social, economic, political, cultural and material differences and conflicts, the relevance and significance of media events may reside not so much in their cohesive function and their symbolic capacity to erase differences, but in their capacity to allow 'for the constructions of a common "we", and of many varied national, ethnic, religious, subcultural and other voicings of that "we"' (Couldry et al., 2010: 12). Key to realizing this potential is the production of geographical knowledge that is grounded in and acknowledges specificity and difference. The montage of city skies lit by fireworks, faceless members of two armed forces engaging in a 'friendly football match' on a field that could be anywhere, an online account highlighting Palestinians' right to live as humans and to enjoy the New Year 'as much as' Europeans do, all promote abstract, unspecific, placeless and thus largely inaccessible understandings of the subject at stake. 'Cosmopolitanism bereft of geographical specificity', Harvey (2001: 211) warns, 'remains abstracted and alienated reason.'

6   Imagining the Self

The stories and images in the news, magazines, newspapers and on television and the Internet constitute central symbolic resources we rely on to make sense of our lives and the world we live in. We also produce our own stories and images, which enable us to recount to ourselves and to others who we are. 'We are all the unofficial biographers of ourselves, for it is only by constructing a story, however loosely strung together, that we are able to form a sense of who we are and of what our future may be' (Thompson, 1995: 210). In this 'symbolic project of the self' (Thompson, 1995), we weave the symbolic materials at our disposal into a narrative of self-identity, in our attempts to establish coherent accounts of who we are.

Media representations play two central roles in this process. First, images, accounts and symbolic content circulating in the media increasingly are becoming central symbolic resources that people draw on in constructing the narrative of the self. People, at least in the global north, increasingly are evaluating and constructing their selves, bodies and relationships on the basis of, and in relation to, images and stories that appear in the media and in public discourse. People may refuse or fail to recognize the influence of media representations on their self-identities and the formation of their self-narratives, for example, many are reluctant to admit that advertising has a major influence on their attitudes or lives (Corner, 2000). However, research shows consistently the centrality and influence of media representations and discourses in shaping people's imaginations, subjectivities, self-identities and self-narratives, alongside non-mediated symbolic materials, such as the reminiscences and stories of family and friends.

Second, in constructing and redefining their identities, individuals repeatedly tell stories that are modified and refashioned continuously. They relate these stories in the course of personal interactions with friends, family, colleagues and acquaintances. Today, they can do this also in mediated forms, for example, on reality TV, Facebook, YouTube, Twitter, blogs or online forums, to both people they know and to unknown audiences. Thus, the process of recounting the story of the self, which underpins the symbolic project of the self, involves drawing on media representations as well as producing mediated self-representations.

The distinction between self-representations of the kind people produce online, for example, on YouTube, Facebook or blogs, and representations whose nature is fundamentally public, such as television programmes or cinema films, is becoming blurred. Private lives are projected publicly: more and more people are making their selves the objects of scrutiny, and engaging in a work of complex, ongoing introspection that involves naming, expressing, talking about, arguing over, negotiating and justifying their emotions. This symbolic project of the self is exercised on various sites and in and through mediated forms. As Illouz (2007) argues in relation to online romantic relationships, the self becomes a public text and performance. Through its projection on to mediated spaces, such as reality TV, Facebook or video and image-sharing sites, the self becomes a domain subject to public gaze.

A considerable body of research explores representation of the self in mediated forms, such as talk shows, online journals and Internet forums. This literature highlights the significance and complex consequences of the transformation of the contemporary public sphere into an arena for the exposition of private lives, emotions and intimacies (Illouz, 2003a, 2007; Manga, 2003; Orgad, 2005; Peck, 1996; Shattuc, 1997; Thompson, 1995; Thumim, 2012). Various studies show how media platforms, such as the Oprah Winfrey show (Illouz, 2003a) or online forums and personal journals (Orgad, 2005), furnish a stage for storytelling and spaces where individuals recount their lives, emotions and identities in relation to issues such as health, gender relations and romantic relationships.

The mediated accounts produced and published by individuals on these sites commonly situate themselves and are perceived as personal, subjective, intimate, confessional, therapeutic and experiential. They have been often understood as separate from, and sometimes antagonistic to, narratives concerning broader 'public' issues (Matthews, 2007). Narratives of 'big', 'public' issues typically include accounts of world politics, financial affairs or the state of the environment. These narratives have been analysed and critiqued predominantly in relation to their *deliberative* function. That is, the interest is in how representations of such 'macro' public issues on sites traditionally associated with the formation of public opinion and rational debate, such as political ads and news, help (or fail to help) to develop a public sphere, a communicative space for the exchange and deliberation of rational ideas. Analyses of individuals' self-representations on sites such as talk shows, blogs and online journals, on the other hand, focus largely on their performative and/or therapeutic function and their modes of *display* (for a distinction between deliberation and display, see Cottle, 2006). These studies focus on the expressive and affective capacities of representations, and their aesthetic, emotional and ritual dimensions.

While scholars acknowledge that the distinction between private and public in contemporary mediated globalized culture is becoming increasingly blurred, analytical studies mostly maintain this division. For the most part, research on representations of issues such as politics, war, public health, finance and the economy is divorced from research on individuals' self-representations of personal suffering or the body, for example. There is, however, some critical work that seeks to challenge this division, for instance, in relation to the genre of talk shows. In an important study of talk shows, Livingstone and Lunt (1994) examine the extent to which, and the ways in which, a genre so centrally focused on the personal and the therapeutic provides a space for the deliberation and exchange of ideas, potentially constituting a Habermasian public sphere. By the same token, Cottle (2006) accounts for the ways in which journalism communicates simultaneously through the modes of 'deliberation' and 'display'. The former, he writes, 'is based on the circulation of information, reasoned accounts, rational arguments, investigation, discussion and debate' (Cottle, 2006: 173), while the latter communicates, among other things, by the presentation of narratives of self, experiential accounts and emotive testimonies. However, as Cottle also acknowledges, much work remains to be done to break down this division and better understand how the media operate within both modes, often simultaneously.

Within this paradigmatic division, the themes discussed in chapters 2, 3, 4 and 5 constitute quintessentially 'public' issues, whose study traditionally has focused on their deliberative role. Research on representations of natural disasters and distant suffering, national conflicts, migration and the world, focuses primarily on how the media, and the news in particular, facilitate and foster (or fail to) informed understanding of the issues, critical debate and deliberation. However, representation of these issues in the contemporary global media, as the earlier chapters in this book show, is never exclusively, or in any way chiefly, 'public', 'rational' or 'deliberative'. Crucially, the presentation and discussion of these issues and how they shape the way we imagine others, ourselves, possible lives and the world are closely related to the intimate, the personal, the emotional, the private, and to stories of the self. The self is often in the foreground of these representations: the story of thousands affected by an earthquake is told through a close-up on the face of a single victim; the story of a nation in conflict is articulated by one of its citizens; migration and its consequences are communicated through the story of a single migrant; the world is explained through the eyes of the individual.

Chapter 6 explores the centrality of the self in media representations. I argue that the self has come to constitute a primary site for the cultivation of a global imagination: imaginings of others, of ourselves, of possible lives and of the world are fed by and constituted through images and narratives of the self. The self furnishes a symbolic 'conduit' for the projection of a broader narrative (about the world, others, ourselves and possible lives). In this process, the self becomes the centre of what is being imagined. For example, the news reported the 2010 floods that devastated Pakistan through the story of a mother and her heroic struggle to survive the suffering inflicted by nature's forces on her and her baby. The story of an individual's struggle makes suffering concrete, while at the same time serving as an exemplar of 'a plurality of situations of misfortune' (Boltanski, 1999: 12). In turn, it constitutes a story of the (modern psychological) self: a tale of the individual's capacities to take control of life and emerge from a calamity, for which the suffering and devastation caused by the floods in Pakistan provides a context.

To explore this theme, in what follows I analyse four representations of self that correspond to the four sites of global imagination explored in the preceding chapters. I show how imaginings of the other, ourselves as the nation, possible lives, and the world, are produced symbolically by focusing on the self and, in turn, how calling us to imagine others, ourselves (as the nation), possible lives, and the world through the self, renders the self the object of the story.

Imagining the Other/Imagining the Self

Thompson (1995: 209) asks: 'in a world where the capacity to experience is no longer linked to the activity of encountering, how can we relate mediated experiences to the practical contexts of our day-to-day-lives?' More specifically, how can we relate to distant others in locales and contexts that are remote from the contexts of our daily lives? The fundamental problem in 'symbolic dislocation' (Thompson, 1995), of how to relate to distant others, is thrown into relief most acutely in the representation of distant suffering. We are confronted daily by representations of suffering occurring miles away. Live broadcasts enable an immediacy and proximity in depictions of others' suffering: mediated images and narratives enable 'presence-at-a-distance' (Peters, 2001: 717) and evoke 'intimacy at a distance' (Thompson, 1995: 219). The symbolic 'stretching' of time and space has the potential to open up people's imagination and expand their horizons, allowing recognition of people unlike themselves, but with whom they share a 'common humanity'.

However, there remains a 'fathomless distance' (Cohen 2001: 169): a physical, temporal, cultural, social, ontological and fundamentally moral space between sufferers and viewer, which the transmission of distant others' suffering as signs on screen, on paper or on the radio enhances. The enormity of the distance between 'us', the viewers, and the 'other', the sufferers, and between 'here' – the zone of safety and 'normality', and 'there' – the zone of danger, chaos and lack of order – is rendered more present and more stark. The viewer is 'sheltered' from and is in a fundamentally different situation from the unfortunate: 'he [sic.] is not by his [sic.] side during his [sic.] agony or torture' (Boltanski, 1999: 153).

As discussed in chapter 2, the issue of the distance between the spectators (predominantly in the west) and distant suffering has provoked lively debate, particularly since the mid-1990s (e.g., Benthall, 1993; Boltanski, 1999; Chouliaraki, 2006; Cohen, 2001; Höijer, 2004; Moeller, 1999; Peters, 2001; Silverstone, 2007; Tester, 2001). How can the representations of suffering, that have become an integral part of contemporary life, overcome this 'fathomless distance' and evoke 'a generalized concern for the "other"' (Boltanski, 1999: xx)? How can we imagine the unimaginable – the suffering experienced by distant others?

In attempting to address these questions, critics and media and NGO practitioners emphasize the need symbolically to 'humanize' sufferers, to represent distant others as human beings with dignity, deserving of recognition, pity and aid. In the symbolic project of 'humanizing' the other, the self has assumed centre-stage: it is through presentations of others as individual agents with humanity, volition and capacity to act, so the argument goes, that the sufferers become humane, and moral proximity can be established between the audience and the distant sufferers (Chouliaraki, 2006). Among the plethora of representations in the media and in NGO communications, the focus is predominantly on the individual, the self, in depictions of distant others. A Save the Children campaign appealing for donations to assist the people of Sierra Leone, by helping to reduce malaria, pneumonia and diarrhoea, presents the story of Temba, a boy of almost two years of age. The UNICEF 'Put it Right' appeal centres on Sreynet, a ten-year-old Cambodian child who is 'forced to beg for money and scavenge through rubbish so she and her sister can eat', and an Oxfam appeal for donations to help thousands of displaced people living in refugee camps, threatened by cholera, acute diarrhoea and other diseases, tells the story of Karo, a young mother in the Eastern Democratic Republic of Congo, who survived a violent raid on her village.

Self-representations, published on new media such as blogs, social media and photo- and video-sharing sites, are the most recent development in this representational paradigm in which the self becomes the locus of the imagination of distant others. Self-representations allow formerly invisible and unheard others to achieve visibility and claim a voice. Such mediated self-representations call for recognition of a denied humanity, for 'symbolic rehabilitation' (Cottle, 2006: 168) and, consequently, for a reallocation and redistribution of symbolic, social, political and material resources. In this process, the self is often made into a public text. In providing a platform for numerous self-presentations, the Internet in particular, highlights the self as an object that can be apprehended through texts that are classified, presented and performed publicly (Illouz, 2007). The self becomes the primary voice through which the other speaks and appears in the global media space.

I want to develop these observations through examining a specific example. *Hometown Baghdad* is an online documentary series of thirty-eight short episodes, recounting the lives of three young Iraqis – Saif, Adel and Ausama – during the Iraq War. It was produced by a group of Baghdad filmmakers and Chat the Planet, a New York-based 'global dialogue company' that also hosts Internet discussion forums. *Hometown Baghdad* premiered in March 2007 on the website, with the final episode broadcast in June 2007. The series was highly acclaimed throughout the world, and was linked to YouTube and hundreds of other websites and blogs. In 2009, it was aired on television channels across the world, including the US Sundance Channel and National Geographic in Asia, Europe, Latin America and Africa.

The series' creators explicitly position the project as a call for recognition of the invisible 'other': 'The brave Iraqi subjects and crew risked their lives every time they turned on a camera to make this series. They did it to share their stories with the world; to make sure that the voices of regular Iraqis did not remain unheard.'[1] The media coverage of the series and the comments from viewers that were posted on the website echo this mission. The personal video diaries of Saif, Adel and Ausama, seen by both western viewers and Iraqis watching in Iraq and in other countries, were regarded as a potent intervention into the American and global imaginations that 'de-others' the other and symbolically rehabilitates the image of the Iraqi people. The comment of an Iraqi viewer, referring to the final episode (posted on 21 June 2007), captures this:

> all the things that u said in this and the feelings u were feeling, i was feeling and wanted to shout to the whole world and let them hear my message, i left baghdad recently and i know and understand everything u feel and i am more than glad that now people know what it is like over there in baghdad and what is really happening. and most importantly they know that we are normal people just like them and we used to live normally until now and we wish a 1000 time everyday that this whole situation is over and we go back again to our real life because we don't deserve this and don't deserve what is happening to us.

This, and other comments posted on the website, discuss viewers' personal feelings, responding to the feelings and emotions displayed by Saif, Adel and Ausama in their video diaries. The short video diary clips are a mix of 'home-made' video diaries and professionally shot footage, and reveal aspects of the characters' intimate, everyday lives: their homes and families, their hobbies (e.g., playing the guitar, playing basketball), their studies, friendships and love relationships. The genre of the video diary presents the other through the presentation of self. It is centrally located within the realm of everyday life and family – key sites of the (American-dominated) psychoanalytical imagining of the self (Illouz, 2007). The thirty-eight episodes, which expose the lives of Saif, Adel and Ausama in war-struck Baghdad, make the characters' emotions objects to be thought of, expressed, talked about, argued over and negotiated. For instance, in the fifth episode entitled 'Songs of Pain', we see Adel in his bedroom, playing the guitar, juxtaposed against images of the destruction surrounding him: 'Playing this loud music and screaming, it's like a therapy . . . it's really helpful when you've expressed yourself with no fear, it gets out a lot of the anger and the negativity.' Thus, Adel endorses, quite literally, the therapeutic ethos of the self, which encourages management of emotions such as rage. Many viewers subsequently discuss, interpret and evaluate Adel's and their own emotions. Commenting on Adel's playing the guitar, a viewer writes:

> With all of the political and religious propaganda being shoved down everyone's throats these days, it's refreshing to see something honest and real . . . just people who want to live normal and prosperous lives, like all human beings. I hope you all keep up on the musical stuff, creativity is such a positive thing to channel anger, sadness, and discontent into. It's overlooked many times by the powerful but is such a strong voice to make a difference with. (posted on 18 April 2007)

Iraqis, continuously demonized as 'evil', stereotyped and symbolically annihilated by mainstream American and international coverage during and after the war (Silverstone, 2007), become the intimates of viewers of *Hometown Baghdad*. The documentary's un-staged filming and editing style, the focus on the spaces of the home and within it the characters' private spaces, the centrality of the family in the characters' personal narratives, the dwelling on their personal relationships and emotions, and the informal glimpses of their everyday lives, all converge to create a 'non-reciprocal intimacy at a distance' (Thompson, 1995). Posts on the website's forum frequently describe Adel, Saif and Ausama as 'new friends'. A viewer's comment on the final episode encapsulates this sense of intimacy:

> Adel ... you are so good-looking, it's mind-blowing, I can't take my eyes off of you:) Please, stay safe because you absolutely must pass these good genes on!:) I already have an Iraqi boyfriend but now I want two:) But in all seriousness, I love your rich, poetic soul and you are such a profound person, what an integrity and wisdom you have! I would love to keep in touch or help you with anything you might need. All of you, guys. Let me know ... You, guys, shine! Shine on!

As this quote illustrates, in this form of mediated intimacy, the self and the other are often fused. The videos and the viewers' responses (published on the website and on viewers' personal blogs that link to the series' site) become a multi-authored public text in which the self is written, performed, negotiated and evaluated, largely in the language of popular psychology and what Ilouz (2007) calls 'emotional capitalism'. Both the 'others' – Adel, Saif and Ausama – in their personal video diaries, and the audience, in posts that are often highly personal and confessional responses, appropriate the ritual discourse of confession, in which 'the speaking subject is also the subject of the statement' (Foucault, 1981: 61). In so doing, they address one another as the listener, making each 'the authority who requires the confession' (Foucault, 1981: 62). This mutual exercise of the confessional discourse seems to dissolve the power relation of oppressor/oppressed, symbolically putting 'us' and 'them', or 'me' and 'you', on a par. A comment posted on the *Hometown Baghdad* website by a US soldier (interestingly on 11 September 2007) shows how the mode of confession enables the poster (the confessor) to construct a sense of a power-free dialogue and a bonding with the other:

> I watched every episode of Hometown Baghdad the moment I heard about it. It pains me to see not just the physical wounds, but the psychological and emotional ones people living in a war-zone endure everyday on my computer screen. However, I have seen these familiar faces in person in a different war-zone. I saw the mysery in Afghanistan. I saw limbs, blood and bombs on the streets. I saw the hurt on the injured, the dead and survivors' faces. I saw their tears. When I was alone, I shed mine. I'm a U.S. Soldier, and I have been around Soldiers of all types of specialties and rank for nearly three years now. The vast majority of them wish no ill harm on Iraqis, Afghans or any other innocent country's civilians. I know our invasion has caused a lot of pain and mysery, but I ask everyone who's watched this, and the Iraqi citizens, to know that most troops sincerely want those people to live in peace. For those who've had their faith and trust in us broken, I am sorry. I just hope and pray that Iraqis will someday view us as good people again, as many did when the war first began. I also hope and pray that we'll all realize we're not that much different from each other. Culture, religion and tradition may differ,

but at our cores, we just want to live in peace, security, freedom, and live a long, happy life with our friends and family. That is the greatest lesson my deployment taught me. That we all want the same things in life. It showed me our common ground. We are all truly brothers and sisters. God Bless Iraqis, – A U.S. Soldier.[2]

Locating the 'big' story of a bloody war between countries in the personal confession of a self to particular distant others (Adel, Ausama and Saif) seems to dissolve power relations, leading to the conclusion that 'we all want the same things in life. We are all truly brothers and sisters.' However, while the American soldier and other viewers commenting on the series website are situated in the privileged position of the authority, which, to draw on Foucault, prescribes, appreciates, judges, punishes, forgives, consoles and reconciles the other's confession, Adel, Ausama and Saif, and the millions of Iraqis who remained in Iraq or were forced to flee the country, cannot command the same authority. This is where the fusion of the self with the other, enabled through such online self-representations, becomes misleading and problematic. For while the self/other intimacy opens up a space for identification and empathy with the distant other, at the same time it fails to preserve the other through difference. That is, it does not enable recognition of the other; not just on the basis of a shared identity with 'us', but, fundamentally, on the basis of the other's radically *different* life conditions, beliefs, fears and desires – the other and the self become one, difference is effaced.

The series concludes with Adel's statement that 'I have spent a lot of time just trying to make sense of this madness and I couldn't. So the only option for me is to live.' Ultimately, this is one of the key messages of the series: the ongoing project of the self, attempting to make sense of the world in which it exists. The narratives of Adel, Saif and Ausama fuse with those of the viewers to become a larger project of writing the self.

This narrative of selfhood is rooted in western and particularly American psychological imagining, in which the self has to be continuously worked upon, negotiated, improved and performed (Illouz, 2007). In contrast, the self in the Middle East, despite slow transformations, is largely obliterated (Saghie, 2001); the collective is much more important than the individual, and empowering the individual is equated with dividing society (Friedman, 1999). For example, in Arabic newspapers, the word 'I' appears only rarely, and autobiography has yet to be established as an independent literary genre (Saghie, 2001). The personal video diaries of Adel, Saif and Ausama reveal little, if anything, of 'the predicament of the individual' (Saghie, 2001) in their society: there seems no tension between the absence of the self and the negative connotations of self in Middle Eastern imagination, and the preoccupation (not to say obsession) with self in western psychological imagination. It is this last that seems to govern the representations of the lives of these three young Iraqis whose telling of their stories through the confessional genre of a personal video-diary is produced to appear 'natural', 'authentic' and 'truthful'. In Foucault's terms, this genre and its confessional mode produce 'truth effects' that support and reproduce the western 'regime of truth' of confession and the psychological self.

The proliferation of new media representations, of the *Hometown Baghdad* type, expands, enhances and complicates the way we imagine distant others and, inextricably, the way we imagine ourselves. On the one hand, they make a powerful call to recognize the others, through their presentation as individual human beings with voice and visibility. Precisely because these representations are stories of the self, they portray the other within the horizon of the viewer, and have the capacity to reduce the 'fathomless gap' between 'them' and 'us', and enable an imaginable 'you' and 'me'. At the same time, these kinds of self-representations subject imagining of the other to the narrative of the self; the self is seen as the primary, if not only, way of expressing and understanding the other. In this process, not only are the larger contexts and power relations within which the self operates suppressed, but also difference is effaced. In the context of *Hometown Baghdad*, for example, the series fails to recognize the possible tensions between its focus on the selves of the three young Iraqis, and their cultural context where the self is not the dominant 'regime of truth'. Thus, paradoxically, while 'selfing' of the other paves a symbolic path to a recognition of the other on the basis of the other's uniqueness and specificity, it simultaneously undermines this recognition, by failing to acknowledge, accept and respect difference.

Imagining the Nation/Imagining the Self

The contesting scripts circulating in the media about the nation work their way into personal thinking and are drawn into narratives of the self. These narratives are often communicated orally in public spaces or in the private, domestic sphere of the home. However, more and more often, they are being produced and performed publicly, on mediated sites. In a culture and media environment saturated with calls to 'broadcast yourself', mediated sites, such as Facebook, video and photo-sharing sites, television talk shows, reality TV and radio programmes, provide a stage for individuals' articulation and reworking of their relations to the nation and, inextricably, to their selves. These narratives are not separate from, or secondary to, the 'macro' imaginary scripts which are constructed and disseminated in the news, in films or television shows, and which feed national and global imaginations; they are all part of this discursive field. The self becomes a central locus for imagining the nation and the articulation of tensions that national imagining invokes.

How are the tensions around the relation to the nation – symbolic distancing, estrangement and attachment, discussed in chapter 3 – articulated, negotiated and performed through the self in the contemporary global media? I address this question by examining Israeli citizens' narratives posted on the Internet in response to photographs posted on Facebook in 2010 by a former Israeli woman soldier, of her posing in front of blindfolded Palestinian prisoners.

These photographs of Eden Aberjil with blindfolded Palestinian prisoners, which Aberjil put into an album entitled 'The Army: The Best time of My Life', provoked heated debate in the Israeli blogsphere and the national media, and condemnation in the international media, resulting in them eventually being removed from Facebook. The official state response was simultaneously condemnation and denial, with the Israeli Defence Force (IDF) insisting that the incident did not reflect 'the spirit of the IDF' and the 'ethical standard to which we [the Israeli nation] all aspire'.[3] Official comments of this kind, not surprisingly, reframed the event in order to underline an unproblematic relation of attachment to the nation and reinforce that the Israeli army was a superior moral entity. Human rights organizations, on the other hand, called for an admission from Israel that the incident reflected a wider practice of abuse of Palestinian prisoners by Israeli soldiers. The human rights organization Shovrim Shtika (Breaking Silence), for example, used the same mediated space of Facebook to post similar pictures of other soldiers posing alongside restrained or dead Palestinian prisoners, to demonstrate the prevalence of this abuse and demand that the military should teach its soldiers that Palestinians are civilians with human rights, and should be treated as human beings.[4]

Both types of official discourse – the Israeli state's on the one hand, human rights organizations' on the other – produced largely crude narratives of the severity (or lack thereof) of the case and its implications. More interesting, and often more complex and ambivalent narratives, emerged from citizens' responses to the event, many posted online.

An example of these is a posting on the blog of Omer Barak (http://omerbarak.com). A month after the Aberjil case, when it had fallen out of the headlines, Barak, a former entertainment journalist writing for Israeli newspapers and working at the time as a content editor for a national commercial television channel, published on his blog a post titled: 'I Am Too

Eden Aberjil'. In this lengthy account (1,746 words), Barak, in a highly confessional style, revisits his experience as a reporter during his conscripted army service in the Palestinian occupied territories. The opening paragraph of the blog confesses that (my translation):

> Since the explosion of Eden Aberjil's affair, I have had this feeling of discomfort in my stomach, as if a huge tumour was sitting there, refusing to go away. 'It's terrible,' I keep saying in daily conversations, 'that there are people like her in our country. It drives me mad'. But I know, though do not fully understand why, that this is not what really bothers me. Last night I jumped out of bed as if stung by a snake, and rushed to look at my old photo albums. There I found precisely what I so much dreaded I would find: that I am too, notwithstanding all possible distinctions, Eden Aberjil.
> [. . .]
> Here I am in a Hummer [military jeep] in the midst of Gaza, smiling a big smile of self-satisfaction. Here I am in Hebron, behind me three Palestinian prisoners, who later were described in the news as 'terrorists'.

Barak goes on to confess his experience as a reporter during his army service, of witnessing Palestinian prisoners being arrested, tied and humiliated, and taking pictures of them – pictures he put in his personal photo album which he now reflexively revisits. Up till that time, his album, the site of personal memory, of the display of self and nationhood, has been a seemingly peaceful and unproblematic site. The mediated instance of Eden Aberjil disrupted this comfort. It triggered an introspective look at the album – a look into the self and its relation to the nation, a look that has now been endowed with distance and strangeness.

This process of self-estrangement, which Barak describes as sobering and giving him 'new eyes', is deeply painful and exposes an extremely precarious self (my translation):

> This transition, from patriot to someone who realizes that his country is fucked up from its very foundation, is extremely painful and takes a long time. Something inside you is broken, it's a bit like in Matrix, because suddenly, 18 years later, you finally see with your eyes . . . with my former eyes – I had no idea of what I was actually seeing back then.

This self-estrangement from self and nation involves confronting the self's relation to the other. Barak reflects on the act of photographing Palestinians as an act of symbolic violence, the exercise of the Orientalist gaze which encapsulates the injustice, violence and suffering inflicted upon the other: 'I do not know what it was, this urge I had, to take out my camera each time I saw a Palestinian. Maybe it's because they are the ultimate Other.'

Barak appropriates a therapeutic narrative to cope with the disruption to his biography: a narrative of evaluation of and complex introspection into the self, in which one of the key tenets is evaluation and comparison of the images of self and the other (Illouz, 2007: 19). He also appropriates the popular film *Matrix*, as a metaphor for his experience of self-realization; like Neo, the hero in *Matrix*, Barak learns that he was constructed and exploited by a huge ideological machinery (his nation-state), and participated in its reproduction. Like Neo, he seeks to break free from this world, to rebel against the machines that created his self. His personal album acts as a mirror of his self-image – an image that is disrupted, made strange and fundamentally questioned. This introspection blurs the boundaries between the normal and the pathological, encapsulated in Barak's acknowledgement, which he repeats at the end of his post, of the resemblance to and collusion between his 'normal' self and the 'pathological' self of Aberjil (my translation):

> I completed my army service and never looked back. I never went back to the occupied territories and have no intention of doing so. Perhaps my decision to focus exclusively on entertainment and the light side of life was influenced by my army experience. I suppose so. Today I perceive myself a left-winger . . . advocating human rights . . . But a look at my photo album exposes the bitter and sad truth: I am, much more than I am willing to admit, still Eden Aberjil.

I am not suggesting that Barak's blog is representative of blogs and self-representations posted following the publication of Eden Aberjil's photos on Facebook. Similar accounts were posted online, of Israeli citizens recounting their experience as soldiers, and negotiating (albeit in less elaborate and reflexive ways), their relation to the nation and the Palestinian other.[5] But there were also postings that augmented Aberjil's narrative, trivializing torture and annihilating the Palestinian other, through a range of discursive practices of denial (Cohen, 2001; Sturken, 2011), emphasizing an unproblematic attachment to nationhood and denying reflexive selfhood.[6] However, what Barak's blog demonstrates is how the imagining of ourselves as a nation and the tensions that this work of imagining involves, are processed in a mediated narrative of the self. The self constitutes a central locus for the negotiation of these contradictions, and contemporary mediated spaces, such as blogs, provide the tools and environments to exercise a narrative of the self. This narrative opens up a reflexive and potentially progressive space for imagination that is more complex, contradictory, precarious and ambivalent than that afforded by public media narratives of the nation, especially in times of conflict. The blog's narrative provides Barak with a structure to achieve symbolic distance and separate the self from the nation. Crucially, it is a political narrative. Contrary to what many lament as the de-politicizing effect of the centrality of the narcissist self, which is seen to be compounded by 'me'-centred online spaces such as blogs and social media, this narrative of the self constitutes a prime structure for politicizing the experience of the self.

At the same time, the contradictions and complexity of the relation to the nation are internalized within the self. They are contained in a story of a self that seeks to correct, manage and improve itself, as if this were completely under the control of and within the capacity of the self. Though Barak's narrative reflexively recognizes the broader ideologies and social structures that conditioned his identity and actions, at the same time his account promotes an individual message of failure of the self and pursuit of self-correction. The political is the personal: political action is privatized in the form of writing the self by confessing on a blog. Ultimately, and unlike the hero of *Matrix* who in the epilogue to the film promises that he will demonstrate to the people imprisoned in the matrix that 'anything is possible', and then flies off into the sky, Barak's narrative reaffirms the self's incapacity to separate from the nation. His narrative is an attempt to reconcile his individuality, however precarious and fragile, within the nation in which it is located.

Imagining Possible Lives/Imagining the Self

The common focus in media debates on migration is the economic, social and political aspects of migration and their policy-related implications. This focus is manifest in political discourse, in news, political adverts and migration-related activists' website, examples which I examined in chapter 4. It appears also in popular culture, for instance, films or celebrities, which blur the distinctions between popular and political culture and between the political and the personal (see the examples of Shakira and Stephen Colbert in chapter 4). Another significant type of representation where the personal and the political converge in constructing an imaginary of migration is that of migrants' self-narratives. Narratives of individual experiences of migration are sometimes mobilized to support the dream narrative, for example, a story of a migrant's 'successful' journey and incorporation into a new society. Other self-narratives endorse the nightmare scenario, recounting experiences of struggles, rejection and exclusion from new societies. Yet other migrant narratives offer more complex and ambivalent stories, exemplified by the Riverbend blog discussed in chapter 4.

News is perhaps the most central site in which the issue of migration is discussed and new media are becoming increasingly central in journalistic reporting of migration. In particular, storytelling and self-narrative forms are being incorporated into journalistic accounts, allowing readers to see and hear migrants speaking for themselves, in the first person. The focus on the self and migrants' own stories challenges the practice that largely, if unconsciously, underpins western journalism, of speaking for and on behalf of the subaltern. Such news stories, which focus on migrants' lives and selves, also challenge the notion that news is a site for rationalist discourse and public elaborations of reason and debate. Rather, they highlight also the expressive capacity of news, its emotional appeal and its focus on the self (based on Cottle, 2006: 172–3), and blur the lines between deliberation and display, public and private, rational and emotional, the political and the personal.

I now examine an example that sheds some light on this observation, in relation to the representation of migration and the self in the news. The international news organization, Christian Science Monitor, chronicled a year in the life of seven-year-old Bill Clinton Hadam, named after the former US president, who had settled with his Congolese family in Atlanta, Georgia. The series, entitled *Little Bill Clinton: A School Year in the Life of a New American*, follows the school year 2008–9, through blogs, multimedia pieces and print stories. It won the 2008 American Education Writers Association Award,[7] an institutional acknowledgement of its positive and informative representation of migration and its trustworthiness and 'truthfulness' (in the Foucauldian sense). The project's leading correspondent, Mary Wiltenburg, explains on the website the two aspects that make the series unusual:

> First, I'll be reporting it in real time, in a variety of media, so you'll be learning about things happening just as I do. That will mean that it unfolds less like a traditional newspaper story, more like a friendship does, over time. Second, the community surrounding us will be involved in telling and discussing it.

From the outset, the reader's relation to Bill and his life is defined in terms of the double promise of intimacy and voice, of 'unmediated' access to his life, of the opportunity for readers to become his intimates through liveness, the ongoing flow of information, and incorporation of his and his community's voices. Against the experience of reading a traditional news story, which freezes experience in time and implies distance between the reader and the other, we are invited to become Bill's friends. The reader is allowed exclusive access to Bill's new life in the US through symbolic (mediated) occupation of the spaces he occupies, meeting his family and his new community, and witnessing his activities.

Like *Hometown Baghdad*, *Little Bill Clinton* utilizes new media platforms to display the migrant self, to invite readers, primarily in the west, to imagine the other as self and develop 'intimacy at a distance'. The project positions itself as transcending the limits of traditional journalism (as implied in the quote above), and as eschewing reflexively the patronizing Orientalist gaze:

> We've been granted intimate access to people's lives and we take the responsibility seriously . . . in fairness to the people who've opened their homes and classrooms to us, to the vital issues their stories raise, and to our readers, we think it's important not to 'protect' subjects in a way that patronizes them or minimizes the challenges they face.[8]

The 'direct' access to Bill and his life, through a story that unfolds over time in multimedia representations, is offered to challenge the practice of speaking for and on behalf of the other (with the colonial implications this brings). The promise of proximity, intimacy and mediated friendship with Bill is predicated on the construction of Bill as a unique individual, whose identity and experience can be neither reduced nor substituted. The use of multimedia, the unfolding of the story over the space of a year, the inclusion of people from Bill's community whose voices and accounts are woven into his story in videos, images and texts, enable the production of a highly detailed, in-depth account that emphasizes the specificity and uniqueness of his identity. It symbolically establishes Bill as 'a friend', one of a kind. His naming after a former president of the US further highlights his distinctiveness.

At the same time, Bill's narrative acts as a representative of the stories of many other refugees, and of the larger social issue of migration in the US. Bill Clinton Hadam's story serves as 'a window on the nation's [America's] refugee programme', to cite the reporter.[9] 'In our globalized world', the reporter adds, 'every war eventually shows up on America's doorstep as kids like Bill.' Thus, our mediated intimate friend, Bill, is emblem of 'what it's like to be a refugee in America',[10] the title used for part 12 of the series.

Frosh (2011b: 390) describes this paradox in media representations of strangers:[11]

> In their voices, faces and bodies individuals are depicted in all their astonishing deictic particularity, their singular indexicality in relation to a unique place and time; it is them, and no other, there, then. And yet these same individuals frequently stand for a broader reality, even encapsulating and embodying entire populations and events of immense scale – catastrophes, conflicts and celebrations – that are not themselves depicted.

News, probably more than any other genre, is caught in this paradox. Journalism is committed to informing the public about issues of significance and interest to the collective. Its exploitation of personal stories and its focus on the self are geared inherently towards generalization: the personal story and the self as windows on society; an individual journey representing a broader issue. However, 'there seems to be a heavy price to pay for turning the individual into an emblem: the erasure of the individual as a singular being, a memorable, unique person – indeed, it can seem but a little way to go from emblem to stereotype' (Frosh, 2011b: 390).

The *Little Bill Clinton* series, at the symbolic level, does precisely this. It criticizes the US 'one-size refugee resettlement' for its failure to meet migrants' divergent and unique needs (episode 12), but reduces the unique identity of Bill Clinton Hadam into a 'one-size-fits-all' identity. It promises that in getting to know this mediated Bill, the viewer will come to understand the issue of migration in America. However, while some aspects of Bill's experience may resemble the experience of other migrants, his singular experience can never capture the plurality of experience of an entire migrant population. Bill's largely positive and upbeat experience of accustoming to life in America suppresses the extremely varied and complex character of migration and what migrants' lives entail. Most notably, it suppresses the misfortunes, the many hurdles and the failed migrations.

Little Bill Clinton is meant to symbolize not only the entire population and experience of migrants to the US. It concurrently embodies the bigger story underpinning the American imagination: a story of the power of individual volition and agency to overcome multiple hurdles and be transformed into a 'new American'. The final episode in the series illustrates the idea of makeover of the self into the desirable identity of an American:

> In 2008, the Monitor began a year-long series that followed Bill (now 11), Igey (now 9), and their parents, as the newly arrived refugee family adjusted to life in the United States. When the project ended in September 2009, their future was uncertain. Today, challenges remain, particularly for Bill's missing sister and nephew – and changes to the family have added new ones. But one thing seems clear: Although the boys won't become citizens for another couple of years, they're Americans now.[12]

Bill's triumph, the narrative's closure tells us, is that he has become one of 'us'. His unique self has been written off by a new self, that of an American. Thus, while the intimate encounter with Bill and his family has invited readers to recognize his otherness, it simultaneously erases this acknowledgement of difference, providing readers with a confirmation of the singular desirable self: the American self.

Imagining the World/Imagining the Self

As discussed in chapter 5, the world is a central spatial construct in the modern imaginary: a space of sameness, of homogeneity transcending geographical, national, cultural, political or economic boundaries, but, simultaneously, a space marked by competition and hierarchies among nations, regions, peoples, cultures, and political, economic and military allegiances. The self is rarely explicit in this imagining of the world. For example, in the world news sections of newspapers or on major international news websites, there is a notable absence of the self in what is presented as representing 'the world'. The televised New Year celebrations, discussed in chapter 5, show 'the world' as a homogeneous space consisting of urban environments inhabited by crowds; little if any focus is given to individual faces or identities. The use of the world map to represent the world (e.g., in news reports and digital earth systems such as Google Earth) is another example of the world's representation as an abstract space, disconnected from the individual and the self.

At the same time, globalization carries the promise, continuously perpetuated in public discourse and media representations, of the individual's connection to the world. Across divergent fields, discourses and genres, individuals are continuously called on to 'embrace' the world and become 'immersed' in the world: 'the world at your fingertips',[13] 'the world has never been closer',[14] 'the world is yours'.[15] Knowing, experiencing and fusing with the world are constructed as ways of knowing and realizing the self. The movie *Eat Pray Love* (2010), starring Julia Roberts, is a useful illustration of this message in popular culture. The film is an adaptation of Elizabeth Gilbert's 2006 memoir of a year-long global search for sustenance and serenity following a painful divorce. In the film, the heroine travels to Italy, where she is shown eating in trattorias and standing amid historic ruins, to India, where she visits an ashram, and to Indonesia, on a therapeutic journey of self-examination and self-realization. The story is based on a formula of '[g]lobe-trotting and soul searching' (Scott, 2010): discovering the world is constructed as enabling discovery of the self and, vice versa, in order to discover the self, it is necessary to discover 'the world'.

This formula is articulated and fuelled by a range of cultural representations, including tourism advertising, novels and memoirs, nature programmes, self-help discourse and its supporting genres and products, Hollywood films and computer-generated virtual environments. It is this last that I focus on here. In particular, I examine Second Life, a multi-user virtual environment, based on computer graphics, simulating an immersive three-dimensional space and compelling animations. Users have to move and navigate these worlds, and sustain their characters in the virtual space. They are represented on screen by avatars, chosen from a predetermined or user-customized menu, which may approximate an (idealized) human form, or may take the form of an animal or inanimate object (Gale, 2009).

This example is different from the representations examined in the previous sections: it is not a self-narrative insofar as it refers to a set of representational practices, signs and forms that constitute a virtual environment rather than a particular media text. Also, at the time of writing, Second Life had attracted only 4 per cent of adult Americans (Pew Internet, 2009) and had recorded even lower numbers of users in other countries, despite enthusiastic forecasts that the majority of active Internet users would have virtual selves by the end of 2011 (Pew Internet, 14 December 2008). However, rather than being totally idiosyncratic or esoteric, I hope to show that Second Life constitutes a compelling site to explore how the imagining of world and self are co-constructed and articulated in the contemporary media environment.

Virtual environments, such as Second Life, can be seen as the most complete fulfilment so far, of the promises of mediation and globalization – to become an 'armchair Columbus' (Billboard, 19 August 1944; see discussion of DuMont television advert in the Introduction), able to access the world, its places and people, at the touch of a button without the need for co-presence. Second Life fulfils the Dumont advertisement's promise of 'a world actually served to you', 'of everything odd, unusual and wonderful', and takes the promise of mediated proximity ('just as though you were on the spot') a step further by putting the user actually on the spot through a screen avatar.

Before moving on, some brief background is needed. Spaces and spatial practices in Second Life are extremely varied, and include city simulations, collaborative workspaces created and employed by corporations such as IBM and BMW, non-profit organizations such as Global Kids and American Cancer Society, fan communities, art spaces, classrooms and others. I clearly cannot capture all or even most of these; nor can they be characterized in a singularly cohesive manner (based on Gordon, 2008: 202). In this chapter, I focus on two aspects of Second Life that shed light on the symbolic co-production of world and self: (1) immersion, embodiment and navigation in the space;[16] and (2) uncertainty, ephemerality and spatial confusion.

Identification, immersion, embodiment and navigation in space

Representation of the world and the self are inseparable in Second Life: worlds appear and exist (symbolically, on the computer screen) through the user's movements, creation, immersion and sustainment of them. Unlike representations where the self (viewer) is separate from the representation, in Second Life and other immersive virtual environments, it is impossible to know a world without being embodied in it. Representations of worlds, therefore, always include and depend on the symbolic presence of self embodied in an avatar. *Knowing* the world is dependent on symbolically *being in it.*

Bardzell and Odom's (2008) ethnographic study of a Gorean community in Second Life sheds light on this aspect. Gorean communities are virtual simulations, based on the fantasy novels about Gor, an alternative world. They simulate a stratified Greco-Roman culture, whose clear social structure dictates the roles and actions of citizens (e.g., dominant masters and submissive slaves). The Gorean world is projected by the avatar, which enacts the drama, for example, through a rite of passage in which a slave completes her training and is inducted into the house of the community:

> Citizens and guests . . . teleport to a welcome area, walk to the ceremonial site, and form a semicircle in hierarchical order around the stage where the ceremonial props (e.g. branding frame, hot iron, water bucket, medicine supplies, and examination cot) are housed and the main actors stand. (Bardzell and Odom, 2008: 254)

The virtual body of the avatar – the projection of the self – is inseparable from the projection of the world. What is more, nearly all the elements, in this 3-D, user-created, virtual world – for example, a waterfall, a house and other objects – were created by other Second Life users (Bardzell and Odom, 2008: 239). Thus, avatars do not simply navigate a pre-constructed world; they also construct buildings and buy and sell land and property in this world.

Studies show that one of the main appeals of Second Life is that it offers an opportunity for the self to connect symbolically, immerse in space and engage in the public life of a virtual community. While some regard this experience of immersion in space as escape from everyday 'first' life into fantastical worlds (e.g., Book, 2003), others regard the immersive qualities of the virtual world facilitated by the avatar's spatial navigation, as offering 'a sense of presence not possible in traditional Web media' (Gordon, 2008: 202). In other words, rather than mere escape, the immersion of self in these virtual environments can be seen as enabling a quality of experience missing in other computer-mediated communication, and also, I would add, in other media experiences and representations, for example, in watching films about 'the world'. The immersive qualities of Second Life seem to suggest a relation between self and world not offered by other media representations, and absent from modern public life. Sennett (1977) famously argued that modern life is characterized by a decay of embodied forms of participation in public life in outdoor spaces, and the disappearance of 'the bond of a crowd' (1977: 4). It has led to withdrawal into private life focused on increasingly narcissistic forms of intimacy and self-absorption. The media are seen as the central forces generating and enhancing this process, for example, in the Frankfurt School's immensely influential view of the culture industries, or in popularized views of such genres as talk shows or reality television shows, as celebrating, fuelling and normalizing the modern 'narcissism epidemic' (Twenge, 16 June 2009).

Second Life seems to proffer precisely what Sennett (1977) argues that public life lacks: participation in the world, engagement in public life and, through the genre of a game, 'the ease, the spirit of play, the kind of discretion that would allow us real and pleasurable relationships with those whom we may never know intimately' (from the book cover of Sennet's (1977) *The Fall of Public Man*). Thus, as a representational space, Second Life could be seen as restoring the connection between self and space, and embodied participation in public life. Contrary to current representations of the world (see chapter 5) that are 'bereft of geographical specificity' and thus remain 'abstracted and alienated reason' (Harvey, 2001: 211), Second Life is characterized by extremely detailed geography and spatial specificity, which, together with the user's avatar representation moving in the virtual space, encourage identification. As Lammes (2008: 260) observes, 'on a very fundamental level an important function of any game is to involve the player in a spatial process and to encourage a strong identification with the spatial dimensions of the game'. Along similar lines, Jenkins (1998), in his early work on video games, argues that such virtual spaces provide children (albeit boys much more than girls) 'complete freedom of movement', and a way to respond to the domestic confinement that characterizes Americans' lives in urban or semi-urban neighbourhoods, driven, among other factors, by parents' fears for children playing in the streets.

On the other hand, Second Life can be seen as the ultimate manifestation of the social problem that Sennett (1977) describes, and which many lament in relation to contemporary media culture: a narcissistic form of intimacy and self-absorption. Immersion in virtual space is immersion in oneself; the exploration of space and the world through compelling 3-D graphic representations is motivated by and furthers an experience that is totally self-centred. Like the experience of Liz, the character played by Julia Roberts in *Eat Pray Love*, who throws herself into the world to find refuge from her failed self through the experience of tourism, Second Life users immerse themselves in the virtual world to explore and realize the self. Similar to the way that the other and self fuse in contemporary representations (see earlier discussion of *Hometown Baghdad* and *Little Bill Clinton* and also chapter 2), so too in Second Life self and other fuse and the distance that is fundamental to the self's recognition of its boundaries and limitations is erased.

An avatar in Second Life is seemingly omnipotent: it can teleport from one world to another, fly, take on another appearance and create worlds at will, at the click of a mouse. Once indoctrinated into the game, the user can pull up maps of the Second Life universe and choose a new location, becoming what Lammes (2008: 267) calls a 'cartographer on tour'. The view is omniscient, 'God-like', which emphasizes a sense of omnipotence. The avatar controls (or rather, the user thinks it controls) its environment, symbolically creating, changing and buying land, and smoothly navigating it. This ability, within the representational space of the game, defeats what Bauman (1998: 12, cited in Gale, 2009: 132) describes as a key consequence of globalization: the notion of a 'full planet', that efforts to 'speed up' have reached their ultimate limit and that there is nowhere left to be conquered. In Second Life, it seems that the planet is never full, and there is always room for further exploration and new places and spaces to conquer. However, Jenkins (2005, cited in Lammes, 2008: 268) reminds us that the centrality of exploring and marking 'new' territories in Second Life and other virtual games is deeply situated in a western tradition, and the colonial project in particular, of the fascination with exploring new worlds.

Uncertainty, ephemerality and spatial confusion

At the same time that the fusion of self and world in the virtual environment of Second Life endows the user with a sense of control and omnipotence, it offers users an opportunity to reimagine themselves as part of a globe that lacks predetermined scripts and assumptions. None of the real world's natural properties need to be retained, although the user can visit and explore real-life spaces, such as the cities of Munich, Amsterdam, Chicago and New York. The user enters a dialectic between 'what is' – 'real-life' geography and world spaces – and 'what if'. While real-life destinations include famous sights, they can also incorporate fantastical elements created by their 'residents' (other Second Life users). 'What if' destinations are fictional by definition, that is, they do not bear any mimetic relation to real places and are listed under the subcategory 'Fantasy' in the destination list. The fantasy destination of Pasithea, for instance, is described as follows:

You are about to enter a world of dreams. You write the story and determine your fate in this fully immersive, multilayered medieval fantasy. Various character role-play groups inhabit the sim – join in as an elf, faun, nymph, merrow or one of many other races.[17]

The representation of space and self in these worlds allows and encourages experiencing:

> a degree of puzzlement about where you are and where you are headed, struggling to gain and maintain a spatial overview to win the game . . . a player is always struggling to get to grips with these rules, therefore experiencing a certain amount of uncertainty that can hardly be described as ordered. (Lammes, 2008: 262–3)

The futuristic texture of the opening 'welcome' capsule alludes to the transgression and violation of frontiers enabled by Second Life. The tutorial for 'new residents' emphasizes the violation of boundaries. Users are instructed to talk to a bird to explore their speech capacities, and are taught how to fly. As the user becomes familiar with the spatial order and rules of the game, navigation becomes easier and smoother, but there remains an inherent sense of spatial uncertainty, of the possibility of losing direction, getting trapped in a building, falling into water, or bumping into another resident. This sense of lack of control over the space and the body in space is amplified by the avatar body encountering codes and norms that determine particular environments. For instance, in the Gorean community, which Bardzell and Odom (2008: 252) researched:

> an avatar playing the slave who is about to step into the water in a Gorean bath house in service to her master is constrained in how she plays the part; that is, by using a sequence of appropriate poseballs, she prostrates her body in prescribed ways to show servitude and submission during role-play. The avatar's body is further dependent on network connection, which can cause the avatar to exhibit abnormal behaviors as a result of lag, rendering bugs, and so on. Accordingly, the body of an Ithaca citizen is the locus of a dialectic: to be one's own person and yet also to be subject to another, as a slave's body is owned by her master.

Another feature that enhances spatial confusion and uncertainty is the interactive affordance provided to the user to construct the world at will. If the user requires a material not accessible in his or her Second Life universe, it can be created using the 'Build' tool, and even sold to other Second Life residents. Representations of the world in Second Life, therefore, are inherently impermanent and ephemeral: features can appear and disappear and the self that is embodied in an avatar is essentially transient.

In sum, on the one hand, Second Life offers a representational space which emphasizes the self's connection to and immersion in the world, and offers a sense of the self's confidence and presence in space intertwined with possibilities for participation in (virtual) public life and a strong spatial identification. On the other hand, a degree of confusion and uncertainty about the world is innate in the experience in Second Life. The sense of omnipotence, achieved through the avatar's control and capacity to move with seemingly no limits, is countered by continuous reminders of the brittleness and transience of the self and the world: what may be symbolically present can disappear in an instant – users are never in full control of their avatars.

Conclusion

The self has become a principal prism through which the other, the nation, possible lives and the world are explained, understood and imagined. In the media environment of the early twenty-first century, the narrative of the self provides a primary script to present the far-away other, to express and negotiate relation to the nation, to articulate the meaning of possible lives opened up by migration and to construct the world.

The preoccupation with self in modern culture and the centrality of self in media representations are often lamented as narcissism and self-absorption, and as leading to the decay of participation in public life, de-politicization of social problems and debasing of culture and taste. To an extent, these claims are valid. As the analysis of *Hometown Baghdad* shows, *imagining the other as self*, at a symbolic level, fuses self and other, thereby effacing difference and failing to acknowledge and respect the other through difference – on the grounds not of their similarity to us, but because their life conditions, needs, imaginations and desires are (sometimes radically) divergent from ours. Thus, viewing the other through the prism of self offers a narcissist form of intimacy rather than recognition of the other as separate and different. The analysis of Omer Barak's blog shows that *imagining one's nation through the self* encourages locating the responsibility for coping with the moral contradictions created by the nation (and nationalism) within the self and developing a sense of self-failure. It deflects attention and respon-sibility from the nation-state and larger societal forces. *Imagining possible lives through the self*, as illustrated by the journalistic project of *Little Bill Clinton*, involves reducing the complexity and diversity of possible lives – the endless possibilities of what new life can entail for different individuals in different contexts – to a one-size-fits-all model. It erases the individual as a singular memorable, and unique person (Frosh, 2011b). Finally, as the case of Second Life reveals, *imagining the world through the self* is entwined with and reinforces a sense of omnipotence and lack of separation between self and space. Thus, rather than opening up the self to know and experience the world in its difference and variety, symbolic exploration of the world through representation centred on the self cultivates an inward self-centred view and experience.

A series of social, cultural and political forces, including the cultural persuasions of therapy, economic productivity and feminism, have converged to make the therapeutic narrative of the self a widely pervasive model in modern western and, particularly, American culture (see Illouz, 2007, for an elaboration). In this narrative, the self must be continuously worked on, negotiated, improved and performed (Illouz, 2007). The danger is that a global imagination sustained by representations that endorse and reproduce this predominantly western, and especially American, narrative of self excludes any other narrative. It suppresses and discounts different perspectives on others and the world we live in and how we make sense of our lives.

At the same time, the self provides an extremely rich, productive and potent symbolic site for the global imagination. *Hometown Baghdad* presents the other as three young people and their day-to-day lives, rather than as an abstract national group cast as 'the enemy'. The others are human beings deserving of recognition, a representation which helps to 'symbolically rehabilitate' (Cottle, 2006) the other, and provides a basis for dialogue and interaction between 'us' and 'them', as illustrated by the comments posted by viewers in response to the series. The self-narrative on Omer Barak's blog provides a structure that allows the writer to negotiate his relationship to his nation and to reflect critically on relations of domination, exploitation and violence towards the other. In seeing himself as the 'other', Barak achieves distance from the self, which allows him to address and to try to redress injustice at the personal level. The narrative of the self in *Little Bill Clinton* opens up different imaginings of what it means to be a migrant and what migrants' possible lives entail. It moves beyond the binary discourse that dominates discussion of migration in the media, to reflect on the specificity of human beings' particular experiences of migration. Lastly, Second Life offers a sense of presence, participation and confidence in the world, identification with and connection to space, which is not always available (or possible) in other representations, and is absent, more generally, in modern public life. The virtual world simultaneously allows and encourages a degree of confusion and uncertainty, which may be seen as echoing the inherently transient, precarious and volatile character of modern life, what Bauman (2000) famously called 'liquid modernity'.

Modern life in the global age presents multiple contradictions, tensions and uncertainties. The narrative of the self, one of the central narratives through which we are called to imagine ourselves, others and the world we live in, provides a structure for articulating and dealing with these contradictions. This chapter shows that it is an essentially dialectical narrative, which provides the valuable potential to expand our imagination, to acknowledge and understand that 'the other', 'the nation', 'possible lives' and 'the world' are complex, ambivalent and more brittle than they may seem. At the same time, it can work to reinforce inwardness, knowing the self rather than the other and the world, and consequently 'the elision of the different to the same', and 'the refusal to recognize the irreducibility in otherness' (Silverstone, 2007: 47).

7   Conclusion
Nothing Gets You Closer Revisited

If one were to design a job advert to recruit a media representation for the contemporary global media space, what would it look like? What would the job specifications for the work of media representation include? I have argued in this book that one of the prime aspects of the work of media representations today is the cultivation of global imagination. Perhaps a recruitment ad for this work might resemble the following:

Job title: Media representation
The global media space is looking for candidates to join a vibrant team of representations and play a key role in shaping, informing and orienting how people see and judge the world, others and themselves, and how they imagine real and possible lives in this global age. The successful applicant will contribute to creating a sense of distant places, people and cultures as relevant and connected to media consumers.

The job involves inviting readers and viewers, through the use of images and narratives, to dislocate. The applicant must have the capacity to symbolically 'disembed' and lift audiences out of their local contexts of interaction, and 'plant' them in remote places, cultures or contexts, creating a sense of being there, of being 'on the spot'. The applicant must be able to demonstrate the ability to create 'intimacy at a distance' in inviting audiences to imagine the world, others and themselves.

No previous experience needed; however, ability to work in a highly complex, competitive and networked global media environment, and to interact and compete with other representations would be desirable.

This imaginary ad provides an entry point to the final chapter of this book, in which I gather together the arguments proposed in the preceding chapters. The ad summarizes the book's argument about central features of the 'work' (Hall, 1997) of media representation in the contemporary media landscape. The chapters in this book have highlighted the essence of media representations as symbolic resources that nourish collective and individual imaginations by constructing certain pictures and stories, which, albeit diverse and often contradictory, converge to create a general understanding of 'the world' and 'of who we are, how we fit together, how we got where we are, and what we might expect from each other in carrying out our collective practices that are constitutive of our way of life' (Gaonkar, 2002: 10).

This imaginary recruitment ad is deliberately couched in the language used in many job ads, which prioritizes (and implicitly valorizes) market-driven competition and success: this framework, as I have argued, is central to how media representations call us to imagine the world and social life today. Though the book has focused on the work of representations in producing meanings primarily from a phenomenological perspective of globalization, and on the ways representations construct and feed the cultural and social dimensions of the experience of globalization, it has demonstrated the centrality of capitalism in this process. In particular, the notion of markets as the organizing principle of social life, feeds and frames in significant ways how the world, and our and others' place in it, are constructed and imagined.

I have engaged with the work of media representation and some of its potential consequences, by analysing current media representations in terms of what they offer, the presuppositions and claims on which they rest, and what they call on their readers to think, feel and perform. Inevitably, it has been possible only to touch on some of the multifarious representations that characterize the contemporary mediated global environment. However, I would suggest that the material reviewed brings to the fore some of the complexities and issues that need to be addressed when studying today's representations.

I have argued that two interrelated practices are particularly central to the work of representation in a global age: symbolic dislocation and the development of intimacy at a distance. The imagining of distant others relies on the invitation issued by media representations to dislocate from one's own here and now and travel to the other's often radically divergent and distant time, place and experience. A central feature of this invitation in today's media, as demonstrated by the account of the trajectory from eighteenth-century representations of the Lisbon earthquake, through the 1985 'We are The World', to its 2010 remake for the Haiti earthquake appeal, is a call to viewers to imagine distant others as intimates, as friends or relatives.

Intimacy at a distance is central also in the imagining of ourselves as 'the nation'. Through symbolic practices of 'flagging', the construction of 'banal nationalism' (Billig, 1995) and the linking of individuals' personal, private and confessional stories and nationhood (Frosh and Wolfsfeld, 2007; Matthews 2007), the nation is imagined and experienced as an intimate and inseparable part of the self. At the same time, symbolic dislocation can work to unsettle the intimate relations between self and nation. The exposure to images and stories of ourselves – the nation – as seen and told by foreign storytellers, such as international news networks or bloggers, may invite symbolic distancing: adoption of a degree of distance from and critical thinking about the nation, about the familiar, and about what 'we', as members of a national people, generally regard as 'normal'. Thus, while symbolic dislocation and the creation of intimacy at a distance may be mutually constitutive and supportive, as illustrated in relation to the imagining of distant others (chapter 2), they may exist in tension, as exemplified by the discussion of the imagining of ourselves (chapter 3), where the proposal made by representations for viewers to 'dislocate' implies de-familiarization, strangeness and opacity, rather than intimacy with the nation.

The capacity to imagine distant events and distant others in locales and contexts that are remote from the contexts in which we live out our daily lives – a capacity that media representations help develop and nourish – is a prerequisite for, and is intertwined with, the ability to imagine possible lives. Representations of migration are one key site where scenarios of possible lives are constructed (chapter 4). Some of these representations are optimistic and utopian ('dream'), others are dystopian and infused with ideas and feelings of danger, threat, disappointment and despair ('nightmare'), yet others are ambivalent, refusing a classification of experiences into the binary structures that seem to govern the debate on migration. In all these scripts, however, intimacy at a distance is a central mode through which representations call on audiences to relate to and think about migrants and migration. Celebrities, video games, social media and blogging sites call on viewers to understand migration – a 'bigger-than-self'[1] issue – by inviting them symbolically (albeit momentarily, and in a pre-planned and produced fashion) into intimate lives and personal experiences of others.

Thus, media representations are symbolic travel agents inviting people to disembed and extend their horizons beyond the self and beyond their locales, to remote places, cultures and people. In so doing, images and stories in the media construct certain 'geographical knowledges' (Harvey, 2001) and 'cartographic consciousnesses' of the world; they offer certain 'maps' and visions of the world, and of how we and others are situated within them. Contemporary representations construct the world simultaneously as a social, economic, political and cultural space of sameness, unity and standardization, and a place marked by competition and divided by deep differences, inequalities and hierarchies of success.

This dual narrative is imbricated in and is being reproduced through the different sites of imagining. *Imagining of distant others* (chapter 2), on the one hand, draws on and plays out a sense of 'common humanity', which endorses a view of the world as a space joined by a common morality, and, on the other hand, is characterized by distance and symbolic annihilation, which reinforces a notion of the world as a place marked by 'hierarchies of life' (Chouliaraki, 2006). *Imagining ourselves* (chapter 3) as a nation displays a continuous tension between a notion of being part of a world of nations joined by common interests and values, and a strong sense of a divide between 'us' and 'the world', perpetuated frequently by claims to the particularity, idiosyncrasy and uniqueness of the nation. *Imagining of possible lives* (chapter 4) is nourished by scripts that reproduce a contradictory view of the world. On the one hand, we have scripts that promote a cosmopolitan view of the world as an interconnected space of hospitality, solidarity and ethics of care and, on the other hand, there are scripts that reinforce a view of a world divided between 'us' and 'them' and predicated on fierce competition, inequality and hostility.

I have shown that this work of media representation, of nourishing a global imagination through symbolic dislocation and invitation to develop intimacy at a distance, is inherently dialectical. It is geared to expanding, or at least carries the promise to expand, symbolic horizons by inviting viewers to imagine new and different worlds, beyond the self. However, in so doing, especially through the development of mediated intimacy and a focus on the personal, it re-centres on the self and promotes an inward, self-centred view and experience. Representations invite viewers to 'meet' distant others, to become their symbolic companions, but, in so doing, fail to recognize the others' difference, the irreducibility of their otherness; some representations cast the other as beyond the pale of recognition and understanding (Silverstone, 2007). In the age of new visibility (Thompson, 2005), representations circulating in the media space expose us to images that formerly would have remained hidden. These images, which may be uncomfortable and disturbing, invite a rethinking of our lives and histories and trigger processes of symbolic distancing and estrangement. At the same time, these same images can produce the opposite result: triggering and reinforcing attachment to and entrenchment in common wisdoms and familiar ways of seeing and thinking. Thus, what at first sight may seem a straightforward 'job description' for media representation (see the imaginary ad above) is actually a highly complex, contradictory and, I would argue, consequential, work.

Putting together a job advert (at least from my experience of working in an advertising agency and universities) is often an opportunity to revisit existing structures, practices and goals, and to think about what it is that we would like a new recruit to add to our environment. What changes to the current job (and by implication the environment in which it is performed) would we like to see in the future? Drawing on the discussion in the book of the representations and scripts available in the current media space, I want to consider three areas of such change in relation to media representations in the twenty-first century.

The Desire to Defeat Distance Revisited

The central project of media representation in a global age is to annihilate distance, to overcome this great obstacle, which, paradoxically, is brought to light and becomes a problem through the act of mediation. The development of intimacy at a distance is a central means and consequence of this project: 'sail with television through vanishing horizons into exciting new worlds' by becoming 'an intimate of the great and near-great' (*Billboard*, 19 August 1944; see the DuMont advert cited in the Introduction). The highly intense and competitive market-driven media environment amplifies and foregrounds the abolition of distance and the development of intimacy as the primary goal of representation. Representations compete over reducing the distance between the audience and the distant other or the distant event: the objective is to 'get you closer' as the Sky ad discussed in the Introduction puts it – the implication being that the closer you get to a mediated object, the better you will understand it.

The notion of getting the viewer closer as representation's chief endeavour is not just a commercial slogan, it is a central component of the imaginary of media and globalization, which frames how we think about and relate to the world, others and ourselves. Distance in this imaginary is seen as a problem, an obstacle, and anything that is perceived to contribute to its creation and maintenance tends to be criticized, de-legitimized and denigrated: the use of rap and hip-hop in a song made for charity, to attract donations to relieve the suffering of Haiti earthquake victims, is seen as alienating, detaching and reducing any chance of intimate connection to the devastation (chapter 2). Foreign media are seen by national media, politicians and citizens as strangers lacking an intimate understanding of the nation and its unique circumstances (chapter 3; and see also Orgad, 2011). Traditional reporting is cast as constrained in its ability to abolish distance between subject and reader, in contrast to multimedia live reporting enabled online, which is cast as an ideal medium that allows its users to develop friendship with the mediated other (chapter 6).

However, as I have argued, the emphasis on symbolically annihilating distance, which seems to be driving the work of media representation, can be positive and enabling, but is also constraining and even repressive. Therefore, rather than starting from the idea of distance as a problem or an obstacle, and then lamenting it and/or looking for symbolic ways to abolish or overcome it, distance can be seen as a powerful stimulant for the exploration of diverse relations to, and more complex understandings of, the world. In other words, rather than eradicating distance, perhaps a more productive project for media representation today would be to acknowledge the inevitability of distance and focus on developing ways to engage and work *with* distance, in order to create fuller and more complex understandings of the world. I propose three specific directions (which are by no means mutually exclusive or exhaustive) that may be informative for this project.

The value of distance

Distance is a significant component in the cultivation of our relations to the other, to the world and to ourselves. It might be useful to recall that professional standards and values of journalism, of objectivity and impartiality, are predicated on and rooted in recognition of the value and merit of distance. It is through a 'bird's-eye view' that news traditionally calls readers to experience and know the world and the other, although, in the current media space, this seems to be changing in significant ways. I have argued in this book, in line with Silverstone (2007), that a degree of distance in the representation of others, rather than complete collusion with the other, is vital for recognizing the other and her difference. Representations should also be able to help cultivate a degree of distance from the self and from ourselves as members of a community: disturbing, painful and threatening as gaining distance from ourselves may be, it is also rewarding and a progressive moral force (see Orgad, 2011).

The value of degrees of proximity and different modes of achieving it

It is useful also to consider how representations can generate varying degrees of proximity through different modes of relation to the mediated event or to the distant other. Can representations invite us to achieve closeness and connection to the mediated distant other in ways other than forming intimacy with them? Boltanski's (1999) discussion of the representation of the unfortunate is helpful here. For a politics of pity to be a politics, Boltanski argues, the sufferers depicted by the media should *not* be intimates:

> [They] must not be characterised in preferential terms. They are neither friends nor enemies. . . . They therefore must be hyper-singularised through an accumulation of the details of suffering and, at the same time, under-qualified: it is he [*sic.*], but it could be someone else; it is the child there who makes us cry, but any other child could have done the same. Around each unfortunate brought forward crowds of replacements . . . Although singular, they are none the less *exemplary*. (1992: 12, emphasis in original)

Boltanski (1999) argues that fundamental to feeding a moral imagination is the construction of the distant other as both particular and generalizable, a specific individual and an emblem of a wider group or phenomenon (see also Frosh, 2011b). Intimate relationships, by contrast, are experienced and perceived as unique, they cannot be replicated; thus, nourishing intimacy at a distance is doomed to fail to enable this dialectic position of the other. To get closer to the mediated other by developing intimacy runs the risk of getting 'too close' (Silverstone, 2007: 48), as exemplified by the representation of the child migrant, in *Little Bill Clinton* (chapter 6), who readers are encouraged to treat as a friend, and whose story is (to use Boltanski's (1999) terms) 'hyper-singularized' but perhaps insufficiently 'under-qualified'.

So what alternative modes of relations (other than intimacy) can be sustained through the media to facilitate a degree of proximity to and to cultivate care for the distant other? Silverstone (2007: 48) proposes the concept of 'proper distance' – 'both close and far', to stress the need for concurrent distance and proximity in how media representations invite us to relate to the mediated other. For Silverstone, proper distance is the path to the development of a moral imagination that is necessary in the mediapolis of the twenty-first century. Proper distance is a theoretical concept which is hard to apply in practice, and which has various shortcomings (whose exploration is not appropriate here; for a critical discussion of the concept, see Dayan, 2007; Chouliaraki and Orgad, 2011); however, it is useful for the present discussion in at least two respects. First, it highlights the danger of intimacy and the 'too close' in media representations, but also stresses the problems of the 'too far' and the 'neither close nor far',[2] which Silverstone discusses. Second, proper distance helps to emphasize that, rather than annihilating distance and/or building maximal proximity, the work of media representation should focus on the symbolic management of distance, which, by definition, is a process of *negotiation* between alternative degrees of distance and proximity.

The value of intimacy at a distance

However critical we may be of intimacy at a distance, we should not be too quick to dismiss its value and significance and, certainly, we should not simply (and simplistically) lament it as narcissism and self-absorption that 'contaminates' the moral imagination. Illouz's (2007) account of the cultural centrality of intimacy in modern life is instructive in this context, as is Thompson's (1995) careful consideration of the multiple implications of mediated intimacy at a distance. Rather than abandoning mediated intimacy, which some critics seem to suggest is the path to pursue, it might be more constructive to consider how some of the pitfalls we observed in relation to the cultivation of intimacy as a mode of relation to the mediated other in current representations may be eschewed.

In his discussion of non-reciprocal intimacy at a distance, Thompson (1995) focuses on the example of fans' relations to distant others such as actors, singers or television presenters. One of the characteristics of these mediated relations, which make them such potent, integral (and intrusive) ingredients in fans' lives, is that they are practised and sustained on an ongoing basis, sometimes over years or even whole lifetimes. This temporal feature of a relation of intimacy established at a distance enables and involves high levels of commitment to the distant other. This contrasts with the type of intimacy that many representations available in today's media invite viewers to develop, which is often *fleeting*. As demonstrated by many of the examples in this book, representations call on viewers momentarily to become intimate with distant others, to imagine them as if they were a friend, a son or a daughter, to connect to, develop an imaginary bond with, and then, usually, forget about and move on.

The consequences of the media's continuous invitation to their audience to engage in these fleeting intimacies at a distance, and the lack of sufficient structures to encourage and sustain longer-term commitment, have yet to be explored. But comparison of many current representations of distant others to the mediated experience of fandom (as discussed by Thompson, 1995), which is predicated on an opposite temporality of long-term ongoing commitment, may be suggestive of one of the reasons why intimacy at a distance in today's media may fail to translate into a meaningful understanding of relation and commitment to, and action for, distant others. In this context, for example, NGOs are realizing that the short-lived character of the intimacy that their communications invite people to develop with distant others has failed to engage and mobilize long-term commitment to the alleviation of distant suffering (Plan UK, 2011). Some NGOs and media seem to be trying to overcome this problem by providing 'follow-up' representations, for instance, television and online programmes revisiting the victims of the Haiti earthquake a year on, or newsletter updates to supporters about how their money is being or has been used to improve the lives of distant sufferers. Such efforts by these organizations and the media may be a step towards enabling the maintenance of a more long-term character of intimacy, and better realization of its value.

The Internet is seen as particularly promising in this context since it provides a more flexible and participatory communicative platform to cultivate intimacy at a distance on an ongoing, long-term basis, for instance, via social media and blogs, which document the lives of distant others over a prolonged period of time. The online environment also offers ways to transform the non-reciprocal feature of intimacy at a distance (characteristic of media in the late twentieth and early twenty-first centuries) into a reciprocal relation. Online representations, especially new media platforms which provide sites for the articulation of 'local imagining', as many examples discussed in the book show, present interesting possibilities for developing intimacies that might translate better into interaction, dialogue and the exchange of ideas and feelings. They can help to enhance recognition and understanding of difference, and contribute to nourishing a richer and more complex global imagination (though, clearly, online communication is not a 'fix' for the limits of non-reciprocal intimacy at a distance, and does not provide magical solutions to the lack of commitment associated with non-reciprocity in 'old' media; nor to the broader crisis of exchange and dialogue in the contemporary public sphere).

Levine's observation of Simmel's thinking is useful to conclude this discussion of media representations and their desire to defeat distance. Levine (1971: xxxivi, cited in Illouz, 2003a: 237–8) argues that 'one of the respects in which worlds, and various forms within the same world, differ from one another is how near and how far they bring objects to the individual'. I am not convinced that there is a singular 'proper' degree of distance or proximity through which we should experience the world, mediated or 'real'. Rather, as cultural forms, media representations should build and allow *different* degrees of distance and proximity, a plurality of positions vis-à-vis the referent, via signs that evoke a *variety* of modes of relation, which would allow us to know and experience the world in more diverse, complex and, I believe, moral, generous and satisfying ways.

The Desire to Remove the Medium Revisited

Media representations continuously propel and sustain the paradoxical sense that mediation – the projection of symbolic representation of distant reality – grants viewers unmediated access to the world (Tomlinson, 1999). The desire to defeat distance and to allow viewers to experience the mediated other through intimacy is intertwined with and accomplished by creating a sense that there is no medium that separates and connects the viewer and the distant event and, thus, that there is no distinction between the mediated world and the world of the viewer. This notion is neatly captured by the comparison discussed in the Introduction to this book, between the 1944 Dumont ad's depiction of a small-sized viewer watching distant events and distant others on a giant television screen, and the 2010 Sky ad's depiction of a viewer and a distant other seemingly occupying the same space, without the medium (television) that facilitates this fusion (and simultaneously separates). This difference between the visual depictions of the medium in these ads is telling in terms of how media technologies figure in today's cultural imagination compared to earlier times, when they were neither ubiquitous nor taken for granted. Tomlinson (2011: 353) explains this difference in his account of the shift from the media culture that emerged in Europe during the 1930s, to today's era of omnipresent media:

> The media and communications technologies of the 1930s can thus be plausibly assimilated to a cultural imaginary in which they share more with transport and delivery systems than with the sort of complex cultural spaces we are used to thinking about today. The connectivity they were expected to provide was as 'highways' for the delivery of machine modernity.
>
> [. . .]
>
> [In this media culture there was] a categorical distinction between this media world and our own, and this is particularly so in terms of the sort of global connectivity the technologies were imagined to afford.

By contrast, the current era of 'complex connectivity' of globalization (Tomlinson, 1999, 2007) is characterized by the presence of media everywhere in our everyday lives, and an increasingly complex network of 'technologies and modalities of cultural contact and flow' (Tomlinson, 2011: 356). Consequently, the distinction between the mediated world and our own has dissolved. An arsenal of techniques and representational practices, some of which have been discussed in the preceding chapters, is being employed to generate this sense of fusion and lack of distinction and to call on viewers to imagine themselves as inhabiting the mediated world. This is illustrated by, for example, the collapse of the mediated distant other and the viewers into a collective 'we', use of images, narratives and sounds that enhance 'authenticity', liveness and twenty-four-hour coverage of events, participatory platforms on which citizens comment and take part in the production of meaning (blogs, video and image-sharing sites, online comment forums), and virtual environments based on computer graphics simulating immersive, three-dimensional spaces.

This enhancement of the relations between the mediated world and the viewer holds significant promise for changing cultural and moral sensibilities and for 'the enlargement of mentality beyond the individual and the solitary self' (Silverstone, 2007: 47, drawing on Kant, 1983, and Arendt, 1977), that is, for the expansion of our horizons of moral relevance (Boltanski, 1999; Chouliaraki, 2006, 2008, 2012; Robertson, 2010; Silverstone, 2007;

Tomlinson, 2011). I have reflected on some of these potentials by analysing particular examples of the ways in which imaginings of distant others, ourselves, possible lives, the world and the self, are enabled and cultivated in the contemporary media space.

However, the lack of distinction between the mediated world and our own, characteristic of the global media culture, entails various dangers, most notably, the failure of many media representations to distinguish between the self and the mediated other and to recognize difference – a central argument that I have developed throughout the book. In the next section, I reflect on another implication of the fusion that contemporary representations invite and encourage, between viewer and the mediated world, and of how symbolically they remove 'traces' of the medium that separates and connects the viewer and the mediated scene.

The Desire for Completeness, Coherence and Closure Revisited

Castoriadis (1987 [1975]: 1–2) criticizes academic accounts for removing 'the scaffolding and cleaning up the area around the building':

> Presenting the result as a systematic polished totality, which in truth it never is . . . can only serve to reinforce in the reader the disastrous illusion towards which he [sic], like all of us, is already naturally inclined, that the edifice was constructed for him [sic] and that he [sic] has only, if he [sic] so desires, to move in and live there.

Though written in relation to a completely different object (academic writing), Castoriadis's (1987 [1975]) warning seems to chime with our discussion of media representations. Media producers invest considerable effort in creating and sustaining the illusion of representations as neat, unproblematic, polished depictions of a world that readers can seamlessly inhabit. However, this illusion, Castoriadis (1987 [1975]) contends, deprives readers of the essential ability to see that the reality is messy and that its representation is always a construction, selective, partial, interpretative and purposive. Certain genres today, such as fictional films or virtual worlds, are designed precisely to create this illusion and to invite viewers to 'move in' to the worlds that they construct. They are fictional by definition and have no mimetic orientation, although sometimes the fictional worlds they build are seen as 'reflecting' (or replacing in the case of some virtual worlds) reality (consider, for instance, how fictional movies are frequently evaluated and reviewed in terms of how adequately they reflect reality).

However, removal of the symbolic 'scaffolding' and the invitation to viewers to 'move in' and live in a constructed 'polished' building are perhaps most central, and most consequential, in 'reflectionist' genres, such as news, reality TV and documentary programmes, which are geared to creating the sense that the stories they tell are a reflection of how things *really* are. The analysis in chapter 5 of news reporting of New Year celebrations vividly illustrates this: though clearly a construction – a carefully edited montage of images of scenes of celebrations from several countries – through the employment of a range of techniques, such news reports construct a story that makes the reflectionist claim that this is how New Year is celebrated across the world, and this is what 'the world' is. The viewer is invited to embrace this coherent 'polished' celebratory narrative and the particular geographical knowledges that it produces, and few, if any, elements muddle this refined story.

Thus, a considerable part of the work of media representation is invested in the creation and perpetuation of a polished account of a world to which viewers are invited and given the impression that they can seamlessly inhabit. At the same time, the conditions of the global 'age of new visibility' (Thompson, 2005) are mounting significant challenges to this investment. The current media environment in which representations contest for visibility, and in which it is increasingly hard to control and contain the flow of information, images and narratives, undermines the notion of representation as reflection. Exposure to multiple storytellers who, in relating their stories of the same event often produce contradictory accounts, renders the notion of neat reflection, and the very possibility of achieving it, highly problematic and contestable, if not impossible and inappropriate. It highlights the messiness of the work of meaning-making and underscores the centrality of the mediator and the medium in the production of reality. Today's environment, in which media representations are produced, circulated and consumed, invites audiences to recognize that rather than being a building ready-made for them to live in, the landscape of the representations that feed personal and collective imaginations is a huge construction site, where versions of the 'truth' and 'reality' are constantly under construction, in ongoing contestation and always at risk of collapsing.

Recognition of this is scary; it challenges one of the fundamental social and cultural roles of representation, which is rooted in the historical mimetic view of representations as reflections: that of proof that something *really* happened (see chapter 1). Representations historically constitute a source of certainty, ontological security, reassurance and comfort – an aspect that has been discussed extensively in the literature, influenced by Durkheim's work. However, in today's complex, competitive, porous and networked media environment, representation is no longer only, necessarily, or predominantly, a source of assurance and confirmation. It becomes a source of anxiety, uncertainty and fragility. Representations compete, challenge and undermine others' claims to 'truthfulness'; different storytellers present visions and claims that may radically unsettle our 'automatism of perception' (Shklovsky's (1991[1929])) and disturb commonsensical geographical knowledges. Media representations, particularly online, can remain incomplete with no ending, undermining the fundamental structure of narrative. It is this challenge to narrative, which is surfacing in the contemporary space of representations, and the possibilities it opens up, that I want to discuss in concluding this chapter.

In developing my argument about the challenge to narrative in contemporary representations, I draw on White's (1981) account of the relationship between historiography and narrative. White (1981) argues that the received wisdom in modern historiography is that narrative is the highest form of historical representation of events, outranking two other historical forms – annals and chronicles – which to different degrees and in different ways have been seen by historians as failing to attain narrativity. Narrative is a discursive form that organizes a sequence of events in a temporal structure, has a central subject, a proper beginning, middle and end, and a coherence that builds towards closure. This structure 'strains to produce the effect of having filled in all the gaps, to put an image of continuity, coherency, and meaning' (White, 1981: 11). By contrast, the non-narrative forms of annals and chronicles (which are different, but whose differences I do not have the space to elaborate on here) are characterized by discontinuity, lack of causal connection between one event and another, loose ends, gaps and, in some cases, lack of information about the identity of the author. Significantly, annals and chronicles do not conclude; they terminate. They leave things unresolved, an unfinished story.

The lack of narrativity in annals and chronicles tends be dismissed by historians as failure; too many loose ends are frustrating and disturbing to the modern story reader's expectations and desire for specific information (White, 1981). However, instead of considering this lack of narrativity a failure, White encourages us to ask what kind of notion of reality leads certain storytellers to refuse narrativity and represent events in a different form.

It is here that White's (1981) argument seems so pregnant for a critical analysis of media representations in today's global age. It is probably fair to argue that narrative governs contemporary representations, fictional, factual and blurring forms. The majority of the examples of representations discussed in this book exhibit the characteristics of a narrative, and representations are often evaluated for producing (or failing to produce) a clear, compelling narrative. But White (1981: 20) asserts (along similar lines to Castoriadis's observation cited earlier) that the completeness and fullness of meaning in the narrative is only a mask; we can only imagine, never experience, events in a narrativized form. In particular, the demand for closure is 'a demand for moral meaning, a demand that sequence of real events be assessed as to their significance as elements of a *moral* drama' (White, 1981: 20, emphasis in original). Narrativity, more generally:

> certainly in factual storytelling and probably in fictional storytelling as well, is intimately related to, if not a function of, the impulse to moralize reality, that is, to identify it with the social system that is the source of any morality that we can imagine. (White, 1981: 14)

The narratives circulating in the media are moralizing; they impose moral judgements on the events that they describe, and identify reality with certain moral authorities, such as religion or Enlightenment thought (chapter 2); the nation (chapter 3), international, cosmopolitan and humanitarian discourses and institutions (chapters 3 to 6), capitalism (chapter 5) and the therapeutic regime of self-help and self-governance (chapter 6). Yet the current media environment, especially (but not only) the online space, facilitates and, some would argue, encourages, the production, and increasing visibility, legitimacy and recognition of representations that refuse narrativity and, by implication, classification, completeness and closure. Recall Riverbend's blog (chapter 4), which is imbued with ambivalence, uncertainty and gaps, and which, like annals and chronicles, does not conclude, but simply terminates. Or the *Hometown Baghdad* website (chapter 6): although each video diary constitutes a mini-narrative, there is no particular structure that links the different videos together, and there is no imposition on the viewer of a certain order in which the events must be watched and understood – it is possible to make sense of any of the videos without necessarily watching the others.[3] The virtual world of Second Life (chapter 6) is perhaps the most vivid non-narrative representation examined in this book: it defeats the modern viewer's need for fullness and continuity in an order of events, and refuses any ranking or hierarchizing of events or places with respect to their significance.

Such non-narrative representations defy coherence, completeness and closure and, in so doing, following White's (1981) argument about the moralizing force of narrativity, they defy moralizing. Two fascinating analyses – of jokes on the Internet about 9/11 terror attacks (Kuipers, 2002) and of Internet sites showing body horrors (Tait, 2008) – exemplify lack of moral framing in online representations. Such representations, Kuipers (2002) and Tait (2008) argue, contrast with narratives circulating in 'mainstream' media, which prescribe specific moral judgements and are couched in moral language about what is acceptable and obligatory and what is not. The representations on these websites deliberately lack any moral framing: visual and textual humour are used to give vent to ambivalence, alienation and annoyance (Kuipers, 2002) and the video clips in Tait's (2008) analysis, which were produced by soldiers, are provided with almost no context other than brief titles or descriptions.

The surfacing of these new types of non-narrative representations is an effective reminder that narration and narrativity, and their impulse for the completeness, coherence and closure so central to the ways that representations call us to imagine the world, are 'the instruments by which the conflicting claims of the imaginary and the real are mediated, arbitrated, or resolved in discourse' (White, 1981: 4–5). Narrative strives to sustain order and establish causality and to suppress contingency and randomness. It gives the world a structure that manipulates its probabilities and makes some events more likely and more important than others (Bauman, 1991). In so doing, narrative effectively prohibits ambivalence, that is, 'the possibility of assigning an object or an event to more than one category' (Bauman, 1991: 1).

This morally suppressive force of narrative is extremely pronounced in current mediated discussions of the global financial crisis. The financial crisis, at least in part, is a story of the failure of existing global structures. It exposes the unsustainability of the capitalist and particularly neo-liberal narrative that 'market functioning trumps all other' (Couldry, 2010: 2), and reveals carelessness, arbitrariness and incoherence in the workings of the 'hegemonic rationality' (Couldry, 2010) of market logic. Yet these 'cracks' in the overriding story of markets as the only valid principle of human organization are reduced. The tensions that challenge the 'neatness' of the capitalist narrative, are suppressed, diffused and fall out. For example, in current media discussions of the global financial crisis, we hear and see relatively little of the consequences of economic restructuring for families and the costs that individuals incur in order to enter and stay in the market.

The dominant narrative of the market continues to be reproduced and reinforced, promoting hierarchies of success (see chapter 5): countries such as Greece are positioned at the bottom of this hierarchy, their entire societies infantilized and ridiculed, depicted as 'stupid', 'lazy ouzo-drinkers', needing to be rescued by the responsible, hard-working, mature north-European partners, embodied by the 'responsible' parental figures of Angela Merkel, Chancellor of Germany ('the mother'), and Nicolas Sarkozy, president of France ('the father').

Certainly we need narratives, and today perhaps more than ever, to cope with the constant uncertainties, fragility and lack of coherence of our 'liquid times' (Bauman, 2007). Narratives work to impose a symbolic order on the modern experience that is fraught with ambivalence and anxieties. We need narratives to help continuously to maintain and repair the reality that we have produced, 'for it consistently breaks down' (Carey, 1992: 30). At the same time, from time to time, 'with fear and regret, [we have to] toss away our authoritative representations of reality and begin to build the world anew' (Carey, 1992: 30). We need symbolic spaces to articulate the contradictions and tensions brought by modern life, and by the 'disembedding' of social relations from local contexts. We need representations that will allow us to live with ambivalence, and to accept incompleteness, lack of closure and discontinuity in the ways in which we represent and imagine the world. Ambivalence, as Giddens (1990) contends, is inherent in the experience of globalization; representations thus have a key role in articulating this experience and providing people with the tools and resources to comprehend the world and social life with ambivalence.

Media representations in the current global age often oust ambivalence from the imagination, making it 'the waste of modernity' (Bauman, 1991: 15). At the same time, the rapid transformations in the media environment, despite their many dangerous and worrying consequences, open up potential spaces for (re)admitting ambivalence into the imagination. They invite us to acknowledge and accept that, rather than fully knowing and understanding the world, ourselves and others, not knowing and not fully understanding are an inevitable feature of life today.

* * *

Some books for children include blank pages for their readers to draw their own images or write their versions of 'what happens next'. I hope that the discussion in *Media Representation and the Global Imagination* has provided some tools and provoked critical thought to enable its readers to fill a blank page with their own critical imagining of how media representation may and should look in the future; to compose their own 'recruitment ads' for media representations in the twenty-first century.

Notes

Introduction

1 The DuMont campaign was aimed at the post-war American public and has a clear cultural and historical specificity, which is not addressed here (see Tichi, 1991). However, the advert encapsulates and, to an extent, sets the terms and suggests metaphors for a wider discourse on television and globalization and, in this respect, seems useful for the Introduction to this book.

2 See Spigel (1992) and Tichi (1991) for discussions of gendered discourses on television in the US, during the war and in the post-war era.

3 For a detailed discussion of these developments, see Illouz (2007).

4 This point is inspired by Shome and Hegde's (2002: 174–5) observation that 'globalization is not a structure already set in place against which we can then place our theories and theorization'.

5 See also Chouliaraki's (2006: 8–11) discussion of the 'merit of example'.

Chapter 1 Media Representation and the Global Imagination: A Framework

1 See <http://www.advertisingarchives.co.uk/searchframe.php>, last accessed 4 May 2011.

2 The panel was hosted by Polis and took place on 26 November 2009 at the London School of Economics and Political Science, UK. Panellists included Jeremy Bowen (BBC), Alan Fisher (Al Jazeera), Sherine Tadros (Al Jazeera English) and Louise Turner (Channel 4). See <http://www.charliebeckett.org/?p=2196#more-2196>, last accessed 4 May 2011.

3 See Macdonald (2003) for a detailed discussion of ideological critique of representation and its weaknesses.

4 See also Macdonald (2003) for a similar point.

5 For example, within the vast literature on online communication of health and illness, much research focuses on the analysis of texts: patients' online journals, messages posted on online support groups, public and commercial health organizations' websites. These representations display significant similarities to 'traditional' discourses and 'old media' (e.g., press, television) representations of health and illness, as well as important divergences from them. However, this connection is hardly made: studies commonly focus on the novelty of online sites, but fail to link their analysis to previous and other media experiences and texts or broader discourses of health and illness (see Orgad, 2005).

6 Even when studies describe representations as 'hybrid', analytically they often demonstrate hybridity as an (often uneven) mix of 'global' and 'local' features.

7 Though both Silverstone (2007) and Chouliaraki (2006) propose a normative view, Silverstone's argument is based on a broad-brush theorizing of morality in the contemporary media space, whereas Chouliaraki's proposes a normative ideal on the basis of 'phronesis' – analysis of particular examples of news reports, to demonstrate their ethical orientations.

Chapter 2 Imagining Others: Representations of Natural Disasters

1 This claim is based on four theoretical debates: (1) linguistics, particularly de Saussure's theory of the dependence of meaning on the relations between different words within a meaning system; (2) theories of language (especially Bakhtin's), which stress that we need difference since we can only construct meaning through dialogue with the other; (3) anthropological arguments about marking difference as the basis of culture; and (4) Lacan's psychoanalytical observation that the infant learns to recognize itself as separate from others (see Hall, 1997, and Pickering, 2001).

2 See: <http://news.bbc.co.uk/onthisday/hi/dates/stories/december/26/ newsid_4631000/4631713.stm>, last accessed 4 May 2011.

3 See: <http://www.cbsnews.com/stories/2010/07/12/world/main6670281. shtml>; and: <http://news.bbc.co.uk/1/hi/8596080.stm>, both URLs last accessed 4 May 2011.

4 See: <http://articles.cnn.com/2005-01-03/world/un.egeland.disasters_1_tsunami-disaster-relief-efforts-egeland?_s=PM:WORLD>, last accessed 4 May 2011.

5 The King of England sent a ship to Portugal with donations (Georgi, 2005). Other countries donated money and offered other kinds of help to Lisbon (Araújo, 2006). While this aid was motivated by philanthropic reasons, it should be remembered that Portugal was an important economic centre, and political and economic interests were responsible for much of the aid provided.

6 Engravings appeared on playing cards, ballads, almanacs, folktales and other illustrated stories that circulated as broadsheets and chapbooks (Sliwinski, 2009: 27). They were widely and cheaply accessible.

7 Compilations of sermons by charismatic preachers are dismissive of the idea that the earthquake was a natural event, e.g., the *Serious Thoughts Occasioned by the Late Earthquake at Lisbon*, written by the Methodist John Wesley, first published in London in 1755 and republished several times before the end of the century (cited in Araújo, 2006: 2), and a similar series of sermons by the Italian Jesuit, Malagrida (Neiman, 2002: 249).

8 Neiman (2002) argues that what turned the Lisbon earthquake into a threat to these religious worldviews was related to the interworking of two developments in the history of rationality. First, the conviction common to the natural sciences and the Enlightenment movement that the universe as a whole is intelligible. Second, a global bourgeois demand for a social order that distributes rewards according to rational principles, that is accessible to all, and applies the same rules to the whole cosmos.

9 See: <http://news.bbc.co.uk/1/hi/world/africa/703958.stm>, last accessed 4 May 2011.

10 Band Aid's 'Do They Know It's Christmas?' and the Live Aid project have been thoroughly discussed in the literature (e.g., Benthall, 1993; Harrison and Palmer, 1986; Richey and Ponte, 2011). I do not rehearse this discussion here, but it complements the analysis in this chapter of 'We Are The World'.

11 'We Are The World' achieved amazing popularity in the west, topping the charts in the US, France, New Zealand, the Netherlands, Norway, Sweden, Switzerland, the UK, Austria and Italy. See: <http://www.ultratop.be/en/showitem.asp?interpret=USA+For+Africa&titel=We+Are+The+World&cat=s>, last accessed 4 May 2011.

12 See: <http://wearetheworldfoundation.org/the-song/>, last accessed 4 May 2011.

13 See: <http://www.darfurisdying.com/aboutgame.html>, last accessed 4 May 2011.

14 Author Reebee Garofalo criticized the 'We're saving our own lives' line, describing it as a 'distasteful element of self-indulgence' (Wikipedia, We Are The World).

15 The Haiti government claims that the money promised by international donors has not materialized. See: <http://news.bbc.co.uk/1/hi/world/americas/8596080.stm>, last accessed 4 May 2011.

16 See: <http://www.bbc.co.uk/news/10593255>; <ehttp://edition.cnn.com/2010/WORLD/americas/07/12/haiti.six.months.later/index.html#fbid=vi5lRoIOElI&wom=fals>, both URLs last accessed 4 May 2011.

17 See: <http://entertainium.org/music/%E2%80%9Cwe-are-the-world-25-for-haiti%E2%80%9D-review/>, last accessed 4 May 2011.

18 See, for example, Pareles (14 February 2010) and *Washington Post* at: <http://www.washingtonpost.com/wp-dyn/content/article/2010/02/02/AR2010020200485.html>, last accessed 4 May 2011.

19 See: <http://www.mtv.com/news/articles/1631768/20100211/story.jhtml>, last accessed 4 May 2011.

20 The director, Paul Haggis, invited a group of Haitian film students to help edit the clip. However, as Hall (1997) and others (Mbembe, 2001; Lau, 2009) observe, victims can be trapped by the stereotype and 're-orientalize' themselves.

21 See: <http://specialagentdalecooper.wordpress.com/2010/02/15/we-are-the-world-25-for-haiti-an-analysis-as-long-as-that-crappy-title-and-the-actual-crappy-song-too/>, last accessed 4 May 2011.

22 Narine (2010) makes a related claim about contemporary films, in which privileged westerners depicted by 'humanitarian celebrities' confront suffering others. These protagonists, he argues, routinely opt to privatize their affective and political responses: they act alone, even as vigilantes, despite their connections.

23 See: <http://www.guardian.co.uk/world/2010/sep/07/pakistan-floods-reza-khan-appeal>, last accessed 4 May 2011.

Chapter 3 Imagining Ourselves: Representations of the Nation

1 However, some critics accuse the show of conserving and reinforcing rather than undermining stereotypical views, e.g., of women, elderly people and immigrants.

2 In their dailiness and use of strategies, such as casual modes of address by television presenters approaching the audience at home, the media establish themselves as 'friends', companions in our daily lives (see also Silverstone, 2007, and Frosh, 2011b, on the companionship of the media).

3 Based on Scannell's (1996) discussion of care structures discussed earlier.

4 TV 5 is a joint venture of Francophone public broadcasters from Europe and Quebec.

5 Juppé was a Member of Parliament from 1995 to 1997. In 2004, he was suspended from politics for a year after a conviction for mishandling public funds.

6 Based on Cohen's (2001: 111) discussion of contextualization and uniqueness as a strategy used in official denial of governments.

7 See, e.g., Blog TV, 6 November 2005; Un Blog de bretagne, 6 November 2005.

8 Some (e.g., Jarvis, 14 November 2005; Schwarz, 9 November 2005) argue that this wave of violence in France triggered the proliferation of blogs by young people from the *banlieues*.

9 See: <http://bouna93.skyblog.com>, last accessed 4 May 2011.

10 See, e.g.: <http://atouteslesvictimes.samizdat.net/?m=200511>, last accessed 4 May 2011.

11 See, e.g.: <http://www.youtube.com/watch?v=3syuyp3Va90>; and <http://news.bbc.co.uk/1/hi/world/europe/4469484.stm>, both URLs last accessed 4 May 2011. Discussions of French rap and hip-hop also made their way to CNN and the *Washington Post* (see also Russell, 2007).

12 As a result of such postings, three French teenagers involved in the riots were arrested on suspicion of inciting violence primarily through blogs, resulting in the 'hardcore' and 'Sarkodead' blogs being suspended (Plunkett, 9 November 2005), although some bloggers who had their blogs removed started new ones (Schwarz, 9 November 2005).

13 'The French Democracy', at: <http://www.youtube.com/watch?v=stu31sz5ivk>, last accessed 4 May 2011.

Chapter 4 Imagining Possible Lives: Representations of Migration

1 For example, accounts produced to deter people from migrating, referring to migration as an experience imagined in the future, versus accounts produced by migrants, describing the act of migrating in the past and the experience of being a migrant in the present.

2 See also the Australian Government's Department of Immigration and Citizenship's website, at: <http://www.immi.gov.au/media/success_stories/>, last accessed 4 May 2011.

3 See: <http://www.unhcr.org/pages/49c3646c74.html>.

4 In the US and some other countries 'alien' is used in the political arena by both sides, to mean migrant, a term which sometimes has pejorative connotations.

5 See, e.g.: <http://www.ynet.co.il/articles/0,7340,L-3387795,00.html>; <http://www.ynet.co.il/articles/0,7340,L-3405989,00.html>, both URLs last accessed 4 May 2011.

6 See: <http://www.chinadaily.com.cn/china/2010-06/27/content_10024861.htm>, last accessed 4 May 2011.

7 See: <http://www.cctv.com/english/special/springfestival2008/20080209/100929.shtml>, last accessed 4 May 2011.

8 See 'Driver's Licenses for Illegal Immigrants' at: <http://www.youtube.com/watch?v=rbyocX-9_mo&feature=player_embedded>, last accessed 4 May 2011.

9 Barrett (10 August 2008).

10 Coalition Against Illegal Immigration (CAII) (2007a).

11 See: <http://www.icedgame.com/> and <http://www.icedgame.com/assets/learn/ICED_Curriculum.pdf>, both URLs last accessed 4 May 2011.

12 Coalition Against Illegal Immigration (CAII) (2007b).

13 See: <http://www.ctv.ca/CTVNews/WFive/20051119/w5_broken_promises_051119/>, last accessed 4 May 2011.

14 Cited in Trotter (21 November 2005).

15 See: <http://annares.wordpress.com/2009/06/05/who-is-notcanada-com/>, last accessed 4 May 2011.

16 See Silverstone's (2007) argument about the blurring of factual and fictional in the realm of American political discourse, in his discussion of the rhetoric of evil.

17 The entries were collected by investigative journalist James Ridgeway (2005) and published in English, as *Baghdad Burning: Girl Blog From Iraq*. The book has been translated and published in numerous countries and languages, has won several awards, and was dramatized on BBC Radio 4.

18 See: <http://www.unhcr.org/cgi-bin/texis/vtx/search?page=search&docid=4a323b686&query=iraqi%20refugees>, last accessed 4 May 2011.

19 This term appeared in a report written by WWF and Oxfam, discussing approaches to tackling climate change. See: <http://www.oxfam.org.uk/resources/policy/climate_change/downloads/common-cause-cultural-values-090910-en.pdf>, last accessed 4 May 2011.

Chapter 5 Imagining the World: Representations of New Year Celebrations

1 Dayan and Katz (1992) identify three basic scripts of media events: contest (e.g., the Olympic Games), conquest (e.g., the first man on the moon) and coronations.

2 This sentiment emerges in other news reports. For example, a 2008 Sky News reporter, at the one minute to midnight mark, says: 'This year, more than any other, the "battle of the bang" is on,' concluding later that 'the place to be is clear . . . no one did it better than Britain'. In Sky's 2009 report, economic prowess again is linked to the celebrations, with the size of the London display discussed in the context of the global recession, imputed to demonstrate London's and the UK's resilience.

3 See: <http://www.youtube.com/watch?v=RKRLBtAtbc8>, last accessed 4 May 2011.

4 See 'CCTV New Year Gala' at: <http://www.cctv.com/english/special/09nygala/english/index.shtml>, last accessed 4 May 2011.

5 There is an emphasis on grandeur and spectacle also in the gala on CCTV International at Christian New Year. Although imbued with idealistic sentiments that depart from the blatant sense of competition and comparison fostered in western international coverage, the CCTV gala employs (and is limited by) many of the traditional western New Year rituals, such as fireworks displays. The theme of global inter-competitiveness, although not explicit, is implicitly practised. In the 2010 gala, for instance, a song entitled 'America, America' is performed by a Chinese artist and glorifies America's vast landscape, but includes implicit references to the differences between the two nations, and the unavoidable competition that these differences produce. See: <http://english.cntv.cn/english/special/09nygala/english/index.shtml>, last accessed 4 May 2011.

6 Ali (2 January 2009).

7 The sheer proliferation of sources producing and disseminating representations does not mean necessarily that the range of meanings generated is diverse and inclusive. Whether the quantitative proliferation of representations in the contemporary mediated space corresponds to, and translates into, qualitative diversity of meanings is a big and important question, which I return to in chapter 7.

Chapter 6 Imagining the Self

1 See: <http://chattheplanet.com/index.php?page=about&cat=83>, last accessed 4 May 2011.

2 See: <http://chattheplanet.com/index.php?page=videos&v=38>, last accessed 4 May 2011.

3 See: <http://www.bbc.co.uk/news/world-middle-east-10997011>, last accessed 4 May 2011.

4 See: <http://www.bbc.co.uk/news/world-middle-east-10997011>, last accessed 4 May 2011.

5 For example, a posting responding to Barak's blog: 'Your post threw me back to the days I was in [the Palestinian refugee camp] Balata when I arrested an Arab in the age of my dad and I shouted at him like an idiot and checked his testacles to see he is not hiding a knife. Till now I feel like vomiting' (at: <http://omerbarak.com/?p=83>, last accessed 4 May 2011).

6 For example, a comment posted on the Hebrew website, *Sachim*, which describes itself as a space for the 'typical politically correct and lacking self-awareness Israeli', and geared towards 'the mainstream, the common, the average':

> The prisoners are sitting comfortable in the shade . . . they are not being tortured or even threatened with guns at their heads and knives at their throats. They do not seem to be beaten up. They are blindfolded because they always blindfold prisoners there, because they tend to escape all the time, forcing the IDF to shoot them, because that's what they want, to be Martyrs . . .
> The blindfolds are even the kind of fabric Yasser Arafat used to wear on his head. They are not blindfolded with bikinis or anything demeaning, rather the contrary . . .
> So what are they complaining about? A girl smiling? Yes I suppose so. Girl smiling must be the greatest insult for them. (<http://sachim.tumblr.com/post/961910853>, last accessed 4 May 2011).

7 Contest entries were limited to stories published or broadcast for the first time during the 2008 calendar year. See: <http://www.ewa.org/site/PageServer?pagename=contest_pastwinners>, last accessed 4 May 2011.

8 See: <http://littlebillclinton.csmonitor.com/littlebillclinton/about/>, last accessed 4 May 2011.

9 Wiltenburg (2009a).

10 Ibid.

11 See also Boltanski (1999) for a related discussion of the paradox of singularity and generalization in the representation of suffering.

12 Wiltenburg (2009b).

13 For example, the UK *Daily Mail* describes a Japanese-developed 3-D TV system that allows users to touch and feel the images that pop out from the screen; see: <http://www.dailymail.co.uk/sciencetech/article-1306700/The-world-fingertips-3DTV-touch-floating-images.html>, last accessed 4 May 2011.

14 For example, the marketing manager of the Internet company AfriConnect described the introduction of the Internet as: 'the world has never been closer to Namwala'. See: <http://www.namwala.com/news/the_world_has_never_been_closer_to_100007.htm>, last accessed 4 May 2011.

15 Originally a Pan American Airways slogan and adopted by several musicians, including Ian Brown and Motörhead, as an album title.

16 My discussion of the self's immersion in the world and its implications is brief; in-depth study of these virtual spaces and users' engagement is needed for a complete understanding of this issue. Here, I highlight just two dialectical aspects that seem particularly pertinent in this context.

17 See: <http://secondlife.com/destination/pasithea-medieval-fantasy-roleplay>, last accessed 4 May 2011.

Chapter 7 Conclusion: Nothing Gets You Closer Revisited
1 See chapter 4, n.19.
2 Examples of 'too far' would include nightmare scripts depicting migrants (see chapter 4) as 'beyond the pale of humanity' (Silverstone, 2007: 48), the invisibility and lack of voice of people of the *banlieues* in the French media (chapter 3), and the images of Palestinian prisoners posted online (chapter 6). To exemplify 'neither close nor far', Silverstone (2007) cites the 'contemporary cult of the celebrity', which simultaneously destroys difference by making the ordinary exceptional, and naturalizes it by making the exceptional ordinary, thus denying the legitimacy of difference. The example of Shakira discussed in chapter 4 is illustrative of the latter.
3 See: <http://chattheplanet.com/index.php?page=videos>, last accessed 4 May 2011.

Bibliography

Aksoy, A., and Robins, K. (2000). Thinking across spaces: Transnational television from Turkey. *European Journal of Cultural Studies*, 3(3): 343–65.

Aksoy, A., and Robins, K. (2002). Banal transnationalism: The difference that television makes. Working paper WPTC-02-08. Retrieved 4 May 2011, from: <http://www.transcomm.ox.ac.uk/working%20papers/WPTC-02-08%20 Robins.pdf>.

Al-Achi, D. (2009). Iraqi refugees release captivating album online. *UNHCR.* Retrieved 4 May 2011, from: <http://www.unhcr.org/cgi-bin/texis/vtx/ search?page =search&docid=4a323b686&query= iraqi%20refugees>.

Ali, M. (2 January 2009). Gaza diary: Welcoming the New Year. *Al Jazeera English.* Retrieved 4 May 2011, from: <http:// english.aljazeera.net/focus/2008/12/2008 123092151692386. html>.

Altheide, D. L. (2007). The mass media and terrorism. *Discourse & Communication,* 1(3): 287–308.

Andén-Papadopoulos, K. (2009). Body horror on the Internet: US soldiers recording the war in Iraq and Afghanistan. *Media, Culture & Society,* 31(6): 921–38.

Anderson, B. (1983). *Imagined Community*. London: Verso.

Appadurai, A. (1996). *Modernity at Large: Cultural Dimensions of Globalization.* Minneapolis, MN: University of Minnesota Press.

Appadurai, A. (2000). Grassroots globalization and the research imagination. *Public Culture,* 12: 1–19.

Araújo, A. C. (2006). The Lisbon earthquake of 1755: Public distress and political propaganda. *e-JPH,* 4(1): 1–11.

Arendt, H. (1977). *Between Past and Future: Eight Exercises in Political Thought.* New York and Harmondsworth: Penguin.

Auffray, A. (8 February 2007). Sarkozy peine à voir les cités de l'intérieur. *Libération,* pp. 2–3.

Baker, P., and McEnery, T. (2005). A corpus-based approach to discourses of refugees and asylum seekers in UN and newspaper texts. *Journal of Language and Politics,* 4(2): 197–226.

Baker, P., and McEnery, T. (2007). Using collocation analysis to reveal the construction of minority groups: The case of refugees, asylum seekers and immigrants in the UK press. *Lancaster EPrints.* Retrieved 4 May 2011, from: <http:// eprints.lancs.ac.uk/602/>.

Bardzell, S., and Odom, W. (2008). The experience of embodied space in virtual worlds: An ethnography of a Second Life community. *Space and Culture,* 11(3): 239–59.

Barrett, J. E. (10 August 2008). Illegal immigration commercial I was in. Retrieved 4 May 2011, from: <http://www.myspace.com/video/vid/40467299#ixzz148rXy6n5>.

Barthes, R. (1977). *Image, Music, Text.* London: Fontana.

Baudrillard, J. (1995). *The Gulf War Did Not Take Place.* Bloomington, IN: Indiana University Press.

Bauman, Z. (1991). *Modernity and Ambivalence.* Cambridge: Polity.

Bauman, Z. (1998). *Globalization.* Cambridge: Polity.

Bauman, Z. (2000). *Liquid Modernity.* Cambridge: Polity.

Bauman, Z. (2007). *Liquid Times: Living in an Age of Uncertainty.* Cambridge: Polity.

Bauman, Z. (2010). *44 Letters from the Liquid Modern World.* Cambridge: Polity.

BBC News. (2004). Thousands die in Asian tsunami. Retrieved 4 May 2011, from: <http://news.bbc.co.uk/onthisday/hi/dates/stories/december/26/newsid_4631000/4631713.stm>.

BBC News. (30 October 2005). In pictures: Paris riot suburb residents. Retrieved 4 May 2011, from: <http:// news.bbc.co.uk/1/shared/spl/hi/picture_gallery/05/europe_paris_riot_suburb_residents/html/1.stm>.

BBC News. (2007). France launches world TV channel. Retrieved 4 May 2011, from: <http://news.bbc.co.uk/1/hi/world/europe/6215170.stm>.

BBC News. (2010a). UN Haiti donor pledges surpass targets at almost $10bn. Retrieved 4 May 2011, from: <http://news.bbc.co.uk/1/hi/8596080.stm>.

BBC News. (2010b). Israeli woman soldier denies Facebook photos wrong-doing. Retrieved 4 May 2011, from: <http://.bbc.co.uk/news/world-middle-east-10997011>.

Beck, U. (2003). Rooted cosmopolitanism: Emerging from a rivalry of distinctions. In U. Beck, N. Sznaider and R. Winter (eds), *Global America: The Cultural Consequences of Globalization* (pp. 15–29). Liverpool: Liverpool University Press.

Beck, U. (2006). *The Cosmopolitan Vision.* Cambridge: Polity.

Bennhold, K. (30 March 2006). French find the villain in protests: The media. *The International Herald Tribune,* p. 3.

Benthall, J. (1993). *Disasters, Relief and the Media.* London: I.B. Tauris.

Berg, C. R. (2002). *Latino Images in Films.* Austin, TX: University of Texas Press.

Billboard. (19 August 1944). You'll Be An Armchair Columbus. Billboard, p. 9.

Billig, M. (1995). *Banal Nationalism.* London: Sage.

Bin, Z. (1998). Popular family television and party ideology: The Spring Festival Eve happy gathering. *Media, Culture & Society,* 20(1): 43–58.

Blog TV. (6 November 2005). Violences urbaines et banlieues sensibles: le grand déballage médiatique. *Blog TV.* Retrieved 4 May 2011, from: <http://www.vip-blog.com/vip/articles/1095112.html>.

Boltanski, L. (1999). *Distant Suffering: Morality, Media and Politics.* Cambridge: Cambridge University Press.

Book, B. (2003). Travelling through cyberspace: Tourism and photography in virtual worlds. *Paper presented at the Still Visions – Changing Lives: International*

Conference on Tourism and Photography, Sheffield Hallam University, Sheffield. Retrieved 4 May 2011, from: <http://papers.ssrn.com/sol3/papers.cfm?abstract_id=538182>.

Bourdais, S. (2004). Télévison: Black blanc beur. *Télérama*.

Bourdieu, P. (2005). The political field, the social science field and the journalistic field. In R. Benson, E. Neveu (eds), *Bourdieu and the Journalistic Field* (pp. 29–47). Cambridge: Polity.

Bradley, S. (2007). Advert aims to deter African immigrants. *Swiss Info*. Retrieved 4 May 2011, from: <http://www.swissinfo.ch/eng/index/Advert_aims_to_deter_African_immigrants.html?cid=6287120>.

Bradshaw, P. (13 December 2002). Dirty Pretty Things. *Guardian*. Retrieved 4 May 2011, from: <http://www.guardian.co.uk/culture/2002/dec/13/artsfeatures.dirtyprettythings >.

Braun, T. E. D., and Radner, J. B. (2005). *The Lisbon Earthquake of 1755: Representations and Reactions*. Oxford: SVEC – Studies on Voltaire and the Eighteenth Century.

Brook, S. (28 February 2006). BBC accused by gay rights group. *Guardian*. Retrieved 4 May 2011, from: <http://www.guardian.co.uk/media/2006/feb/28/bbc.broadcasting>.

Brosius, H. B., and Eps, P. (1995). Prototyping through key events: News selection in the case of violence against aliens and asylum seekers in Germany. *European Journal of Communication*, 10: 391–412.

Buchanan, S., Grillo, B., and Threadgold, T. (2003). What's the story? Results from a research into the media coverage of refugees and asylum seekers in the UK. London: Article 19. Retrieved 4 May 2011, from: <http://www.article19.org/data/files/pdfs/publications/refugees-what-s-the-story-.pdf>.

Calhoun, C. (2007). *Nations Matter: Citizenship, Solidarity and the Cosmopolitan Dream* (E-book). Abingdon: Routledge.

Calhoun, C. (2008). The idea of emergency: Humanitarian action and global (dis)order. In D. Fassin (ed.), *States of Emergency* (pp. 18–39). Cambridge, MA: Zone Books.

Campani, G. (2001). Migrants and media: The Italian case. In R. King and N. Wood (eds), *Media and Migration* (pp. 38–52). London: Routledge.

Carey, J. W. (1992). *Communication as Culture: Essays on Media and Society*. New York: Routledge.

Castells, M. (2001). *The Internet Galaxy: Reflections on the Internet, Business, and Society*. Oxford: Oxford University Press.

Castells, M. (2009). *Communication Power*. Oxford: Oxford University Press.

Castoriadis, C. (1987 [1975]). *The Imaginary Institution of Society*. Cambridge: Polity.

CCTV International. (2008). Song for the rural migrant workers. Retrieved 4 May 2011, from: <http://www.cctv.com/english/special/springfestival2008/20080209/100929.shtml>.

Cepeda, M. E. (2003). Shakira as the idealized, transnational citizen: A case study of Colombianidad in transition. *Latino Studies*, 1(2): 211–32.

Cesselesse, C. (11 July 2010). Haiti recovery bogged down 6 months after quake. *CBS News*. Retrieved 4 May 2011, from: <http://www.cbsnews.com/stories/2010/07/12/world/main6670281.shtml>.

Chang, L. T. (2008). *Factory Girls: From Village to City in a Changing China*. New York: Spiegel & Grau.

Children Now. (2009). Media impacts children's self-image and how they see others. Retrieved 4 May 2011, from: <http://www.childrennow.org/index.php/learn/media_messages_about_race_class_gender/>.

China Daily. (16 December 2005). French riots film proves popular. *China Daily*.

China Daily. (2010). China's 'floating population' exceeds 210m. *China Daily*. Retrieved 4 May 2011, from: <http://www.chinadaily.com.cn/china/2010-06/27/content_10024861.htm>.

Chouliaraki, L. (2006). *The Spectatorship of Suffering*. London: Sage.

Chouliaraki, L. (2008). Media as moral education: Mediation and action. *Media, Culture & Society*, 30(6): 831–52.

Chouliaraki, L. (2010). Post-humanitarianism: Humanitarian communication beyond a politics of pity. *International Journal of Cultural Studies*, 13(2): 107–26.

Chouliaraki, L. (2012). *The Ironic Spectator: Solidarity in the Age of Post-Humanitarianism*. Cambridge: Polity.

Chouliaraki, L. and Orgad, S. (eds), (2011). Proper distance: Mediation, ethics, otherness. *International Journal of Cultural Studies*, 14(4): 341–5.

Christian Science Monitor. (n.d.). About this project. Retrieved 4 May 2011, from: <http://littlebillclinton.csmonitor.com/littlebillclinton/about/>.

CNN Insight. (5 November 2005). Riots in France. Retrieved 4 May 2011, from: <http://transcripts.cnn.com/TRANSCRIPTS/0511/07/i_ins.01.html>.

CNN. (29 November 2005). De Villepin interview: Full text. Retrieved 4 May 2011, from: <http://www.edition.cnn.com/2005/WORLD/europe/11/29/dev-illepin.text/index.hml>.

CNN World. (10 March 2011). World must 'wake up to disasters'. *CNN World*. Retrieved 4 May 2011, from: <http://articles.cnn.com/2005-01-03/world/ un. egeland.disasters_1_tsunami-disaster-relief-efforts-egeland?_s = PM:WORLD>.

Coalition Against Illegal Immigration (CAII). (2007a). About the coalition against illegal immigration. *CAII*. Retrieved 4 May 2011, from: <http://www.uncooperativeblogger.wordpress.com/about/>.

Coalition Against Illegal Immigration (CAII). (2007b). ICE'd the video game. *CAII*. Retrieved 4 May 2011, from: <http://www.uncooperativeblogger.word-press.com/2007/07/11/iced-the-video-game/>.

Cohen, A. (1985). *The Symbolic Construction of Community*. Chichester and London: Ellis Harwood and Tavistock.

Cohen, S. (1996). Crime and politics: Spot the difference. *The British Journal of Sociology*, 47(1): 1–21.

Cohen, S. (2001). *States of Denial: Knowing about Atrocities and Suffering*. Cambridge: Polity.

Cole, R. (1 January 2011). Revellers round the world welcome in 2011. *Sky News*. Retrieved 4 May 2011, from: <http://news.sky.com/skynews/ Home/World-News/Fireworks-in-Sydney-Taipei-Dubai-And-London-As-World-Welcomes-In-2011/Article/201101115875784>.

Cooper, D. (2010). 'We Are The World 25 For Haiti': An analysis as long as that crappy title and the actual crappy song, too. *Special Agent Dale Cooper*. Retrieved 4 May 2011, from: <http://specialagentdalecooper.wordpress.com/2010/02/15/ we - are - the - world - 25 - for - haiti - an - analysis - as - long - as - that - crappy - title-and-the-actual-crappy-song-too/>.

Corner, J. (2000). Influence: The contested core of media research. In J. Curran and M. Gurevitch (eds), *Mass Media and Society*, 3rd edn (pp. 376–97). London: Arnold.

Cottle, S. (2006). *Mediatized Conflict*. Maidenhead: Open University Press.

Couldry, N. (2003). *Media Rituals: A Critical Approach*. London: Routledge.

Couldry, N. (2010). *Why Voice Matters: Culture and Politics after Neoliberalism*. London: Sage.

Couldry, N., Hepp, A., and Krotz, F. (2010). *Media Events in a Global Age*. London: Routledge.

Curran, J., and Park, M. J. (2000). *De-Westernizing Media Studies*. London: Routledge.

Dajani, J. (11 November 2005). In France's dark hour, Palestinian media stand by their longtime ally. *New America Media*. Retrieved 4 May 2011, from: <http:// news.newamericamedia.org/news/view_article.html?article_id=f9c5a25d3c758 d5871a956076602017d>.

Davila, A. (2001). *Latinos, Inc.: The Marketing and Making of a People*. Berkeley, CA: University of California Press.

Dayan, D. (2007). On morality, distance and the other: Roger Silverstone's *Media and Morality*. *International Journal of Communication*, 1: 113–22.

Dayan, D., and Katz, E. (1992). *Media Events: The Broadcasting of History*. Harvard, MA: Harvard University Press.

de Beer, P. (14 November 2005). The message in France's explosion. *Open Democracy*. Retrieved 4 May 2011, from: <http://www.opendemocracy.net/ globalization-institutions_government/banlieues_3021.jsp>.

Debord, G. (1994). *The Society of the Spectacle*. New York: Zone Books.

Derrida, J. (1972). *Positions*. Chicago, IL: University of Chicago Press.

D'Haen, T. (2006). On how not to be Lisbon if you want to be modern – Dutch reactions to the Lisbon earthquake. *European Review*, 14(3): 351–8.

Dickey, C. (21 November 2005). Europe's time bomb: Will unrest spread? *Newsweek,* 21.

Ditzian, E. (2010). 'We Are The World' director Paul Haggis recalls video-shoot 'chaos'. *MTV*. Retrieved 4 May 2011, from: <http://www.mtv.com/news/arti-cles/1631768/we-world-director-paul-haggis-recalls-videoshoot-chaos.jhtml>.

Dogra, N. (2006). 'Reading NGOs visually' – Implications of visual images for NGO management. *Journal of International Development*, 19(2): 161–71.

Dogra, N. (2012). *Representations of Global Poverty: Aid, Development and International NGOs*. London: I.B. Tauris.

Dorfman, A., and Mattelart, A. (1975). *How to Read Donald Duck: Imperialist Ideology in the Disney Comic*. New York: International General Editions.

Doyle, M. (10 March 2011). Quake-stricken Haiti bears scars six months on. *BBC News*. Retrieved 4 May 2011, from: <http://www.bbc.co.uk/news/10593255>.

Dyer, R. (1977). *Gays and Film*. London: British Film Institute.

Dyer, R. (1986). *Heavenly Bodies: Film Stars and Society*. Basingstoke: Macmillan.

Economist. (30 November 2006). Everybody wants one now. Retrieved 4 May 2011, from: <http://www.economist.com/node/8356337>.

Elias, N., and Lemish, D. (2009). Spinning the web of identity: The roles of the Internet in the lives of immigrant adolescents. *New Media & Society*, 11(4): 533–51.

Entman, R. M. (1993). Framing: Toward clarification of a fractured paradigm. *Journal of Communication*, 43(4): 51–8.

Espejo Cala, C. (2005). Spanish news pamphlets on the 1755 earthquake: Trade strategies of the printers of Seville. In T. E. D. Braun and J. B. Radner (eds), *The Lisbon Earthquake of 1755. Representations and Reactions* (pp. 66–80). Oxford: SVEC – Studies on Voltaire and the Eighteenth Century.

European Broadcasting Union. (8–9 June 2006). *Cultural Diversity*, Report from the 2006 Plenary Assembly of the Human Resources Managers Group. Retrieved 4 May 2011, from: <http://www.ebu.ch/en/union/under_banners/HR_plenary_assembly_2006_day2.php>.

Feagin, S., and Maynard, P. (1997). *Aesthetics*. Oxford: Oxford University Press.

Fiske, J. (1987). *Television Culture*. London: Routledge.

Fix, M., Papademetriou, D. G., Batalova, J., Terrazas, A., Lin, S. Y.-Y., and Mittelstadt, M. (2009). *Migration and the Global Recession*, Migration Policy Institute. A report commissioned by the BBC World Service. Retrieved 4 May 2011, from: <http://news.bbc.co.uk/1/shared/bsp/hi/pdfs/08_09_09_migration.pdf>.

Flew, T. (2007). *Understanding Global Media*. Basingstoke and New York: Palgrave Macmillan.

Forgacs, D. (2001). African immigration on film: *Pummaro'* and the limits of vicarious representation. In R. King and H. Wood (eds), *Media and Migration: Constructions of Mobility and Difference* (pp. 83–94). London: Routledge.

Foucault, M. (1980). *Power-knowledge: Selected Interviews and Other Writings, 1972–1977*. Brighton: Harvester Press.

Foucault, M. (1981). *The History of Sexuality, Vol. 1*. Harmondsworth: Penguin.

Friedman, T. (1999). *The Lexus and the Olive Tree*. New York: Farrar, Straus & Giroux.

Friedman, T. (2005). *The World is Flat: A Brief History of the Twenty-First Century*. New York: Farrar, Straus & Giroux.

Froidevaux, G. (1989). *Représentation et Modernité*. Paris: Corti.

Frosh, P. (2011a). Framing pictures, picturing frames: Visual metaphors in political communications research. *Journal of Communication Inquiry*, 35(2): 91–114

Frosh, P. (2011b). Phatic morality: Television and proper distance. *International Journal of Cultural Studies*, 14(4): 383–400.

Frosh, P. (forthcoming). *The Poetics of Media: Imagination and Communication*. Cambridge: Polity.

Frosh, P., and Wolfsfeld, G. (2007). ImagiNation: News discourse, nationhood and civil society. *Media, Culture & Society*, 29(1): 105–29.

Furedi, F. (2005). *Politics of Fear*. London: Continuum.

Gale, P. (2004). The refugee crisis and fear: Populist politics and media discourse. *Journal of Sociology*, 40(4): 321–40.

Gale, T. (2009). Urban beaches, virtual worlds and 'the end of tourism'. *Mobilities*, 4(1): 119–38.

Ganley, E. (12 November 2005). French media using less rioting footage. *Editor & Publisher*. Retrieved 10 March, 2012, from: <http://www.editorandpublisher. com/PrintArticle/French-Media-Using-Less-Rioting-Footage>.

Gaonkar, D. P. (2002). Toward new imaginaries: An introduction. *Public Culture*, 14(1): 1–19.

Georgi, M. (2005). The Lisbon earthquake and scientific knowledge in the British public sphere. In T. E. D. Braun and J. B. Radner (eds), *The Lisbon Earthquake of 1755. Representations and Reactions* (pp. 81–96). Oxford: SVEC – Studies on Voltaire and the Eighteenth Century.

Ghazi, J. (9 November 2005). French unrest – Arab media report riot manifesto, recall Algerian revolution. *New America Media*. Retrieved 4 March, 2011, from: <http://news.newamericamedia.org/news/view_article.html?article_id=138a8f4 4f3f7ae44f0a9a99d7204987>.

Giddens, A. (1990). *The Consequences of Modernity*. Cambridge: Polity.

Gilbert, G., and Bauder, H. (2005). Representations of labor migration in Guatemalan and American media. Retrieved 4 May 2011, from: <http://www. geography.ryerson.ca/hbauder/Immigrant%20Labour/latinAmericanMigration. pdf>.

Gill, R. (2007). *Gender and the Media*. Cambridge: Polity.

Gillespie, M., and Toynbee, J. (eds). (2006). *Analysing Media Texts*. Berkshire: Open University Press.

Gilroy, P. (2004). *After Empire: Melancholia or Convivial Culture*. London: Routledge.

Giroux, H. A. (2001). *The Mouse that Roared: Disney and the End of Innocence*. Lanham, MD: Rowman & Littlefield.

Gordon, C. (1980). *Power-Knowledge: Selected Interviews and Other Writings, 1972–1977*. Brighton: Harvester Press.

Gordon, E. (2008). The geography of virtual worlds: An introduction. *Space and Culture*, 11(3): 200–3.

Green, A. (23 December 2005). Why we'll never win the war on terror. *Daily Mail*. Retrieved 4 May 2011, from: <http://www.migrationwatchuk.org/pressArticle/38>.

Hall, S. (1997). *Representation: Cultural Representations and Signifying Practices*. London: Sage.

Hallin, D. C. (1986). *The Uncensored War: The Media and Vietnam*. Oxford: Oxford University Press.

Harding, J. (2006). Color blind. *Columbia Journalism Review*, July/Aug.

Hargreaves, A. G. (2001). Media effects and ethnic relations in Britain and France In R. King and H. Wood (eds), *Media and Migration: Constructions of Mobility and Difference* (pp. 23–37). London: Routledge.

Hargreaves, A. G., and Mahdjoub, D. (1997). Satellite television viewing among ethnic minorities in France. *European Journal of Communication*, 12(4): 459–77.

Hargreaves, A., and Perotti, A. (1993). The representation of French television of immigrants and ethnic minorities. *New Community*, 19(2): 251–61.

Harrison, P., and Palmer, R. (1986). *News Out of Africa: Biafra to Band Aid*. London: Shipman.

Harvey, D. (2001). *Spaces of Capital: Towards a Critical Geography*. Edinburgh: Edinburgh University Press.

Held, D. (1980). *Introduction to Critical Theory: Horkheimer to Habermas*. Cambridge: Polity.

Herman, E. S., and McChesney, R. W. (2001). *The Global Media: The New Missioners of Corporate Capitalism*. London: Continuum.

Hiller, H. H. (2004). New ties, old ties and lost ties: The use of the Internet in diaspora. *New Media & Society*, 6(6): 731–52.

Höijer, B. (2004). The discourse of global compassion: The audience and media reporting of human suffering. *Media, Culture & Society*, 26(4) : 513–31.

Hubert-Rodier, J. (25 November 2005). Intégration: l'image ternie d'un mythe français. *Les Echos*, p. 30.

Ignatieff, M. (1998). *The Warrior's Honor: Ethnic War and the Modern Conscience*. New York: Metropolitan Books.

Illouz, E. (2003a). *Oprah Winfrey and the Glamour of Misery: An Essay on Popular Culture*. New York: Columbia University Press.

Illouz, E. (2003b). From the Lisbon disaster to Oprah Winfrey: Suffering as identity in the era of globalization. In U. Beck, N. Sznaider and R. Winter (eds), *Global America: The Cultural Consequences of Globalization* (pp. 189–205). Liverpool: Liverpool University Press.

Illouz, E. (2007). *Cold Intimacies: The Making of Emotional Capitalism*. Cambridge: Polity.

Illouz, E. (2009). Emotions, consumption, imagination: A new research agenda. *Journal of Consumer Culture*, 9(3): 377–413.

Jarvis, J. (14 November 2005). Media: Chaos spreads from the web to the streets: The French riots have exposed how little we can control new media, as both sides of the conflict use the web for their own ends. *Guardian*, p. 3.

Jenkins, H. (1998). Complete freedom of movement: Video games as gendered play space. In J. Cassell and H. Jenkins (eds), *From Barbie to Mortal Kombat: Gender and Computer Games* (pp. 262–97). Cambridge, MA: MIT Press.

Jenkins, H. (2005). Computer and narrative. In D. Herman, M. Jahn and M.-L. Ryan (eds), *Routledge Encyclopedia of Narrative Theory* (pp. 80–2). London: Routledge.

Johnson, J. K. (2008). *American Advertising in Poland: A Study of Cultural Interactions Since 1990*. Jefferson, NC: McFarland.

Kant, I. (1983). *Perpetual Peace and Other Essays*. Indianapolis, IN: Hackett.

Karanfil, G. (2007). Satellite television and its discontents: Reflections on the experiences of Turkish-Australian lives. *Continuum*, 21(1): 59–69.

Kaye, R. (2001). 'Blaming the victim': An analysis of press representation of refugees and asylum-seekers in the United Kingdom in the 1990s. In R. King and N. Wood (eds), *Media and Migration: Constructions of Mobility and Difference* (pp. 53–70). London: Routledge.

Ki-moon, B. (10 July 2007). We should welcome the dawn of the migration age. *Guardian*. Retrieved 4 May 2011, from: <http://www.guardian.co.uk/commentisfree/2007/jul/10/comment.globalisation?INTCMP=SRCH>.

King, R., and Wood, N. (2001). *Media and Migration: Constructions of Mobility and Difference*. London: Routledge.

Kristof, N. D. (23 February 2005). The secret genocide archive. *The New York Times*. Retrieved 4 May 2011, from: <http://www.nytimes.com/2005/02/23/opinion/23kristof.html?_r=1>.

Kuipers, G. (2002). Media culture and Internet disaster jokes: Bin Laden and the attack on the World Trade Center. *European Journal of Cultural Studies*, 5(4): 450–70.

Lacey, N. (2009). *Image and Representation: Key Concepts in Media Studies*, 2nd edn. Basingstoke: Macmillan.

Laing, R. D. (1990 [1967]). *The Politics of Experience and the Bird of Paradise*. London: Penguin.

Lamagna, M. (13 February 2010). 'We Are the World: 25 for Haiti' review. *Entertainium*. Retrieved 4 May 2011, from: <http://entertainium.org/music/%E2%80%9Cwe-are-the-world-25-for-haiti%E2%80%9D-review/>.

Lammes, S. (2008). Spatial regimes of the digital playground: Cultural functions of spatial practices in computer games. *Space and Culture*, 11(3): 260–72.

Langmia, K. (2008). *The Internet and the Construction of the Immigrant Public Sphere*. Lanham, MD: University Press of America.

Latham, K. (2009). Media, the Olympics and the search for the 'Real China'. *The China Quarterly*, 197: 25–43.

Lau, L. (2009). Re-Orientalism: The perpetration and development of Orientalism by Orientals. *Modern Asian Studies*, 43(2): 571–90.

LCI. (8 November 2005). Les appels au calme restent sans effet. Retrieved 4 May 2011, from: <http://tf1.lci.fr/infos/france/2005/0,,3261201,00-appels-calme-restent-sanseffet.html>.

Lee, C.-C., Man Chan, J., Pan, Z., and So, C. Y. K. (2000). National prisms of a 'global media event'. In J. Curran and M. Gurevitch (eds), *Mass Media and Society*, 3rd edn. (pp. 295–309). London: Arnold.

Leser, E. (15 November 2005). Banlieues: les médias américains sans complaisance; Télévisions et journaux ont pointé du doigt, parfois avec virulence, l'échec de l'intégration des immigrés et la montée de l'islamisme en France. *Le Monde*.

Levine, D. N. (1971). *On Individuality and Social Forms: Selected Writings of Georg Simmel*. Chicago, IL: University of Chicago Press.

Li, Y. (20 May 2009). Digital storytelling as participatory media practice for empowerment: The case of the Chinese immigrants in the San Gabriel Valley. *Paper presented at the annual meeting of the International Communication Association*, Chicago, IL. Retrieved 4 May 2011, from: <http://www.allacademic.com/meta/p300927_index.html>.

Lidchi, H. (1993). All in the Choosing Eye: Charity, Representation and the Developing World. Unpublished PhD thesis. Milton Keynes: The Open University.

Liebes, T., and Kampf, Z. (2009). From black and white to shades of gray: Palestinians in the Israeli media during the Second Intifada. *International Journal of Press/Politics*, 14 (4): 434–53.

Livingstone, S., and Lunt, P. (1994). *Talk on Television: Audience Participation and Public Debate*. London: Routledge.

Lu, X. (2009). Ritual, television, and state ideology: Rereading CCTV's 2006 *Spring Festival Gala*. In Y. Zhu and C. Berry (eds), *TV China* (pp. 111–25). Bloomington, IN: Indiana University Press.

Ludwig, C. (2006). Re-Imagined in translation: Sliding signs, hybrid representation and mis-recognition in the American, British and French press coverage of the November 2005 crise des Banlieues. Unpublished MSc dissertation. London School of Economics and Political Science, London.

Lull, J. (1991). *China Turned On: Television, Reform, and Resistance*. London: Routledge.

Macdonald, M. (2003). *Exploring Media Discourse*. London: Arnold.

McGee, M. (2005). *Self-Help, Inc: Makeover Culture in American Life*. Oxford: Oxford University Press.

Machin, D., and Van Leeuwen, T. (2007). *Global Media Discourse: A Critical Introduction*. London and New York: Routledge.

Manga, J. E. (2003). *Talking Trash: The Cultural Politics of Daytime TV Talk Shows*. New York and London: New York University Press.

Matheson, D., and Allan, S. (2007). Truth in a war zone: The role of warblogs in Iraq. In S. Maltby and R. Keeble (eds), *Communicating War: Memory, Military and Media* (pp. 75–89). Bury St Edmunds: Arima.

Mattelart, T. (2006). French television confronts urban revolts. *Global Media and Communication*, 2(2): 243–50.

Matthews, N. (2007). Confessions to a new public: Video Nation shorts. *Media, Culture & Society*, 29(3): 435–48.

Mbembe, A. (2001). *On the Postcolony*. Berkeley, CA: University of California Press.

Media Awareness Network. (2010). Hurricane Katrina and the 'two-photo controversy'. Retrieved 4 May 2011, from: <http://www.media-awareness.ca/english/resources/educational/teachable_moments/katrina_2_photo.cfm>.

Media Diversity Institute. (2008). The role of media in promotion of intercultural learning. Report to Council of Europe's Intercultural Cities Programme. Retrieved 4 May 2011, from: <http://www.coe.int/t/dg4/cultureheritage/culture/cities/mediapack.pdf>.

Meng, B. (2011). From steamed bun to grass mud horse: E Gao as alternative political discourse on the Chinese Internet. *Global Media and Communication*, 7(1): 33–51.

Milner, K. (2000). Flashback 1984: Portrait of a famine. *BBC News*. Retrieved 4 May 2011, from: <http://news.bbc.co.uk/1/hi/world/africa/703958.stm>.

Moeller, S. (1999). *Compassion Fatigue: How the Media Sell Misery, War, and Death*. New York: Routledge.

Morley, D. (2004). Broadcasting and the construction of the national family. In R. C. Allen and A. Hill (eds), *The Television Studies Reader* (pp. 418–41). London: Routledge.

Mummery, J., and Rodan, D. (2007). Discursive Australia: Refugees, Australianness, and the Australian public sphere. *Continuum: Journal of Media and Cultural Studies*, 21(3): 347–60.

Narine, N. (2010). Global trauma and the cinematic network society. *Critical Studies in Media Communication*, 27(3): 209–34.

Nash, K. (2008). Global citizenship as show business: The cultural politics of 'Make Poverty History'. *Media, Culture & Society*, 30(1): 167–81.

Neiman, S. (2002). *Evil in Modern Thought*. Princeton, NJ: Princeton University Press.

News Xchange. (2005). 24-hour news: Rolling news and big events, Session Transcript. Retrieved 4 May 2011, from: <http://www.newsxchange.org/newsx2005/rolling_news_01_05.html>.

Nordbruch, G. (2005). The Arab media on the unrest in France. *Qantara.de*. Retrieved 4 May 2011, from: <http://www.qantara.de/webcom/show_article.php/_c-478/_nr-359/i.html>.

Nossek, H. (2004). Our news and their news: The role of national identity in the coverage of foreign news. *Journalism*, 5(3): 343–68.

Ōmae, K. (1995). *The End of the Nation State: The Rise of Regional Economies*. London: HarperCollins.

Orgad, S. (2005). *Storytelling Online: Talking Breast Cancer on the Internet*. New York: Peter Lang.

Orgad, S. (2008). 'Have you seen Bloomberg?': Satellite news channels as agents of the new visibility. *Global Media and Communication*, 4(3): 301–27.

Orgad, S. (2009a). The survivor in contemporary culture and public discourse: A genealogy. *The Communication Review*, 12(2): 132–61.

Orgad, S. (2009b). Watching how others watch us: The Israeli media's treatment of international coverage of the Gaza war. *The Communication Review*, 12(3): 250–61.

Orgad, S. (2011). Proper distance from ourselves: The potential for estrangement in the mediapolis. *International Journal of Cultural Studies*, 14(4): 401–21.

Palmer, E. (2 November 2005). Paris riots. *CBS News*. Retrieved 4 May 2011, from: <http://www.cbsnews.com/video/watch/?id=1005986n&tag=related; photovideo>.

Pan, Z. (2010). Enacting the family-nation on a global stage: An analysis of CCTV's spring festival gala. In M. Curtin and H. Shah (eds), *Re-Orienting Global Communication: India and China Beyond Borders* (pp. 240–59). Urbana-Champaign, IL: University of Illinois Press.

Pareles, J. (14 February 2010). For Haiti, they are the remake. *New York Times*. Retrieved 4 May 2011, from: <http://www.nytimes.com/2010/02/15/arts/music/15notebook.html>.

Peck, J. (1996). The mediated talking cure: Therapeutic framing of autobiography in TV talk shows. In S. Smith and J. Watson (eds), *Getting a Life: Everyday Uses of Autobiography* (pp. 134–55). Minneapolis, MN: University of Minnesota Press.

Pégard, C. (16 November 2005). Après l'incendie? Le bloc-notes politique de Catherine Pégard. *Le Point*.

Peri, Y. (1999). The media and collective memory of Yitzhak Rabin's remembrance. *Journal of Communication*, 49(3): 106–24.

Peters, J. D. (2001). Witnessing. *Media, Culture & Society*, 23(6): 707–23.

Petley, J. (2003). War without death: Responses to distant suffering. *Journal for Crime, Conflict and the Media*, 1(1): 72–85.

Pew Internet. (14 December 2008). The future of the Internet III. Retrieved 4 May 2011, from: <http://www.pewinternet.org/~/media//Files/Reports/2008/PIP_FutureInternet3.pdf.pdf>.

Pew Internet. (2009). Trend data. Retrieved 4 May 2011, from: <http://www.pewinternet.org/Trend-Data/Online-Activites-Total.aspx>.

Philo, G., and Beattie, L. (1999). Race, migration and media. In G. Philo (ed.), *Message Received: Glasgow Media Group Research 1993–1998* (pp. 171–96). Harlow: Longman.

Pickering, M. (2001). *Stereotyping: The Politics of Representation*. New York: Palgrave.

Plan UK. (8 February 2011). *Unnatural Disasters: Compassion versus Complexity in the Media's Reporting of Humanitarian Emergencies*, Media Symposium. London: Commonwealth Club.

Plunkett, J. (9 November 2005). French bloggers held after Paris riots. *Guardian*.

Poggioli, S. (2009). French minorities push for equality post-Obama. *NPR*. Retrieved 4 May 2011, from: <http://www.npr.org/templates/story/story.php?storyId=99298290>.

Rainie, L., and Anderson, J. (2008). Scenario 5: The evolution of augmented reality and virtual reality. *Pew Internet*. Retrieved 4 May 2011, from: <http://www.pewinternet.org/Reports/2008/The-Future-of-the-Internet-III/8-Scenario-5-The-Evolution-of-Augmented-Reality-and-Virtual-Reality.aspx?r=1>.

Rajaram, P. K. (2002). Humanitarianism and representations of the refugee. *Journal of Refugee Studies*, 15(3): 247–64.

Randall, C. (8 November 2005). Anarchy and fear spread to holiday regions. *Daily Telegraph*, p. 4.

Redden, G. (2007). Makeover morality and consumer culture. In D. Heller (ed.), *Makeover Television: Realities Remodelled* (pp. 150–64). New York: I. B. Tauris.

Reinhardt, M., Edwards, H., and Duganne, E. (2007). *Beautiful Suffering*. Chicago, IL: Chicago University Press.

Reuters. (9 November 2005). Coverage of riots in world press hurts French pride. Retrieved 4 May 2011, from: <http://archive.gulfnews.com/articles/05/11/09/191339.html>.

Richebois, V. (24 November 2005). Les rapports ambivalents des cités avec les medias. *Les Echos,* p. 12.

Richey, L. A., and Ponte, S. (2011). *Brand Aid: Shopping Well to Save the World*. Minneapolis, MN: University of Minnesota Press.

Ridgeway, J. (ed) (2005). *Baghdad Burning: Girl Blog From Iraq*. New York: Feminist Press.

Robertson, A. (2010). *Mediated Cosmopolitanism: The World of Television News*. Cambridge: Polity.

Robertson, R. (2009). Differentiational reductionism and the missing link in Albert's approach to globalization theory. *International Political Sociology*, 3(1): 119–22.

Roeh, I., and Cohen, A. (1992). One of the bloodiest days: A comparative analysis of open and closed television news. *Journal of Communication*, 42(2): 43–55.

Rose, G. (2001). *Visual Methodologies: An Introduction to the Interpretation of Visual Material*. London: Sage.

Rose, N. (1990). *Governing the Soul: The Shaping of the Private Self*. London and New York: Routledge.

Rosello, M. (1998). Representing illegal immigrants in France: From clandestins to l'affaire des sans-papiers de Saint-Bernard. *Journal of European Studies*, 28(109–10): 137–51.

Rosello, M. (2001). Protection or hospitality: The young man and the illegal immigrant in *La Promesse*. In R. King and H. Wood (eds), *Media and Migration: Constructions of Mobility and Difference* (pp. 71–82). London: Routledge.

Rukszto, K. (2006). The other heritage minutes: Satirical reactions to Canadian nationalism. *TOPIA: Canadian Journal of Cultural Studies*, 14: 73–91.

Russell, A. (2007). Digital communication networks and the journalistic field: The 2005 French riots. *Critical Studies in Media Communication*, 24(4): 285–302.

Saghie, H. (2001). *The Predicament of the Individual in the Middle East*. London: Saqi Books.

Said, E. (2003 [1978]). *Orientalism*. London: Penguin.

Saussure, F. D. (1974). *A Course in General Linguistics*. London: Duckworth.

Scannell, P. (1996). *Radio, Television & Modern Life*. Cambridge, MA: Blackwell.

Scannell, P., and Cardiff, D. (1991). *A Social History of British Broadcasting: Serving the Nation, 1923–1939*. Oxford: Blackwell.

Schiller, D. (1999). *Digital Capitalism: Networking the Global Market System*. Cambridge, MA: MIT Press.

Schlesinger, P. (1987 [1978]). *Putting Reality Together: BBC News*. New York: Methuen & Co.

Schudson, M. (2002). What's unusual about covering politics as usual? In B. Zelizer and S. Allan (eds), *Journalism After September 11* (pp. 36–47). New York: Routledge.

Schwarz, G. (9 November 2005). Sur les blogs, des jeunes banlieusards libèrent leur parole. *Agence France Presse*.

Scott, A. O. (12 August 2010). Globe-trotting and soul-searching. *New York Times*. Retrieved 4 May 2011, from: <http://movies.nytimes.com/2010/08/13/movies/13eat.html>.

Sennett, R. (1977). *The Fall of Public Man*. Cambridge: Cambridge University Press.

Sennett, R. (1994). *Flesh and Stone: The Body and the City in Western Civilization*. London: Penguin.

Seu, B. I., and Orgad, S. (in progress). *Mediated Humanitarian Knowledge: Audiences' Responses and Moral Actions*.

Shattuc, J. (1997). *The Talking Cure: TV Talk Shows and Women*. New York and London: Routledge.

Shklovsky, V. (1991 [1929]). *Theory of Prose*. Champaign, IL: Dalkey Archive Press.

Shome, R., and Hegde, R. S. (2002). Culture, communication, and the challenge of globalization. *Critical Studies in Media Communication*, 19(2): 172–89.

Silverstone, R. (1994). *Television and Everyday Life*. London and New York: Routledge.

Silverstone, R. (1999). *Why Study the Media?* London: Sage.

Silverstone, R. (2007). *Media and Morality: On the Rise of the Mediapolis*. Cambridge: Polity.

Sisler, V. (2008). Digital Arabs: Representation in video games. *European Journal of Cultural Studies*, 11(2): 203–20.

Sliwinski, S. (2009). The aesthetics of human rights. *Culture, Theory & Critique*, 50(1): 23–39.

Smith, D. A. (5 February 2006). Playing with fire. *Observer*. Retrieved 4 May 2011, from: <http://www.guardian.co.uk/world/2006/feb/05/france.features>.

Smith, M., and Yanacopulos, H. (2004). The public faces of development: An introduction. *Journal of International Development*, 16(5): 657–64.

Sontag, S. (2003). *Regarding the Pain of Others*. New York: Farrar, Straus and Giroux.

Speers, T. (2001). Welcome or over reaction? Refugees and asylum seekers in the Welsh media. *Wales Media Forum*. Retrieved 4 May 2011, from: <http://reposi tory.forcedmigration.org/show_metadata.jsp?pid=fmo: 3208>.

Spigel, L. (1992). *Make Room for TV: Television and the Family Ideal in Postwar America*. Chicago. IL: University of Chicago Press.

Spivak, G. (1988). Can the subaltern speak? In C. Nelson and L. Grossberg (eds), *Marxism and the Interpretation of Culture* (pp. 271–313). Urbana, IL: University of Illinois Press.

Sreberny, A. (1999). *Include Me In*. London: Broadcasting Standards Commission in conjunction with the Independent Television Commission.

Sreberny, A. (2000). The global and the local in international communica- tions. In J. Curran and M. Gurevitch (eds), *Mass Media and Society*, 3rd edn (pp. 93–119). London: Arnold.

Stallabrass, J. (2010). Solidarity or spectacle? War photography in the *Guardian*. *Paper presented at the MeCSSA 2010 conference*, London: London School of Economics and Political Science.

Sturken, M. (2011). Comfort, irony, and trivialization: The mediation of torture. *International Journal of Cultural Studies*, 14(4): 423–40.

Sun, W. (2008). *Maid In China: Media, Morality, and the Cultural Politics of Boundaries*. London: Routledge.

Swissinfo. (30 November 2007). Advert aims to deter African immigrants. Retrieved 4 May 2011, from: <http://www.swissinfo.ch/eng/index/Advert_ aims_to_deter_African_immigrants.html?cid=6287120>.

Tait, S. (2008). Pornographies of violence? Internet spectatorship on body horror. *Critical Studies in Media Communication*, 25(1): 91–111.

Taylor, C. (2002). Modern Social Imaginaries. *Public Culture*, 14(1): 91–124.

ter Wal, J. (1996). The social representation of immigrants: The *Pantanella* issue in the pages of *La Repubblica*. *Journal of Ethnic and Migration Studies*, 22(1): 39–66.

Tester, K. (2001). *Compassion, Morality and the Media*. Philadelphia, PA: Open University Press.

Thompson, J. B. (1984). *Studies in the Theory of Ideology*. Cambridge: Polity.

Thompson, J. B. (1995). *The Media and Modernity: A Social Theory of the Media*. Cambridge: Polity.

Thompson, J. B. (2005). The new visibility. *Theory, Culture & Society*, 22(6): 31–51.

Thumim, N. (2012). *Self-representation and Digital Culture*. Basingstoke: Palgrave Macmillan.

Thussu, D. K. (2009). *Internationalizing Media Studies*. London and New York: Routledge.

Tichi, C. (1991). *Electronic Hearth: Creating an American Television Culture*. New York: Oxford University Press.

Tomlinson, J. (1991). *Cultural Imperialism: A Critical Introduction*. London: Pinter Publishers.

Tomlinson, J. (1999). *Globalization and Culture*. Cambridge: Polity.

Tomlinson, J. (2007). Globalization and Cultural Analysis. In D. Held and A. McGrew (eds), *Globalization Theory: Approaches and Controversies* (pp. 148–68). Cambridge: Polity.

Tomlinson, J. (2011). Beyond connection: Cultural cosmopolitan and ubiquitous media. *International Journal of Cultural Studies*, 14(4): 347–61.

Trotter, M. (21 November 2005). Broken promises. *CTV News*. Retrieved 4 May 2011, from: <http://www.ctv.ca/CTVNews/WFive/20051119/w5_broken_promises_051119/>.

Tulloch, J. (2006). *One Day in July: Experiencing 7/7*. London: Little Brown.

Twenge, J. M. (16 June 2009). The narcissism epidemic: The 'normal' narcissism of reality TV. *Psychology Today*. Retrieved 4 May 2011, from: <http://www.psychologytoday.com/blog/the-narcissism-epidemic/200906/the-normal-narcissism-reality-tv>.

UNHCR. (n.d.). Prominent Refugees. *UNHCR*. Retrieved 4 May 2011, from: <http://www.unhcr.org/pages/49c3646c74.html>.

Van Dijk, T. (2000). New(s) racism: A discourse analytical approach. In S. Cottle (ed.), *Ethnic Minorities and the Media* (pp. 33–49). Buckingham, UK, and Philadelphia, PA: Open University Press.

Voltaire, F. M. A. (1911 [1756]). *Poème sur le désastre de Lisbonne*. Indianapolis, IN: Liberty Fund. Retrieved 4 May 2011, from: <http://oll.libertyfund.org/?option=com_staticxt&staticfile=show.php%3Ftitle=349&chapter=28298&layout=html&Itemid=27>.

Waisbord, S. (2002). Journalism, risk and patriotism. In B. Zelizer and S. Allan (eds), *Journalism After September 11* (pp. 201–19). New York: Routledge.

Wall, M. (2005). 'Blogs of war': Weblogs as news. *Journalism*, 6(2): 153–72.

Walton, D. N. (1996). Practical reasoning and the structure of fear appeal arguments. *Philosophy & Rhetoric*, 29(4): 301–13.

Wang, G. (2010). *De-Westernizing Communication Research: Altering Questions and Changing Frameworks*. London and New York: Routledge.

Warner, M. (2002). Publics and counterpublics. *Public Culture*, 14(1): 49–90.

Watson, I. (12 July 2010). Six months after quake, Haiti still suffers. *CNN*. Retrieved 4 May 2011, from: <http://edition.cnn.com/2010/WORLD/americas / 07 / 12 / haiti . six . months . later / index.html#fbid=vi5lRoIOElI&wom=false>.

White, H. (1981). The value of narrativity in the representation of reality. In W. J. T. Mitchell (ed.), *On Narrative* (pp. 1–23). Chicago, IL, and London: University of Chicago Press.

Wikipedia. (n.d.). Others [Lost]. Retrieved 4 May 2011, from: <http://en.wikipedia.org/wiki/Others_(Lost)>.

Wikipedia. (n.d.). We Are The World. Retrieved 4 May 2011, from: <http://en.m.wikipedia.org/wiki/We_Are_the_World#_>.

Willsher, K. (5 November 2005). A country in flames . . . French cities teeter on the edge of anarchy. *Daily Telegraph*. Retrieved 4 May 2011, from: <http://

www.telegraph.co.uk/news/worldnews/europe/france/1502361/A-country-in-flames-French-cities-teeter-on-the-edge-of-anarchy.html>.

Wiltenburg, M. (2009a). What's it like to be a refugee in America? Retrieved 4 May 2011, from: <http://littlebillclinton.csmonitor.com/littlebillclinton/2009/07/14/what-its-like-to-be-a-refugee-in-america/>.

Wiltenburg, M. (2009b). Refugee comfort zone: Olympic training and US citizenship for newborns. Retrieved 4 May 2011, from: <http://littlebillclinton.csmonitor.com/littlebillclinton/2010/12/22/refugee-comfort-zone-olympic-training-and-us-citizenship-for-newborns/>.

Witte, K. (1994). Fear control and danger control: A test of the Extended Parallel Process Model (EPPM). *Communication Monographs*, 61: 113–34.

Wood, H., and Skeggs, B. (2004). Note on ethical scenarios of self on British reality TV. *Feminist Media Studies*, 4(2): 205–8.

Zandberg, E., and Neiger, M. (2005). Between the nation and the profession: Journalists as members of contradicting communities. *Media, Culture & Society*, 27(1): 131–42.

Zhang, L. (2002). Urban experiences and social belonging among Chinese rural migrants. In P. Link, R. P. Madsen and P. G. Pickowicz (eds), *Popular China: Unofficial Culture in a Globalizing Society* (pp. 275–99). Oxford: Rowman & Littlefield.

Zirinski, R. (2005). *Ad-Hoc Arabism: Advertising, Culture, and Technology in Saudi Arabia*. New York: Peter Lang.

Zuma, J. (2010). South Africa: Let the real media debate begin. AllAfrica.com. Retrieved 4 May 2011, from: <http://allafrica.com/stories/201008140001.html>.

Index